FLY FISHING

FLY FISHING

E. DONNALL THOMAS Jr.

WITH PHOTOGRAPHS BY R. VALENTINE ATKINSON

Outside
BOOKS

W. W. NORTON & COMPANY
NEW YORK • LONDON

For information about permission to reproduce selections from this book, write to
Permissions, W. W. Norton & Company, Inc.
500 Fifth Avenue, New York, NY 10110

The text of this book is composed in Perpetua
with the display set in Monkey
Project Management by Julie Stillman
Composition by Sylvie Vidrine
Manufacturing by Dai Nippon Printing Company
Map illustrations by Janet Fredericks

Book design by Bill Harvey

Library of Congress Cataloging-in-Publication Data

Thomas, E. Donnall.
    Fly fishing / E. Donnall Thomas Jr.
        p. cm. -- (Outside adventure travel)
    "An Outside book."
    Includes bibliographical references and index.

    1. Fly Fishing. I. Title. II. Series.
SH456.T487 2001
799.1'24--dc21

                                            2001032954

ISBN 0-393-32073-1 (pbk.)

W. W. Norton & Company, Inc., 500 Fifth Avenue, New York, N.Y. 10110
www.wwnorton.com
W. W. Norton & Company Ltd., Castle House, 75/76 Wells Street, London W1T 3QT, England

1 2 3 4 5 6 7 8 9 0

Photograph on page 6: A pair of blue trevally, Christmas Island, South Pacific.

To Jeff and Elaine

ACKNOWLEDGMENTS

Itinerant writers can't bum their way around the world without considerable help from their friends. I wish to express my deep appreciation to the following individuals, each of whom contributed in a significant way to this book: Jim Babb, Liz and Alton Bain, Ray Barry, Andrei Belayev, Doug and Olga Borland, Tom Brady, Pierre Candido, Mike Darland, Don Davis, Jim DeBernardinas, Walter Ehrlich, Shawn Feliciano, Mike Freeman, Rick Gaffney, Alex Gonzales, Ernie Holland, Mike Heusner, Ed Hughes, Hank Ingram, Bradd Johnson, Julie King, Paul Kinney, Cory Mattson, Dick LeBlond, Bob and Denise May, Howard McKinney, Steve McGrath, Marguerite Miles, Blanca Moreno, Laurie Morrow, Dick Negley, Joel Rahming, Adam Redford, Robin Reeve, Matt Schuster, Doug and Hillary Sheldon, and Russell Tharin.

Thanks Nicole Youngbauer for help with research and manuscript preparation.

Finally, special thanks to my wife, Lori Thomas, whose contributions should be obvious throughout this book.

Different versions of some of the material in this volume have appeared in a number of publications including *Gray's Sporting Journal* (Chapters 4 and 13), *Sports Afield* (Chapters 2, 11, and 14), *Fly Fishing Salt Waters* (Chapters 9, 10, and 11), *Alaska* (Chapter 10), *Fly Rod & Reel* (Chapter 7), and *Southwest Fly Fishing* (Chapter 5). I appreciate the opportunity to rework this material for inclusion in the text.

CONTENTS

INTRODUCTION

Fly-fishing literature contains plenty of how-to books, detailed volumes devoted to the technical aspects of catching fish under a variety of circumstances both general and specific. This is not one of them. In the first place, presenting a truly comprehensive review of angling methods and fly patterns useful in each location would require that every chapter become a book of its own. Furthermore, I don't possess the necessary knowledge. Although I can speak

with confidence about some of these destinations (I've lived in Alaska and Montana for 30 years), I've enjoyed only brief visits to others. Because I hate the false ring of undeserved authority in print, I've declined to indulge in it myself. Finally, technical writing distracts from what I regard as this book's truly important themes: people, places, sights, natural history, food, company, water, and, of course, fish and the magic that occurs when anglers encounter them in special places.

This doesn't mean that I've deliberately offered a text devoid of information. Inquisitive anglers with limited experience in certain aspects of fly fishing's complex scope should be able to pick up a few worthwhile pointers in each chapter. And I've tried to provide authoritative references that offer more detailed instruction to those who

seek it. That's the best I choose to do.

Angling also contains its share of where-to books, detailed destination-specific volumes that tell readers where to eat and sleep, what road to drive down, and what rock to cast from once you arrive. Despite the appearance of the table of contents, this isn't one of those books either. Again, providing that kind of encyclopedic area knowledge would require book-length treatment of every chapter. And although it might be possible for one angling enthusiast to know a destination or two that well, I don't know anyone who possesses that level of personal experience with regard to all the locations outlined in this book, and I frankly don't think it's possible to do so. I have written about what I've seen and done, and once again tried to provide useful references for the interested reader who wishes to expand upon that scope of knowledge about any given destination. Finally, a sort of Heisenberg's uncertainty principle operates here. In reporting minute details concerning remote locations, one makes them less remote de facto. For some of the destinations described in this book—Midway Atoll and Los Roques, for example—access is so controlled that such concerns scarcely matter. But when it comes to the more accessible locations in North America, readers should plan on discovering

Opposite: Dawn on the Henry's Fork of the Snake River, Idaho. Above: Rainbow trout.

the details of their own wilderness fishing themselves. That's half the fun, if not more, anyway.

So let's call this a why-to angling book. Not *why fish*—I'll leave that Big Question to wiser philosophers. (Interested parties might begin with *Moby-Dick*.) The real question before the house is, *Why travel* to do it? Although only the rare or unimaginative reader will be unable to find interesting angling within a few hours' drive of home, most of us who have fallen under fly fishing's spell eventually feel the urge to experience new challenges. That impulse doesn't necessarily have to take one halfway around the world. Here in Montana, for example, I've spent several years stubbornly exploring warmwater fly-fishing opportunities for bass and pike in the trout angler's equivalent of the Holy Land. But sometimes you just have to get out of Dodge, and when you do you might as well take your fly rod.

The traveling angler's interest in distant destinations often begins with the intrigue of new species and fly-fishing techniques, a relatively modern phenomenon. Historically, fly-rod anglers didn't care about much of anything other than trout and salmon, a collective case of tunnel vision that didn't begin to clear until little more than a generation ago. Nothing illustrates the way attitudes have changed within the once hidebound fly-fishing community like the recent explosion of

interest in salt water, a theme reflected in the selection of destinations described in this book, slightly over half of which focus upon angling in the marine environment. I intend no slight toward more traditional venues. I simply believe in my heart that the sea represents the new frontier.

But as fascinating as the fish and fishing might prove to be, another theme underlies this text. The most rewarding elements of a trip to a far-flung fly-rod destination often have nothing to do with angling at all. I've never felt comfortable divorcing any outdoor experience from the circumstances in which it takes place, considerations that include not just fish and water but intangibles of foreign culture and natural history. So forgive me if I seem to spend more time talking about food and birds than mayflies. I've simply followed an elemental principle of the writer's craft and concentrated on what left the deepest impressions.

ABOUT THIS BOOK

It's hard to provide vivid impressions of a locale without firsthand experience. Therefore, the narrative portion of each chapter reflects time I've spent on the water there myself, without making any effort to be comprehensive. Other portions of the chapter address practical considerations of interest to the angler considering a visit.

Above: Saltwater fisherman checking tackle, Bahamas. Opposite: Early morning fishing for browns, Petrohue River, southern Chile.

AT A GLANCE

Each chapter contains a brief synopsis, titled At a Glance, designed to give a nuts-and bolts impression of a place from the angler's perspective. It contains the following items:

Species. A brief listing of the principal game fish likely to interest visiting anglers. Others might well be available, at least at certain times of year.

Tackle. A brief overview of rods, reels, lines, leaders, and ancillary equipment likely to prove useful. Primarily intended as a guideline and a reminder of certain destination-specific items.

Flies. Suggestions refer to the basic pattern lists recommended in Appendix B for each of a half-dozen common angling situations, plus destination-specific favorites. Such short lists invariably inspire debate, often impassioned even when friendly. I simply felt it reasonable to relate what has worked

for me. Such abbreviated lists cannot be comprehensive and they are not meant to be.

Prime Time. The generally accepted optimum time for fly-rod anglers to visit, based on consensus and personal experience. Excellent fishing might be available during other months as well.

Conservation Issues. Quick notes identifying possible environmental threats to each unique fishery.

Price Range. Prices change constantly, so I've shied away from listing exact dollar amounts. The price range notations are meant primarily to suggest expense relative to other destinations. The price ranges given are for a week of guided fishing at a typical lodge or with comparable accommodations. I've attempted to factor transportation costs from the mainland United States into each

estimate. Anglers traveling on their own and fishing without a guide can expect to cut these figures by 30 to 50 percent. Again, the principal value of these estimates is comparative.

Staging City. Where to fly into to begin the trip.

Heads Up. Briefly alerts readers to possible health and safety risks. More detailed information follows in the What to Expect section of each chapter and Appendix A.

WHAT TO EXPECT

This section provides a subjective overview of the angling experience and local culture. It also contains practical information about travel, clothing, activities for nonfishing companions, and climate, as well as a review of area-specific health and safety issues that includes references to detailed discussions of these topics in Appendix A.

CONTACTS

I've tried to accomplish two purposes under the Contacts heading. The first is to provide a sampling of local fishing lodges, guides, and outfitters; I've made no effort to be comprehensive. For those listed by name, I've either had personal experience with them or had detailed discussions with reliable friends sufficient for me to offer a recommendation. Some areas with well-developed angling resources offer numerous

additional options, and failure to list them by name implies lack of familiarity rather than disapproval. I've provided direct contact information whenever I've dealt directly with the lodge or outfitter. For additional contacts and for a sampling of other types of services, readers should consult Appendix C.

Also in the Contacts section, I've provided information on resources that might be of particular interest to anglers planning unguided visits on their own.

RECOMMENDED READING

Admittedly this represents a hodgepodge. Whenever appropriate, I've tried to list at least one authoritative book on fishing methods pertinent to the location as well as an area-specific fly-fishing guide if available: the how-to and where-to mentioned earlier. Although these books necessarily vary in readability, some are extremely useful. Stephen and Kim Vletas's *Bahamas Fly-Fishing Guide*, for example, is among the most definitive works of its kind. The rest of the listings represent a mixture of everything from natural history to fiction. Focused anglers might wonder, *Why bother?*, but that's the way I think about travel. No one, for example, should fish the Florida backcountry without reading Peter Matthiessen's *Killing Mister Watson*.

APPENDICES

I've included three appendices. The longest, Appendix A, Health & Safety, reflects my own medical background. Anglers face unique potential health hazards, especially when they travel to exotic destinations, and I'm frankly unaware of any other attempt to organize a body of information that addresses these issues in quite such detail. I hope that anglers will find this discussion useful no matter where they plan to fish.

Although obviously not intended to be comprehensive, Appendix B, Tackle & Flies, reflects my experience as an angler who travels frequently to out-of-the-way places where resources can be limited. Think of it as a guide to getting by with less.

Finally, Appendix C, Booking Agencies, lists booking and travel agencies that specialize in serving fly-fishing clientele. This is a resource for anglers who wish to learn of as many options as possible for a given destination while planning a trip. I've worked in various capacities with most of the agencies, some more happily than others. All are regarded as reputable within the fly-fishing community.

Opposite: Fishing for South Island (New Zealand) brown trout. Above: The Sorrano River, Torres del Paine, southern Chile. Overleaf: Bonefish water, Joulters Flat, South Andros, Bahamas.

Christmas Island

As I approached. . .a glimmer of bonefish tails rose to catch the morning sun

The all-day downwind trek to Lone Palm isn't for the faint of heart. Surrounded by the world's largest coral atoll, Christmas Island's interior lagoon consists of a vast mosaic of flats, beaches, and channels nearly devoid of landmarks. The lagoon's potential for spatial confusion nearly led to the death of two members of Captain James Cook's crew who became lost while hunting turtles, and things haven't changed much since. But a single palm tree rises from a sandy spit in the middle of the lagoon, and a driver with local knowledge can get a truck there from the island's main road system. Given my taste for solitude and virgin water, it didn't take me long to decide I needed to spend a day fishing all the way across the lagoon with the wind at my back, aiming for an evening pickup by vehicle at that lonely landmark.

Needless to say, this adventure took place in the days before GPS. The guides and staff back at the Captain Cook Hotel expressed some

A 10-pound bonefish. Such larger bones live in deeper water and cruise the flats only for brief periods.

CHRISTMAS ISLAND

reservations: Even if I could find my way across the lagoon, I'd have to swim deep channels to reach Lone Palm. Undaunted—another way of saying stupid, it sometimes turns out—I loaded my daypack with drinking water and bonefish flies and set out the following morning.

Shimmering waves of equatorial heat hid my one and only landmark as I started across the first long flat, but I still felt confident of my ability to make my rendezvous at the end of the day. And in typical Christmas Island fashion, the fish didn't give me an opportunity to worry for long. As I approached a gap between two sandy spits, a glimmer of bonefish tails rose to catch the morning sun. I dropped a small Crazy Charlie in front of the school and watched the water boil as a trio of fish raced for the fly in the uniquely aggressive style I'd come to expect from Pacific bones. It took me an hour—and a half-dozen more fish—to work my way through the cut, by which time I was no longer sure I really wanted anyone to pick me up. Ever.

STRADDLING BOTH THE EQUATOR and the international date line, the remote island nation of Kiribati (pronounced *Kiribass,* by the way) includes nearly 2 million square miles within its borders, of which barely 300 constitute dry land. The largest of the country's 33 islands, Christmas lies over 2,000 miles east of the capital on Tarawa and 1,200 miles south of Honolulu. Christmas has always enjoyed a sense of isolation, even by the demanding standards of the mid-Pacific. When legendary British sea captain James Cook sailed into the island's lee on Christmas Eve 1777, his crew found it uninhabited, and the island's original Gilbertese name—Abakiroro—means "Far Away Island."

During the 19th century, Christmas served first as an occasional source of water, coconuts, and turtle meat for Pacific whalers and merchant vessels. Later, various commercial interests exploited its supply of pearls, shells, bird plumes, and guano, arousing casual imperial interest from the usual suspects, including, briefly, the United

---

AT A GLANCE

SPECIES Bonefish, trevally (giant and blue), wahoo, barracuda, tuna (yellowfin and skipjack), sharks

TACKLE 7–8-weight rods for bonefish and small trevally, 12-weights for giant trevally and bluewater species; floating lines; 10# tippet for bonefish, 15# for trevally and offshore species, wire for barracuda and sharks

FLIES Basic flats and bluewater selections

PRIME TIME Year-round

CONSERVATION ISSUES Depletion of offshore fish stocks by commercial harvest

PRICE RANGE $2,500–$3,500

STAGING CITY Honolulu, Hawaii

HEADS UP Christmas sits just north of the equator, and at this latitude the sun can be brutal

A driver with local knowledge takes anglers to Christmas Island's vast, featureless interior lagoon.

States. Britain finally claimed Christmas as part of the Gilbert and Ellice Islands in 1888. Throughout this period, the island remained largely uninhabited except for small temporary work forces. It also enjoyed some measure of revenge upon its various exploiters, accumulating a remarkable number of shipwrecks along its treacherous windward shore.

Christmas' desolation ended with the arrival of a renegade French priest named Rougier, who, in distinctly unclerical fashion, flat out bought the place in 1907 using funds swindled from a naïve friend. Rougier turned the island into a vast coconut farm, importing a large, ethnically diverse work force in the process, most of whom endured abysmal treatment. After a generation of wrangling back and forth between French and British legal authorities, none of whom seemed able to control Rougier, Christmas eventually

wound up safely under British administrative authority and permanently inhabited at last, predominantly by Gilbertese workers.

Enter the Second World War and our fellow Americans, absent since a final squabble with the British over guano rights in the late 1800s. Because of the island's apparent strategic importance, American forces—this time with the full approval of British authorities—constructed a 7,000-foot-long runway on the northeast corner of the island. Although the anticipated Japanese invasion never took place, the airstrip American military forces constructed allows air transportation to and from the island today.

What relevance is the island's complex history to modern anglers? Simply stated, it's hard to imagine why locals should bother being civil to outside visitors. Collectively, we took what the island had to offer and left little in return except junk, nuclear fallout (Britain touched off a couple of H-bomb tests nearby during the '50s), and irrelevant conflict. But remarkably, the island's Gilbertese inhabitants impressed me as some of the world's most hospitable people during my initial visits 20 years ago. Granted, I was among the first outside anglers to explore Christmas and there have been changes since, but the island remains a profoundly pleasant place despite everything, perhaps more so than we deserve.

OUT IN THE MIDDLE OF THE LAGOON, I finally came to the first deep channel. I've always been comfortable in the water, so the swim itself didn't look worrisome, even though I was burdened by a small pack and fly rod. The problem was that I'd done some historical research after an earlier visit, and I couldn't forget the following excerpt from the log of Midshipman James Trevenen, describing a fishing expedition into the lagoon during Cook's pioneering voyage:

On every side of us swam Sharks innumerable and so voracious that they bit our oars and rudder and I actually struck my hanger two inches into the back of one whilst he had the rudder between his teeth. The boats fishing for Cavallies and etc. in Shallow water, carried long pikes to keep the Sharks from the Bait.

Furthermore, I'd already noticed that the locals seemed to represent the only subsistence maritime culture I'd ever encountered in which no one ever went in the water, no doubt with good reason.

But there I stood, too far along on my way to Lone Palm to consider turning back. Trying to extinguish the relentless *Jaws* theme from my brain, I cinched down the straps on my pack and waded in, sidearming my way along with one hand while I gripped my fly rod rather desperately with the other. "Sharks innumerable," I remembered young Master Trevenen observing, and God knows

Arrival at Christmas Island. Even customs is a fairly casual affair.

I'd seen plenty during earlier forays into the lagoon by boat. But not this time; it must have been my lucky day.

As terra firma goes, the next little spit of coral sand wasn't much, but it felt like the Garden of Eden when I finally reached it. And I'd scarcely had time to shake off like a dog when the next school of bonefish appeared. By the time I'd finished with them, a big trevally arrived at the edge of the nearest drop-off, and I considered the three minutes the fish took to break me off a minor victory in its own right. By then, I was finally ready to wipe off my polarized glasses with a few precious drops of fresh water and start looking for Lone Palm, which remained nowhere to be seen.

Sure, it was out there somewhere in all that refractive heat, but the failure of a relied-upon landmark to appear on schedule always arouses a certain trepidation. Or at least it should. Trouble was, yet another school of bones had just appeared, and the choice between worry and fish proved delightfully easy. Besides, the school lay in the same direction as Lone Palm. Sort of.

Two hours and a whole bunch of bonefish later, I had to admit that it was time to cover some ground...or, more properly, some coral. It takes a lot to get me to walk past tailing bonefish, but the thought of spending the night curled up on a patch of sand with a dwindling supply of drinking water finally did the trick. Hiking past all those fish hurt, but finally I managed to make out the delicate outline of a single palm tree silhouetted against the late-afternoon sun. With that out of the way, I slowed down and fished my way home, picking off another dozen bonefish before declaring "No mas!" and stumbling up the sand toward the fading outline of the truck.

The driver seemed glad to see me. He spoke no English and I spoke no Gilbertese, but he smiled the kind of smile you never see anywhere but on Christmas Island as we pantomimed our way through the essentials: *The day had been good, there had been lots of fish, I was crazy.*

Full agreement from me on all counts.

WHAT TO EXPECT

ANGLING

Christmas has changed since I first visited 20 years ago. Back then, services were bare-bones minimum and guiding virtually undeveloped. Of course, exploring on one's own was part of the island's appeal in those days. Today, visiting anglers can expect better boats and knowledgeable English-speaking guides, practically unheard of in the early days. Philosophically, I suppose increased angling efficiency has come at the price of a certain lost innocence, for which we have only ourselves to blame.

But make no mistake about it Christmas remains a truly remote destination, with more inshore water than a legion of anglers could fish in a lifetime. The island remains sparsely inhabited, and anglers with an urge to explore can still find vast reaches of virtually unfished water.

Bonefish are the island's premier fly-rod quarry. Christmas' reputation for lots of small bonefish is true only in part. Yeah, there are a lot of 2- and 3-pound bones, but there are plenty of bigger fish as well. Anglers in search of big fish and willing to sacrifice some numbers should concentrate on deeper water near the edges of the flats, where, with patience, they should enjoy lots of opportunities at 6- to 8-pound bones. And I've seen plenty larger than that.

In contrast to some Caribbean destinations, almost all flats fishing on Christmas takes place on foot—a real plus for those who share my passion for wading. The island's windward shore consists of long sand beaches with beautiful ocean flats extending between the beach and the protective barrier reef. These flats offer great fishing for medium-size bones in a spectacular setting. Anglers interested in something new and different can wade out to the reef at low tide and cast into the deep water beyond. Expect to hook a lot of fish, land a few, and struggle to identify most of those. The island's central lagoon consists of a vast maze of sand

Above: Some good bonefish flies, Crazy Charlies, Gotchas, and Bonefish Specials. Opposite: By boat to remote bonefish flats.

Christmas Island idyll: bonefish flats as far as the eye can see, but not another angler in sight.

beaches, channels, and flats that support a truly amazing population of bonefish. At times they seem to be everywhere, and anglers new to the area must learn to walk past fish sulking in backwaters and concentrate their efforts on active flats where wind and tide have attracted actively feeding fish. Milkfish, which do not strike flies, abound in the lagoon. Anglers unfamiliar with this bonefish look-alike must learn to distinguish it from the real thing by its dark eye and the prominent outline of its tail.

When actively feeding in wind-driven or tidal current, Christmas bonefish are seldom selective, and aggressive strikes are the rule. Most anglers could fish their entire stay with a white Crazy Charlie and never need another bonefish pattern. Coral heads abound especially on the ocean flats, making an abrasion-resistant fluorocarbon leader a plus. Needless to say, high-quality polarized glasses are essential, as are tough flats wading boots adequate to protect feet from sharp coral fragments.

Christmas Island waters contain excellent numbers of trevally, both giant *ulua* and smaller blues. As always, big trevally are great tackle busters and it's impossible to rig too heavily for this demanding species. Since GTs show up periodically along the edges of bonefish flats, it pays to have a heavy rod rigged and ready whenever possible. Anglers specifically interested in targeting *ulua* can team up and cast teaser plugs along the reef, hoping for a shot with the fly at whatever appears from the depths to chase the teaser.

Local waters produce some huge Pacific barracuda. Offshore, conventional-tackle anglers have long enjoyed excellent fishing for wahoo and tuna. Fly-rod possibilities for these species remain largely unexplored. Anglers wishing to tackle bluewater species can arrange offshore charters on a daily basis at modest additional cost.

MAN-O'-WAR BIRDS

Many of the mid-Pacific's pelagic seabirds can survive for long periods on the open ocean without making landfall. But all must come ashore to breed and nest, a biological necessity that turns isolated atolls like Christmas Island into areas of intense bird concentration. Of the approximately 20 species of birds known to nest on Christmas, none is as likely to attract attention—occasionally unwanted—from anglers as the greater frigate bird.

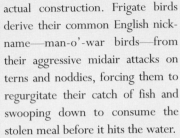

Fregata minor to scientists, *'iwa* to Hawaiians, *eitei* to the Gilbertese, these striking marine predators sport wingspans of over 7 feet. Males display an inflatable crimson throat sac while courting. Capable of gliding without apparent effort on ocean air currents, the frigate bird has a stately, graceful flight pattern that inspires many of the movements in traditional Gilbertese dance (which visitors should have a chance to enjoy during regular performances at the Captain Cook). In contrast to most avian species, females gather the materials for their clumsy nests while males perform the actual construction. Frigate birds derive their common English nickname—man-o'-war birds—from their aggressive midair attacks on terns and noddies, forcing them to regurgitate their catch of fish and swooping down to consume the stolen meal before it hits the water.

For better or worse, Christmas Island anglers are likely to see more frigate birds at close range than they wish. Easily attracted by surface disturbances, they often trail anglers across flats (to the consternation of bonefish) and materialize out of nowhere to attack surface poppers, which sometimes makes trevally fishing difficult if not impossible. Because hooking a frigate bird on a fly turns out to be no fun for either bird or angler, Christmas veterans soon learn to retrieve and move on at the first sign of those long, dark wings overhead.

Because Christmas lies so close to the equator, there is little seasonal variation in water conditions, making it one of the few places in the world to offer good flats fishing year-round. This makes Christmas an especially attractive flats destination for anglers eager for a break from midwinter weather but appropriately wary of cold fronts in the Caribbean.

Island dress remains ultimately informal. In terms of clothing, the only caveat is to pack plenty of lightweight long-sleeved shirts and pants to protect skin from the sun even while actively wading. Supplex garments are ideal for this purpose. Brimmed hats are essential for sun protection, and they'll also help you spot fish by reducing glare.

LAY OF THE LAND

Two small new hotels have been built on Christmas since I stayed at the original Captain Cook back in the early exploratory days: Joe and Eddie's Lodge and the Mini-London Hotel. But services and accommodations remain limited, and most visiting anglers opt for a full-service package provided by one of the booking agencies listed in Appendix C.

Those wishing to tackle the island on their own can find good fishing by foot from the road system, but the availability of rental vehicles is not always reliable. Consult the Air Kiribati office in advance.

Although sharks can excite the imagination,

the biggest health threat visitors face lies overhead, not underwater. At Christmas Island's low latitude, sunburn is a threat any time of day, any month of the year. Water quality at the Captain Cook is good; exercise caution when drinking from unreliable sources. The prevailing easterly winds keep bugs down across most of the island, and I've never had a problem with them except for occasional biting flies in the lagoon. Seasickness shouldn't be a problem in the lagoon's protected waters, although susceptible individuals venturing offshore should take appropriate precautions. Seafood forms a staple (and highly welcome) part of the local diet. Although ciguatera poisoning remains a theoretical concern, I'm not aware of any problems among visiting anglers. Visitors preparing fish on their own should heed local advice. The Centers for Disease Control (CDC) does not consider malaria prophylaxis necessary for visitors to Christmas Island. (See Appendix A for further information.)

Ancillary activities include bird watching (make time for the regular guided trip to the bird sanctuary on Cook Island) and bicycling. The reef offers interesting snorkeling opportunities, but my own experiences there—against local advice—have all been terminated prematurely by sharks.

CONTACTS

Because of limited services and accommodations, most visitors opt for one of the full-service fishing packages offered through booking agencies such as Fishabout or Frontiers as listed in Appendix C.
AIR KIRIBATI
888-800-8144

RECOMMENDED READING

■ *THE CHRISTMAS ISLAND STORY*, Eric E. Bailey (1977. Out of print. Stacey International.) Concise guide to the island's intricate history.

A 72-pound giant trevally for dinner. They grow to over 100 pounds and make for a demanding fight requiring heavy tackle.

■ *A VOYAGE TO THE PACIFIC OCEAN*, Captain James Cook and Captain James King (1784. Out of print. Stockdale and Fielding.) Cook—the Great Navigator—enjoyed one of the most remarkable careers in the history of exploration.
■ *THE LIFE OF CAPTAIN JAMES COOK*, John C. Beaglehole (1992. $24.95. Stanford University Press.) For those who sensibly don't feel like wrestling with the original version.
■ *FLY FISHING FOR BONEFISH*, Dick Brown (1993. $35.00. The Lyons Press.) An excellent species-specific guide to Christmas Island's signature game fish.

Opposite: Stalking bonefish on the Paris Island Flats, composed of hard coral and white coral sand.

The Missouri Headwaters

This divine little lick of clear water
is alive with trout every inch of the way

The banks of the creek lay awash in fall colors so beautiful I found it hard to concentrate on the water. Still waiting for the season's first frost to bring it to its knees, the grass stood tall in autumn yellow. But it was the willows that really caught the eye. Their leaves had turned a lush shade of maroon reminiscent of candlelight shining through a glass of cabernet. It takes a lot of scenery to make me forget about fishing, yet there I stood, knee-deep in one

of my favorite trout streams, concentrating on foliage rather than fish like a wide-eyed tourist.

But not for long. Despite the low angle of the sun, the stream ran so clear I could easily see fish holding in the current, biding their time as if they were the ones who had taken the afternoon off. They didn't seem to be doing much of anything, but if you can see fish in this stream they are bound to be feeding on something. With no surface activity to guide me, I tied on a Bead-Head

Fishing from a riverboat on the Big Hole. Hiring a boat and guide opens up larger rivers to anglers.

MONTANA

Big Hole River

Gallatin River

Bozeman

Billings

Madison River

Yellowstone River

IDAHO

YELLOWSTONE NAT'L PARK

WYOMING

Hare's Ear and went to work.

Granted, work might be something of a misnomer when used to describe standing in gorgeous water casting a 3-weight to a pool stuffed with fish. *Work* was what I had fled from an hour before. But I felt focused on the tricky business of getting the nymph down to the fish without spooking them, which required at least a measure of concentration. And *work* is a relative concept after all; compared to my earlier immersion in the scenery, the demands of accurate presentation almost resembled the real thing.

I needed several casts to get a measure of the drift and the nymph's rate of sink, all of which I worked out several yards downstream from the fish. Finally, I extended my reach and let the leader settle over the heart of the holding water. I quickly lost track of the fly, but when I saw one of the fish move purposefully from its lie, I raised the rod tip and came up fast against a lively rainbow.

Trout always seem more vigorous late in the season, although I don't know whether their enthusiasm on the end of a line represents a response to changing water temperature or general fitness after a long summer of easy living. But ours is not to reason why, especially with a hot trout on the end of a light line. The fish showed no hesitation about going airborne and I felt privileged to enjoy the show. When I finally guided the rainbow into the shallows and backed the hook from its lip, it flicked its tail and magically disappeared into the crystalline current.

As I stood up, a kingfisher rounded the bend downstream and headed across the pool. Off in the distance, the murmur of machinery rose above the sound of the creek as an ambitious farmer tried to coax a final cutting of alfalfa from a field. A muskrat emerged from the water on the opposite bank, jaws working against a mouthful of cattails as its auburn guard hairs

---

AT A GLANCE

SPECIES Rainbow, brown, and cutthroat trout; whitefish; occasional brook trout and grayling

TACKLE 3–4-weight rods for spring creeks, 5–6-weights for larger rivers; floating lines for most fishing; sink-tips for heavy nymphs and streamers in larger waters

FLIES Basic trout selection; caddis fly imitations beginning in May; giant stonefly nymphs and duns from late May–early July; dry hopper imitations from late July– mid-September; large streamers (Muddler Minnows, Woolly Buggers) for lakes and larger rivers

PRIME TIME May–October; some spring creeks and tailwater fisheries remain productive all year

CONSERVATION ISSUES Whirling disease, streamside development, dewatering by competing water users during dry summers, declining stocks of native cutthroat and grayling

PRICE RANGE Less than $1,500–$2,500

STAGING CITY Bozeman, Montana

HEADS UP Snakes are active along rocky banks in warm weather; don't put hands or feet anywhere you can't inspect visually

beaded in the sun. Then the kingfisher saw me and flared, and as I tracked its erratic flight up and away into the brilliant blue sky I realized how much more good trout streams have to offer than the sum of their fish.

Casting to big browns on the Madison River, one of America's favorite trout streams.

This was my home, and I wouldn't have traded it for another anywhere in the world.

MONTANA IS VAST COUNTRY, but simply describing it as the fourth-largest state in the nation doesn't begin to suggest the variety of interesting water it contains. In the northwest corner of the state, the broad-shouldered Kootenai holds some of the country's largest rainbows. Down in Custer country, the Bighorn represents one of America's most celebrated tailwater fisheries. Even the eastern prairies hold fish, from oversized trout in obscure spring-fed stock ponds to largely unheralded warmwater species such as smallmouth bass and pike.

Despite this embarrassment of riches, the heart of the Montana angling experience remains concentrated where the headwaters of the Missouri river system tumble down from the Yellowstone plateau. Lewis and Clark fell under the spell of this country in 1803, just as I did a century and a half later. Ask me to identify the best place in the world to fish day after day and I would point out simply that I voted with my feet. Montana remains my home with good reason.

I'm hardly the first fly-rod enthusiast to structure life around Montana's fishing possibilities. A generation ago, pioneers such as Dan Bailey, Joe Brooks, and Bud Lilly championed what are now Montana's Blue Ribbon streams and created a new American trout fishing manifesto in the process. Recognizing that what had worked for generations on eastern waters would not necessarily apply out west, they developed innovative techniques we take for granted nowadays: big nymphs, hair-wing dry flies, fishing from specially designed riverboats and rafts. If Montana hadn't provided such an appealing proving ground, fly fishing might never have progressed west of the Battenkill.

And they championed the waters as well as the fish. The resource might have seemed unlimited 50 years ago, but Montana's early anglers were perceptive enough to know better. From dams to dewatering to streamside development, Montanans have traditionally displayed a stubborn spirit of activism in the face of threats to their favorite trout streams. Although no one can claim ideal results, Montana waters have fared better than those in most other western states, thanks in large measure to the foresight of an earlier generation of anglers.

You can catch trout somewhere in just about every state in the Union. How much better can the fishing in Montana really be? Any

The early morning mist is burning off the Gallatin River just outside Yellowstone Park.

answer has to be subjective, but I would suggest up front that the issue goes beyond size and numbers of trout, even though the headwaters of the Missouri and the Yellowstone offer plenty of both. The streams look as appealing as the country they run through. Wildlife abounds. And despite modest population increases and a recent flurry of development, Montana still feels different from the rest of the country: older, wiser, more accommodating. In short, it would be a great place to visit even if there weren't any fish.

IT WAS THE SECOND WEEK of December and Lori, my old friend Dick LeBlond, and I were standing beside Nelson's Spring Creek, one of Montana's most celebrated trout streams. This divine little

lick of clear water rises on a working ranch and flows across private property for a mile or so before it dumps into the Yellowstone, and the water is alive with trout every inch of the way. During the summer, anglers fish it by reservation only, some having reserved years in advance.

But by the time the snow flies, the prime-time frenzy is done for the year. The parking area stood empty the morning we arrived, and when Dick walked up to the house to confirm his standing invitation to fish the creek during the off-season, there was no one there to greet him but an indifferent mongrel. "What do you think?" I asked when Dick trudged back to the truck.

"Let's go fishing," he suggested with a shrug, and that was good enough for us, even though the weather seemed more conducive to

CAPTAIN CLARK'S TROUT

Now that the Missouri headwaters have earned a reputation as a world-famous angling destination, it's easy to forget that the browns and rainbows responsible for most of the fuss are aliens. The rainbows originated west of the Continental Divide, where they shared biologic origins with modern Pacific salmon; the browns hailed from Europe and the British Isles. When Lewis and Clark first explored the area, the only trout they encountered was the beautiful, fragile species that now bears the name of one of the expedition's leaders: *Oncorhynchus clarki,* the cutthroat.

Here's what Meriwether Lewis had to say about the results of the fishing on the Missouri on June 13, 1805:

Goodrich had caught a half dozen very fine trout. . . These trout (caught in the Falls) are from sixteen to twenty three inches in length, precisely resemble our mountain or speckled trout in form and position of their fins, but the specks are of a deep black instead of the red or gold color of those common to the U. States. These are furnished long, sharp teeth on the palate and tongue, and generally a small dash of red on each side behind the front ventral fin. The flesh is of a pale yellowish red, or when in good order, of a rose pink.

As usual, Lewis offers an uncannily accurate description of a species unknown then to American naturalists east of the Mississippi.

Time and progress have not been kind to Captain Clark's trout. Although many of the cutthroat's problems in Montana today stem from habitat compromise by logging and mining, anglers must bear some responsibility themselves. The cutthroat simply can't compete with more aggressive browns and rainbows, species that have largely displaced it from much of its historic range. The cutthroat's decline simply demonstrates the potential cost of trying to make the natural world conform to our own idea of what's best, even when we act with good intentions.

Cutthroats still inhabit higher drainages in the Missouri headwaters, where Montana manages them on a catch-and-release basis. Savoring that rose-pink flesh as Lewis and Clark once did might be a pleasure of the past, but anglers can still enjoy the cutthroat both as a game fish and as a legacy of the original American West.

---

decoying ducks than casting to wary trout.

I drove down to the edge of the field and parked according to Dick's directions. Large, wet snowflakes dropped straight down from the sky, making the world beyond the windshield look like a Christmas card. *You can do this,* I told myself even though I wasn't sure I believed it.

We struggled into our boots and pulled on our vests and started across the pasture toward the thin gray line of steam that marked the creek's course. A flock of mallards materialized above the cottonwoods and descended toward the water with wings set and cold air whistling through their primaries. We all stopped to track their progress until they saw us and strained their way back into the snow overhead. Suddenly it was difficult to avoid imagining that there had been some mistake, that we had arrived at the wrong address on the wrong day by accident.

Once the ducks disappeared, we walked on across the frozen field until we stood beside the stream. The water slipped lazily along, so sterile and indifferent in the monochromatic world of winter that it was hard to suppress a sense of futility. There were no insects, nor was there any of the sensual urgency one expects from an active trout stream.

Then suddenly, there were the fish. At the head of the first pool, a lazy wake pushed its way across the channel, and when I concentrated I could see a dark shape beneath the surface, a brown trout substantial enough to demand immediate attention. Then a second disturbance appeared followed by another, until we stood looking at a riot of activity that reminded me of schooled bonefish working skinny water on a falling tide. "What do you suppose that's all about?" I wondered.

"Beats me," Dick replied.

"There sure are a lot of fish out there," Lori pointed out as we slid down the bank toward the water.

From creek level, I could finally appreciate the presence of insects on the surface. Excruciatingly tiny midges swarmed about the surface of the creek. I searched through my vest until I found an appropriate imitation, but I felt foolish as soon as I tied the fly to the tippet and even more foolish when it fell to the water. Whatever was happening out there did not involve fly patterns the size of commas, and there was no point pretending otherwise just because we happened to be fishing a spring creek famous for its sophisticated fish.

"Aw, hell," Dick finally suggested. "Try something big and nasty." That sounded like a wonderfully irreverent idea to me. I clipped off the midge and replaced it with a Woolly Bugger, and then I handed the rod to Lori and walked up the bank. The time had come to let someone else enjoy an opportunity to look foolish.

Lori is a lovely woman, but she was bundled up in layers of clothing topped off by a heavy wool vest. The bulk of this outfit and her thick mane of honey-colored hair made her look like a grizzly as she waded into the current and began to cast. Suddenly the sight of her consumed by determination forged one of those defining moments when you understand exactly why you love someone. I desperately wanted her to catch one of the big trout cruising around the pool because she looked like she deserved a good fish more than any angler I'd ever seen.

A 3-weight rod is not the ideal tool for handling a bulky streamer under the best of circumstances. As Lori eased across the current and began to cast, the cold and the size of the fly and the improbable delicacy of the water made the whole effort look like something out of a Saturday-morning cartoon show. Then the streamer plopped down in the middle of the cruising fish. As soon as she started to strip the line, the rod tip went down hard and a brown the size of my arm broke water in front of her as Dick and I swore together in amazement.

Because of my own laziness and skepticism, the rod was still rigged with a gossamer tippet left over from my earlier effort with the midge. Flush with excitement at the sight of the largest trout she had ever hooked, Lori clamped down on the line as soon as the fish started to run and that was that. Then she was laughing at the emptiness in front of her where the fish had been and we were laughing with her. There was no sense of loss because there had never been any sense of possession.

"That fish had to be over five pounds," I said, and Dick agreed. Lori was already searching through her vest for another streamer, and Dick suddenly seemed very interested in getting his

Float fishing a stretch of the Yellowstone River north of Yellowstone Park.

own gear assembled. Two rods were about all the little pool could handle, so I settled in on the bank to spot fish and offer advice. Lori was soon fast to another huge brown that came unbuttoned after a long fight. While she was occupied in the lower reaches of the pool, Dick landed and released a pair of smaller fish in the riffle at its head. Clearly something unusual was going on. Perhaps the fish had simply lost their senses after too many long winter nights and fallen victim to cabin fever like the rest of us.

After another 30 minutes of craziness, the pool just couldn't take it any longer. The cruising fish disappeared, and Lori and Dick reeled in their lines and climbed back up the bank where we all tried to make sense of what had taken place. Despite the size of the fish and the childish delight of finding them in such an unlikely mood, it was hard to ignore the idea that we had been taking advantage of something.

Back at the truck, I disassembled the rod and climbed into the cab and let the warmth of the heater flow across my hands. My beard was full of ice, and when I pressed my face against the comfort of Lori's neck she squiggled reflexively against the unexpected chill. Then Dick appeared out of the snow and climbed into the passenger side of the cab to share the warmth of the heater. He had taken another fish or two as well, but he agreed that there was nothing left for us any longer. We had found trout during the middle of a Montana winter, and today, that was enough.

WHAT TO EXPECT
ANGLING

Although Montana offers numerous lesser-known fishing opportunities in out-of-the-way places, the state's most famous waters lie in the area bounded approximately by Livingston, Yellowstone National Park, West Yellowstone, and Twin Bridges, including the Big Hole, Madison, Jefferson, Gallatin, Beaverhead, and Yellowstone Rivers. Although anglers certainly might wish to consider a side trip to the Glacier area or one of the famous tailwater stretches of the Big Horn or Missouri, the fishing is so good in the area described above that most first-time visitors will enjoy concentrating their efforts there.

Browns and rainbows coexist throughout most of the area's larger drainages, and anglers can generally expect to catch both species from the same water. Smaller mountain tributaries and the upper reaches of rivers such as the Yellowstone still contain significant populations of native cutthroats, which might well be the most beautiful freshwater game fish in North America. Like the arctic grayling, Montana's native cutthroats are now protected. Whitefish thrive in larger streams, and nymph fishermen will likely encounter more of them than they wish. Some high-country ponds and lakes contain introduced brook trout.

The brave at heart can find fishing opportunities year-round wherever there is open water, but the season really gets going in May, when caddis hatches start to appear and waters have not yet started to rise from spring runoff. The world-famous salmon fly hatch begins in early June on the Big Hole and Madison, and despite this annual event's hype and attendant crowds it still represents a unique opportunity to catch big trout on the surface. Early summer heralds orderly hatches of mayflies, and hoppers provide fast action during late summer, especially on smaller water. Streamers can take big fish any time of year, especially during the fall when browns begin to spawn. Montana insect hatches are complex, especially on the spring creeks. Consult Contacts or local fly shops for expanded information and recommendations.

Of the destinations reviewed in this book, none offers better opportunities for self-guided

Changing flies at a secluded bend on a small tributary of the Yellowstone River.

angling exploration. Public access points dot Montana's Blue Ribbon streams, and the state's Stream Access Law guarantees the right to float almost all the best water. Although some of the area's famous spring creeks lie on private property, local fly shops can usually arrange access for reasonable daily rates.

Access to a boat greatly enhances fishing opportunities along larger streams and rivers in this area. Obviously, hiring a qualified guide offers the easiest means to enjoy these waters by boat. For those with their own craft and a basic

shops can provide current information regarding water conditions and safety.

Mountain weather can deteriorate quickly and nights can be cold at higher elevations even during summer months. Expect wide daily temperature fluctuations and dress in layers, with light woolens available to ward off evening chill. Take both hip and chest waders if space allows, as well as comfortable hiking boots if you plan to explore backcountry waters.

Yellowstone National Park makes an attractive side-trip destination and offers rewarding fishing opportunities in a spectacular setting. While crowds choke the Park's road system during peak summer months, anglers willing to do a little hiking can still find relatively uncrowded water, and the traffic thins out considerably after Labor Day. Because of the park's unique natural beauty and abundant wildlife, it's really a shame to travel to the area without visiting.

LAY OF THE LAND

Anglers arriving by air generally fly into Bozeman, the closest major airport. Accommodations range from deluxe private lodges to roadside camping in numerous public campgrounds. Most of the area's smaller communities (Livingston, Gardiner, West Yellowstone, Twin Bridges, Dillon, Ennis) contain numerous motels and restaurants that cater to anglers during peak season. And in contrast to many secluded destinations where fly tackle is all but unavailable, all these towns contain superb fly shops that can provide state-of-the-art equipment and local advice.

Both black and grizzly bears roam the mountains near Yellowstone National Park. Because they are often habituated to human presence, these bears can cause more problems than their wilderness counterparts. Rattlesnakes

level of whitewater experience, most of these streams offer relatively tame boating. The Yankee Jim Canyon section of the upper Yellowstone is one notable exception, and on water downstream from dams, such as the Beaverhead, boaters must watch for rapidly rising water levels. Local fly

Above: Jewel-like rainbow taken from a float-tube on a pond in Montana's Paradise Valley. Opposite: Fishing the tail of a pool, Armstrong's Spring Creek, with the Absaroka Range in the background.

Brown trout taken on the Madison between Yellowstone Park and Hebgen Lake.

CONTACTS

YELLOWSTONE VALLEY RANCH
422 South Main
Livingston, MT 59047
800-626-3526
www.destinations-ltd.com
A beautiful full-service lodge on the Yellowstone River that offers opportunities to sample everything from big-water float trips to private ponds and spring creeks.

GEORGE ANDERSEN'S YELLOWSTONE ANGLER
Box 660
Livingston, MT 59047
406-222-7130
www.yellowstoneangler.com
A definitively stocked fly shop that also provides guide service and spring creek access.

DAN BAILEY'S FLY SHOP
209 W. Park, P.O. Box 1019
Livingston, MT 59047
800-356-4052, 406-222-1673
www.dan-bailey.com
An institution in the annals of American fly fishing.

MONTANA DEPARTMENT OF COMMERCE
800-847-4868
General tourism information.

MONTANA DEPARTMENT OF FISH, WILDLIFE AND PARKS
Region 3
406-994-4042
www.fwp.state.mt.us
Area-specific fishing information.

frequent rocky outcroppings and high grass along stream banks during warm summer months. Mosquitoes can be unpleasant at lower elevations. Untreated water from backcountry sources can transmit giardiasis. (See Appendix A for further information.)

Ancillary activities include whitewater canoeing and rafting, climbing, hiking, camping, horseback riding, wildlife viewing, and photography.

RECOMMENDED READING

■ *JOURNALS OF LEWIS AND CLARK,* edited by John Bakeless (1964. $4.50. Mentor Books.) An absolutely essential historical perspective.
■ *LEWIS AND CLARK: PIONEERING NATURALISTS,* Paul Russell Cutright (1989. $24.95. University of Nebraska Press.) Annotated material from the journals that reminds us what amazing observers Lewis and Clark really were.

Prime water on the Big Hole River near its confluence with the Wise River.

■ *MONTANA*, Clark Spence (1978. W.W. Norton.) Concise regional history.

■ *MONTANA TIME*, John Barsness (1992. Out of print. Lyons & Burford.) Wonderful personal angling reflections by a true Montanan.

■ *FLYFISHER'S GUIDE TO MONTANA*, Greg Thomas (1997. $26.95. Wilderness Adventure Press.) Definitive practical guide to Montana's fisheries.

■ *DREAM FISH AND ROAD TRIPS*, E. Donnall Thomas Jr. (1996. $22.95. The Lyons Press.) One of the book's three sections is devoted exclusively to Montana. Reading it won't teach you anything practical, but it will explain why I live here.

■ *KNEE DEEP IN MONTANA'S TROUT STREAMS*, John Holt (1996. $16.95. Pruett Publishing Co.) Not many angling writers combine practical information with great reading. John does.

■ *SPRING CREEK*, Nick Lyons (1995. $11.00. Atlantic Monthly Press.) Lyons and Montana; what more need I say?

■ *GREAT PLAINS*, Ian Frazier (1990. $13.95. Penguin.) Most visitors bypass the prairies and head for the mountain scenery. Frazier knows better.

■ *ROADSIDE GEOLOGY OF MONTANA*, David Alt and Donald W. Hyndman (1986. $20.00. Mountain Press Publishing Co.) How did the Grand Canyon of the Yellowstone become grand? This book tells all.

Los Roques

From conch to 'cuda,
Los Roques' flats teem with vitality

Despite a long, rewarding relationship with the human bosom, I've occasionally found its appearance little more than a distraction even in its finest form, at least while engaged in the pursuit of more elusive pleasures. Like bonefish.

Getting to the site of this delightful conflict had proved a minor challenge, testing my one-beer Spanish to its limits. Perpetually rusty, my language skills falter south of the border until the first cold *cerveza* flows, at which point I enjoy a brief period of verbal ebullience. Unfortunately, the second beer is usually a killer. I'd downed two back in the Caracas airport, which reduced me to gestures and infinitives, a state of fluency sufficient to let me realize our flight to Los Roques had been inexplicably cancelled, but wholly unsuited to the problem's solution.

Fortunately for our party, after a year in Caracas as a high school exchange student, my

At the Caribbean's southern limit, Los Roques offers long pristine beaches and big bonefish by the score.

CURAÇAO   ISLAS LOS ROQUES

BONAIRE BASIN   ISLA DE MARGARITA

ISLA LA TORTUGA

Caracas ★

VENEZUELA

daughter Jenny spoke machine gun Spanish, the kind that gets in your face and takes no prisoners. Between the two of us, we convinced the diffident clerk behind the desk that his well-practiced *"No hablo ingles"* wasn't going to get him off the hook. After an hour of frenzied negotiation, we found ourselves airborne above the Caribbean, our only hope being that the pilot's destination matched our own.

As indeed it did. Now as the warm Venezuelan sun began to sink toward the western horizon, Lori and I hopped over the side of our old friend Alex Gonzales' skiff on the upwind side of one of Los Roques' long sandy beaches. Although it was well past the hour when most guides and clients return to the dock, Alex understood our visceral need to fish until the bitter end, and the smooth white bottom just beyond the shoreline offered an opportunity to see fish even in the failing light. With a cheerful wave, Alex promised to pick us up a mile down the beach at dark, and then he headed back across the channel to attend to business on Grand Roque.

As we rounded a rocky point, we found ourselves in the middle of a party of visitors from Caracas who had evidently arrived by yacht. After a quick double take, I made a point of studying the water while Lori's eyes remained fixed on the beach ahead. "Unless I'm mistaken," she finally observed, "none of the señoritas are wearing bikini tops."

"What señoritas?" I replied innocently.

"Yeah, right," she snorted back, but before these circumstances could arouse any serious marital discord, I spotted a long gray shape cruising along the sand just beyond the slap of the waves. Since gallantry and discretion suddenly seemed the order of the day, I pointed out the fish to Lori and stepped back to watch her cast... among other things.

At least one of us was still capable of concentrating on the water. The stiff breeze we'd battled all day had fallen off at last, and her first double haul unfolded like a sweet, lazy dream. The fish darted toward the fly as soon as it settled toward the bottom, and when she struck back with her

AT A GLANCE

SPECIES Bonefish, tarpon, horse-eye and bar jacks, blue runners, snook, barracuda, snapper, permit

TACKLE 7–8-weight rods for bonefish, 10-weights for tarpon and big jacks; floating lines; 10–12# tippet for all species; heavy-monofilament shock tippet for jacks and tarpon, wire for barracuda

FLIES Basic flats and backcountry selections; include plenty of crab patterns for bonefish, and surface poppers for jacks

PRIME TIME February–May

CONSERVATION ISSUES Remarkably few, thanks to Los Roques' geographic isolation and status as a national park

PRICE RANGE $2,500–$3,500

STAGING CITY Caracas, Venezuela

HEADS UP Street crime is a common problem in Caracas

Top: Easy living on Grand Roque. Above: A Venezuelan horse-eye jack; their power can make even a seasoned saltwater angler nervous (see box, page 42).

and the sense of satisfaction amply compensated for all the miles we'd traveled to experience it.

"What a beautiful fish," Lori murmured as the freshly released bone flicked its tail and slid away toward deeper water.

"What fish?" I replied with mock indifference as I stared up the beach toward the picnic in progress, an indiscretion that earned me a shower of salt water from Lori's foot. Then we shared a laugh and started on our way once more.

SITUATED SOME 100 MILES NORTH of Caracas in the Lesser Antilles, Los Roques consists of a remote tropical archipelago inhabited full time by almost no one. When I first heard tales of Venezuelan bonefish a decade ago, the idea of fishing this remote corner of the Caribbean intrigued me at once. But before I could arrange a trip to the area, I began to hear disturbing rumors of organizational incompetence and difficult tides and wrote the place off my wish list for several years. Then my father, enjoying a well-deserved share of post-Nobel Prize (Medicine, 1990) celebrity, received an invitation to lecture in Venezuela. His hosts kindly arranged for my parents to fish at Los Roques, and they returned with stories of vast, pristine flats and big bonefish by the score. Jenny's subsequent stint as a student in Caracas provided an ideal excuse for a multigenerational expedition to Venezuela. After all the conflicting reports I'd heard, I wanted answers even more than I wanted bonefish. Would the real Los Roques please stand up?

Several days into that first trip, I felt qualified to address some of the reservations I'd heard about our destination. The first—lots of small bonefish—proved easy to dismiss. I don't doubt that the immense complex of flats and beaches surrounding home base on Grand Roque holds some 2-pound bonefish, but we sure had trouble finding them. Most of the fish we caught weighed between 5 and 7 pounds. I landed several 8-pounders and broke off larger specimens. We cast to double-digit

line hand the rod tip bucked and she let out a war whoop that brought an appreciative round of smiles from our unexpected audience. Big bonefish seem to defy physics on the end of light line, and even after a lot of years and a lot of bones the sense of disbelief we shared during that first long run felt incomparable, a sea level jump into the angler's equivalent of hyperspace. Forget the fish itself, a glistening 7-pounder that eventually lay quietly across Lori's outstretched hand. The explosion of strength and the scream of the reel were what really counted. That was what we had come for and that was what the sea had given us,

A bonefish guide prompts his "sport" to retrieve line. High wind, strong tides, and complex terrain demand intimate knowledge of the water, and that demands that you hire an experienced guide.

bones every day, and my father landed a solid 10-pound fish that looked as if it had been raised on steroids. Enough said about *that.*

As for charges of disorganization and incompetent guides, I can report only what we experienced firsthand. After several seasons working for other lodge operators, Walter Ehrlich and Alex Gonzales broke away and established their Pez Raton Lodge to offer clients the kind of experience a venue as vast and complex as Los Roques demands. I found them as savvy and enthusiastic as any flats guides I've ever fished with, the kind of people whose company I enjoyed even more at the end of a long day than at the beginning. Although I imagine every kid on Grand Roque has worked as a guide at some time, lack of competence was simply not an issue at Pez Raton. High wind, strong tides, and complex terrain demand

intimate knowledge of the water in order to find a quarry as fickle as bonefish, but Alex and Walter provided just that kind of expertise.

Los Roques' reputation for challenging fishing conditions proved better founded. We experienced plenty of wind and relatively brisk tides, requiring sound casting technique. I didn't find this a problem and caught plenty of bonefish to prove it, but I would suggest that Los Roques is better suited to intermediate to advanced saltwater anglers than to beginners.

Los Roques offers a number of unique attractions as a bonefish destination, including a tremendous variety of shallow-water habitat. We stalked tailing schools of bonefish in skinny water and cast at big cruising singles in the surf. We waded isolated pancake flats in the middle of the central lagoon, picked our way through mangrove channels, and chased bones down long, pristine beaches that appeared to stretch away forever toward the indefinite blue horizon. We strained our eyes against eelgrass bottoms and spotted fish on white sand so smooth and pure you could easily see fish in 8 feet of water. We anchored up for lunch next to vast muds and caught fish backhanding weighted Clousers into the milk water while we ate our sandwiches. In short, I know no other destination that offers such a splendid variety of bonefishing experiences.

And for those who share my preference for stalking bones on foot, Los Roques offers unrivaled wading opportunities. The area's apparently endless supply of hard-bottomed ocean flats offers limitless opportunities to take the chase to the fish on foot. And from conch to 'cuda, Los Roques' flats teem with a vitality that guarantees the observant angler's attention between fish.

Of course, bones aren't the only species of game fish that inhabit the islands' fertile inshore waters. The area does hold permit, but they frequent the flats only during high autumn tides. Tarpon numbers fluctuate with the unpredictable arrival and departure of sardines. During a recent return trip, I spent an afternoon targeting tarpon rolling in the surf, where I took fish in the 40- to 60-pound range. The area supports vast, aggressive schools of bar jacks, horse-eyes, and blue runners, and we've enjoyed furious action sight-casting to

JACKS OF ALL TRADES

The family *Carangidae* represents a diverse group of predatory fishes distributed about both the Atlantic and Pacific, including such well-known game fish as permit, amberjacks, pompano, and roosterfish. For some reason, the true jacks (genus *Caranx*) have never enjoyed wide popularity among fly-rod anglers, which I've always found surprising, as they strike flies readily and fight as hard pound for pound as nearly any fish in the sea. I know few destinations better suited to the proof of this opinion than Los Roques.

Bar jacks *(Caranx ruber)* and blue runners *(Caranx crysos)* run in large schools near rocky outcroppings and the edges of bonefish flats. Hunting in packs like wolves, they often work schools of hapless baitfish into such a frenzy that they leap ashore in desperate attempts to escape. Such disturbances are often visible at great distances, and anglers who can catch up with the fish should expect prompt strikes on virtually any streamer or popper pitched into the melee.

Although extremely vigorous on light tackle, representatives of these two species seldom weigh more than 5 or 6 pounds. The Atlantic horse-eye *(Caranx latus)* is the real heavyweight of the clan, with specimens over 30 pounds common in Venezuelan waters. Schools of horse-eyes frequent rock formations near deep water, where the trained eye can often spot their characteristic golden flash well beneath the surface. Horse-eyes readily take large surface poppers. Unlike most jacks, horse-eyes lack sharp teeth, so they can be taken without wire leaders. Long casts and fast retrieves offer the best chance of drawing a strike, especially when aided by a second angler casting a teaser plug with a spinning rod.

The sight of a big horse-eye jack accelerating toward a fly on the surface can make even a seasoned saltwater angler nervous, and the wild run that inevitably follows a hookup can test strong fly tackle to its limits. Visitors to Los Roques should plan to devote some time to the pursuit of these splendid, underappreciated game fish.

schools of jacks hammering baitfish in shallow water. Incidental to the pursuit of these fly-rod standards, I've taken a variety of interesting species at Los Roques, ranging from barracuda to mutton snapper to mackerel.

Despite the stiff breeze, I found a 7-weight rod perfectly adequate for all my bonefishing needs, primarily because we usually managed to fish downwind. I did appreciate my 10-weight when it came time to target fast-moving schools of jacks, especially horse-eyes, which can exceed 30 pounds and are strong enough to challenge any permit tackle. Otherwise, gearing up for Los Roques is a straightforward affair. All you need is a pair of tough, comfortable wading boots, high-quality polarized glasses, and great quantities of enthusiasm.

Especially the latter.

FOR YEARS, THE SPANISH term for bonefish—*pez raton*—translated literally as "rat fish," left me mystified. I frankly failed to understand the allusion. One day Alex reminded me that *raton* also means "mouse," and as I watched a trio of gray shapes working toward me against the tide I had to agree that they darted and scurried about just like mice crossing a bare hardwood floor. Easing across the sand to intercept the fish, I watched them appear and disappear by magic as the axis of their bodies fluctuated in relationship to the sun. Finally I realized I had drawn as close as I was going to get and shot an ambitious crosswind cast in their direction.

Estimating leads accurately under such conditions always proves difficult. When the fly hit the water a dozen feet in front of the fish, I rated my effort as good but by no means great. Fortunately, bones as aggressive as those at Los Roques have a way of making up for occasional lapses in accuracy. I hesitated for a moment after the cast to let the fish close upon the fly's position, and at the first quick strip from my line hand one veered off course and pounced.

At the first sting of the hook, the fish turned

A wire tippet is the order of the day when going after barracuda.

and accelerated for deep water. The slack line between my left hand and the reel shot toward the lower guide in a riot of loops and coils that threatened to throw a lethal half hitch around the rod butt. Somehow the line managed to find its way to freedom, leaving me to enjoy the sound of the drag and the naked energy of that first great run. I knew the fish was big, but as the backing began to evaporate from the reel I finally realized that it might just be a bit *too* big. I tightened the drag another click and added a bit of palm without apparent effect. Finally there was nothing left to do but set off across the sand in pursuit.

For better or worse, I'll never know whether that fish would have spooled me. A lone mangrove shoot rose from the water at the distant edge of the flat and whether by accident or design, the fish seemed intent on reaching it. I broke into a high-stepping trot to try to decrease the angle between the line and the obstruction, to no avail. The fish shot around the snag like a skier on a slalom course and the line went dead and that was all.

Bonefish are plentiful on the flats surrounding Los Roques, including plenty of 6- to 8-pounders.

"What happened?" Lori cried above the sound of the wind as I reeled in the remains of the wreckage.

"He found the only snag on the flat!" I yelled back. And that was the end of the postmortem, as Lori went on point and began to false-cast toward a glimmer of tails rising above the surface in front of her. The rest of my explanation would have to wait, for Los Roques is a place you go to fish rather than to talk about fishing.

And isn't that the best kind of destination of all?

WHAT TO EXPECT

ANGLING

In a fit of good judgment, the Venezuelan government made the Los Roques archipelago a national park years ago. The resulting ban on development and most commercial fishing helps ensure its unique ambience in perpetuity. Grand Roque, the only settlement in the islands, remains little more than a spruced-up fishing village. Visitors can stay at any one of a number of small *posadas,* most of which cater to divers and windsurfers. Although I've caught fish wading on my own along Grand Roque's shore, you'll need to travel by boat to fish the vast surrounding waters. Staying at Pez Raton or one of the other fishing lodges on the island offers the best opportunity to explore the area and enjoy the fishing.

Bonefish and jack species abound in local waters throughout the year. March, April, and May are traditionally the most popular fishing months. Our initial visit took place in May, but I've subsequently enjoyed great fishing during winter months as well. October and November are the best months for permit but, as noted, high tides then can make flats fishing difficult, and Los Roques does not enjoy a reputation as a permit destination. Tarpon come and go unpredictably with the baitfish.

Although I've devoted all my efforts in Venezuela to the flats fishing at Los Roques, other fly-rod opportunities abound. Estuaries along the Caribbean such as Rio Chico support good numbers of small tarpon and snook. Inland lakes and rivers provide exciting fishing for exotic freshwater species such as peacock bass and payara. Excellent billfish opportunities can be found in the blue water off the coast at La Guaira.

Flats anglers should wear hats and long-sleeved, fast-drying clothing adequate to provide sun protection. High-quality flats wading boots and polarized glasses are essential.

LAY OF THE LAND

Most trips to Venezuela begin in Caracas. Regularly scheduled jet service to Caracas on United or American Airlines originates in Miami and Houston. Depending on connections, most visitors overnight in Caracas either coming or going. Regular air service links Caracas to Los Roques, and most lodges include these flights in their basic fishing package. Warning: Departure times can be unreliable!

Caracas is a sprawling metropolis that abundantly illustrates the gulf between Latin America's rich and poor. The city contains excellent restaurants and museums. Touring Caracas with friends, we found its inhabitants unfailingly gracious, although street crime, occasionally violent, warrants a level of caution. The international airport lies some distance from town, and visitors in transit to remote fishing destinations can save time by planning overnight stays in one of the numerous hotels close to the airport. Venezuela's relatively robust, oil-driven economy makes it substantially more expensive to visit than many South American countries.

Street crime remains a problem in Caracas but not on Grand Roque. Tap water is safe on the island and in major hotels in Caracas, but exercise caution elsewhere. Sunburn is a constant threat at this latitude. Biting insects are not a problem in the islands. The Centers for Disease Control (CDC) recommends malaria prophylaxis for visitors to low-lying areas on the Venezuelan mainland. (See Appendix A for further information.)

Dress on Grand Roque is strictly casual, but take one set of presentable clothing for nights out in Caracas where, as in many Latin American cities, moderately formal dress standards apply.

Ancillary activities include excellent snorkeling, diving, beachcombing, and windsurfing.

CONTACTS

PEZ RATON LODGE
Contact Alex Gonzales directly by FAX (011-582-

A very nice bonefish. Los Roques' especially aggressive bonefish will veer toward even poorly aimed casts.

975-0355) or e-mail pezratonfishing@cantv.net, or book through Frontiers (see Appendix C).

RECOMMENDED READING

■ *FLY-FISHING THE FLATS*, Barry and Cathy Beck (1999. $39.95. Stackpole Books.) An excellent general reference, and the Becks are well acquainted with Los Roques.

■ *FLY FISHING FOR BONEFISH*, Dick Brown (1993. $35.00. The Lyons Press.) An authoritative species-specific guide to Los Roques' premier game fish.

Tierra del Fuego

I began to feel the sense of wonder Charles Darwin must have experienced when he passed through the Strait of Magellan

I knew Buenos Aires by reputation as a charming, vibrant city, but our first impressions left little to support this view.

The fault lay with us. En route to Tierra del Fuego to explore new fishing opportunities, my friend Dick LeBlond and I arrived at the Miami airport only to discover that our attempt to save a few bucks by booking on an obscure Paraguayan carrier had backfired badly. The airline had declared bankruptcy and grounded all flights. A helpful clerk at a neighboring counter suggested that United Airlines might honor our tickets. The United agent initially looked at us as if we had attempted to purchase fares with Monopoly money, but after some pleading and a few phone calls, we were on our way. By the time we finally touched down in BA, we were so happy to be there that not even the fatigue incurred during the long flight could keep us down. We were ready to see the city.

Author Tom McGuane (center) and Patagonia founder Yvon Chouinard (right) with guide along the Rio Grande.

ARGENTINA

CHILE

Strait of Magellan

ATLANTIC

Rio Grande

Rio Grande

TIERRA DEL FUEGO

The city, however, was not ready to see us. As we headed out of the hotel that afternoon, the streets stood eerily deserted, shops and galleries shuttered and boarded as if against an approaching storm. We wondered briefly if we had landed in the middle of an unannounced civil war. Unable to find a place to eat, we finally gave up and went to a matinee showing of *Schindler's List,* a splendid piece of cinema that nonetheless left us in a somber mood poorly suited to the exploration of one of our hemisphere's great capitals.

Of course, we had simply forgotten about the sacred Latin tradition of the siesta, an institution no country exercises as religiously as Argentina. When we finally emerged from the theater early that evening, the recently deserted streets stood choked with throngs of people obviously engaged in celebration. It took us a while to realize that the occasion was nothing more extraordinary than nightfall in Buenos Aires. We spent the rest of the evening wandering from one restaurant veranda to the next, visiting, people watching, and stuffing ourselves pleasantly with great food. When the effects of

our long travel day finally caught up with us and we headed back to our hotel, I had the feeling that the city was just beginning to wake up. And why not? It was only midnight.

The following morning, our flight south left us feeling as if we had suddenly been transported from Paris to Alaska's north slope. The barren, windswept hills of Tierra del Fuego could not have contrasted more sharply with the urban bustle we had just left behind. As we descended toward the gateway outpost of Rio Grande, I noted the complete absence of small-craft facilities along the Atlantic shore, a nearly certain indication of brutal conditions at sea. We were obviously entering wild and lonely country, and I had to admit that Tierra del Fuego looked like my kind of place.

During the drive inland through the foothills toward the sprawling Estancia San Jose ranch, I studied the legendary Rio Grande through the window as it turned from a brackish tidal slough into a rugged semblance of a trout stream. The banks stood bare of vegetation, and

---

AT A GLANCE

SPECIES Sea-run browns and native rainbows

TACKLE 8–9-weight rods with high-capacity reels; floating and sinking-tip lines with 12# tippet; twist-on lead to vary rate of sink

FLIES Basic anadromous selection, weighted and unweighted

PRIME TIME February–March

CONSERVATION ISSUES Unintentional introduction of deleterious exotic species and fish pathogens

PRICE RANGE $3,500+

STAGING CITY Buenos Aires, Brazil

HEADS UP Risk of hypothermia in cold waters

the wind pushed the current backward into little standing waves driven by enough muscle to challenge any fly line. Then a herd of wild guanacos galloped across the road in front of our car. Fleet, shaggy beasts the height of cow elk, they looked like props left over from a *Star Wars* set. A flock of flamingos appeared over the river, pink plumage glistening in the midday sun. As ashy-headed geese rose in a vortex from a nearby field, I began to feel the sense of wonder Charles Darwin must have experienced when he passed through the Strait of Magellan aboard the *Beagle.* "Can you believe this?" I finally asked Dick incredulously.

"No," he mumbled back.

Good, I thought, because I couldn't either.

At least in theory we had come as anglers and not as naturalists, and by the time we reached our quarters and visited with hosts Pierre Candido and Tom Brady, I found myself more interested in what lay beneath the river's surface than above. For the Rio Grande might be the best place in the world to catch giant sea-run brown trout, or *plateados* as these splendid fish are known locally. As a rule, I seldom leave home to fish for trout, simply because I don't need to travel to do what I can do in my own backyard. But these trout were different: hopelessly oversized versions of our familiar browns, brawny and beautiful, packed with the extra measure of vigor salmonids always acquire when they've spent some time at sea.

The following morning, I stood tucked in the lee of a wooded bank, studying the current as the Rio Grande tumbled gracefully past toward the sea. The Estancia San Jose is the last ranch upstream before the unmarked Chilean border, and in contrast to some better-known fishing lodges farther downriver, it contains enough terrain and vegetation to offer some protection

WHERE'S THE BEEF?

In contrast to Americans, Argentines don't just eat. They *dine,* and unless you happen to be a vegetarian, the cuisine and the enthusiasm that accompany it should provide nearly as many memories as the fish.

The abundance of red meat on the typical Argentine table should come as no surprise, as the country is one of the world's largest beef exporters. Fortunately, quality matches quantity, and with all due respect to my many Montana ranching friends I have to say that the Argentines know how to make beef—and lamb, for that matter— better than anyone else in the world. Visitors can expect the opportunity to consume it in staggering quantities.

A brief vocabulary will help introduce the visitor to the world of Argentine beef. *Lomo* refers to various prime cuts of loin, and the term is ubiquitous on menus for breakfast, lunch, and dinner. *Bife de costilla* corresponds to our T-bone. *Asado* means "roast," and in Argentina the term applies to a style of cooking as well as to a cut of meat. An *asado* usually takes place outdoors, as in an American barbecue, and the "roast" can involve most of a cow. *Jugoso* means "rare," *a punto* "medium," and *bien hecho* "well done." In my opinion, most Argentine beef is too good to justify anything but *jugosa.*

It would seem criminal to dine on such great beef without an appropriate wine to accompany it. Fortunately, Argentina's underrated wine producers offer both wide selection and quality at bargain prices, including such familiar varietals as cabernet sauvignon, merlot, and pinot noir.

Enjoy.

The Rio Grande is an angler-friendly river, easy to wade and free of obstructions. But there is always the wind.

against the island's relentless winds. I started to tie on a deliciously ugly Egg-Sucking Leech, but Tom convinced me to try one of his sparsely tied Atlantic salmon flies. Easing into the water, I positioned myself so that I could quarter my cast downstream with the wind. This arrangement didn't lend itself to classic presentation, but when battling the elements one learns to be creative. As I worked my 7-weight furiously against the wind on my back cast, I knew full well that I looked like an American barbarian rather than a dignified visiting angler. At least the delicate little number on the end of my tippet suggested decorum, a concession I hoped would not be lost upon the *plateados*.

The pursuit of anadromous fish often requires a nearly impossible level of faith, driven by the knowledge that even the best waters can

lie barren on any given day. With no hatches or signs of surface-feeding activity to rouse the spirit, a cold, dark stream like the Rio Grande can challenge anyone's enthusiasm. Of course, Dick had landed a small bright *plateado* in the dark the night before, and Tom assured us we should be fishing the peak of the run, but still. Bracing myself against the wind, I summoned forth the tenacity I developed as a kid on the steelhead streams of the Pacific Northwest and began to work the water with a vengeance, hoping against hope, awaiting the Great Perhaps.

FEW VERTEBRATE SPECIES have dispersed to the far-flung corners of the earth as successfully as *Salmo trutta*, the brown trout. From the icy waters of New Zealand's South Island to the

A magical evening on the Rio Grande; these two anglers took 15 big browns.

highlands of the Transvaal, browns have essentially reproduced the outlines of the former British empire, establishing thriving populations across more lines of latitude and longitude than any other game fish I know. Much of their success in these new habitats derives from their adaptability and predatory vigor. But the cosmopolitan brown owes no small debt to the enthusiasm of its admirers, who often went to remarkable lengths to introduce the species to new waters far removed from its original Old World home. Here in the United States, browns have been an angling staple for so long that we tend to forget they originated on the other side of the Atlantic.

In Tierra del Fuego, the brown trout's equivalent of Johnny Appleseed came in the form of one John Goodall, an obsessed Anglo-Argentine who refused to take no for an answer. Rainbows and brook trout arrived in Argentina shortly after the turn of the century, but early brown trout introductions failed. In the 1930s, Goodall, using stocks imported from Chile—

derived in turn from Germany by way of the United States—established breeding populations in a number of Argentine waters. And on Tierra del Fuego, the browns not only thrived but also returned to the sea to develop outlandish size and vigor, a biologic trick duplicated only in the northern British Isles and certain drainages in New Zealand and Chile.

Today, angling for the legendary *plateados* remains anything but a casual undertaking. Tierra del Fuego lies a long way from anywhere, as navigators have appreciated since the age of Ferdinand Magellan. The next stop south is Antarctica. The landscape greets the eye harshly at first, evoking a sense of loneliness appropriate to the wildest reaches of Alaska. And the wind seems sent by capricious gods to scour the face of the earth.

But it doesn't take long to begin to appreciate the beauty of the terrain. A hodgepodge of indigenous species and hardy imports, the flora quickly begins to haunt the imagination. The birdlife covers the spectrum, from penguins to parrots. And the people of Tierra del Fuego demonstrate the kind of enthusiastic hospitality unique to residents of lonely places who habitually regard the occasional visitor as a godsend rather than a pain in the ass.

And then there are the fish.

BACK STREAMSIDE, I've finally worked out the precarious vectors of wind and drift. The fly is sweeping delicately through the sweet spot just above the river's smooth gravel floor when the line hesitates and I haul back as if my life depended upon the outcome of the strike. At the touch of the hook the fish kicks back and goes airborne, nearly a yard of metal-bright iridescence suspended in the oblique rays of the low morning sun. *Plateado:* Now I get it.

Sometimes, the first encounter with a new game fish disappoints when you finally manage to get one on the end of a line. After all, not everything can live up to its advance billing. But this fish is the real thing, big enough to challenge the rod's spine and packing plenty of punch to test the reserves of my reel. As I study my dwindling line supply, Dick whoops downstream and raises his rod tip against another fish's first mad run. For the moment, I've forgotten all about the geese and the parrots, the guanacos and the haunted light spilling over the horizon from the nearby South Atlantic. This is what we have come for, and the fish seem worth every bit of effort required to experience them.

In Tierra del Fuego, a lamb dinner does not mean chops or ragout. It means, well...a lamb. By the time we finally return to base that night, numb and pleasantly exhausted, Pierre has the whole damn thing turning slowly on a spit over the coals to remind us just how many calories we've expended and how hungry we really are. By now, I should know better than to rehydrate with wine after a long day afield, but Pierre has a sampling of Argentina's splendid reds laid out on the table and the selection proves irresistible. Before long we've ripped into the lamb like wolves and

Tom McGuane with a 25-pound sea-run brown trout, for which the lower Rio Grande is famous.

raised our glasses in unison to the fish.

As always, to the fish.

WHAT TO EXPECT

ANGLING

Extending to latitude 55 degrees south, Tierra del Fuego is the world's southernmost landmass outside Antarctica. Chile and Argentina share the island, divided by a rather arbitrary border running north and south. Brook trout, rainbows, and Pacific salmon are all found on the Chilean side, which I have fished only inadvertently, when I wandered across the unmarked border one day during an ambitious upstream hike from the Estancia San Jose. The Rio Grande is by far the most productive stream in the area. Although many aspects of the *plateados'* life cycle remain a mystery, some fish no doubt stop short and spawn in the lower reaches of the river. Nonetheless, I enjoyed fishing the upper river because it offers pleasant wading, and the trees along the banks afford some shelter from the wind.

Despite its harsh surroundings, the Rio

Wind dryer following a shower. The autumn weather is brisk and windy, so light woolens and windbreakers are in order.

Grande turns out to be a remarkably angler-friendly river, easy to wade and free of obstructions. In its upper reaches, it's easy to cross the main river on foot, at least in chest waders. Although a sturdy 7-weight outfit will handle the fish, high winds make it easier to cast with 8- or 9-weight tackle. The largest fish we took on our visit weighed around 15 pounds, but 30-pound browns run the river, so reels should contain at least 200 yards of backing. Sea-run browns are not selective and at times they will hit nearly anything; dedicated top-water enthusiasts have even taken them on dry flies.

Peak runs take place during the southern autumn, February and March. The weather is pleasantly brisk at this time of year. Visitors should expect plenty of wind and dress accordingly, with light woolens and windbreakers appropriate to fall in the mountain West.

Overloading your rod by one or two line weights will make casting easier under inevitable windy conditions.

LAY OF THE LAND

Flights to Buenos Aires are long and somewhat costly. Only one time zone separates Argentina from our own East Coast, so jet lag doesn't pose a problem despite the length of the flight. Although it's possible to connect through directly to Rio Grande, Buenos Aires is one of the world's loveliest and most entertaining cities, and I can't imagine visiting Tierra del Fuego without overnighting there both coming and going.

Few special health concerns apply to visitors to Argentina. Fingerless wool gloves and neoprene chest waders will increase comfort levels during long days on the water. (See Appendix A for further information.)

In common with many isolated island ecosystems, Tierra del Fuego supports an unusual mixture of wildlife, both indigenous and introduced. The lower reaches of the Rio Grande pass through flat, largely treeless terrain reminiscent of Alaskan tundra. Farther upstream, the river descends through rolling hills covered with relatively dense foliage. Flamingos frequent the river bottom while vast flocks of ashy-headed geese cover the fields, and Andean condors soar overhead. Patagonian foxes prowl the brush and guanacos, the largest members of the llama family, roam freely across the open plains.

Ancillary activities include horseback riding, wildlife viewing, and photography.

Kau-Tapen Lodge, located well downstream of Estancia San Jose, is the oldest fly-fishing operation in the area.

CONTACTS

ESTANCIA SAN JOSE

Located high upstream on the Rio Grande, the stretch of river on this working ranch offers easy wading and terrain protection from incessant winds.

TOON KEN LODGE

www.angleradventures.com
TIERRADELFUEGO/TDF.htm
Located on the Estancia San Julio, this lodge offers unspoiled access to a large section of the middle Rio Grande.

KAU-TAPEN LODGE

www.frontierstrvl.com
Located still farther downstream, Kau-Tapen is the oldest fly-fishing operation in the area. More big *plateados* probably come from this stretch of the river than any other, but visiting anglers should expect plenty of wind.

RECOMMENDED READING

- *IN PATAGONIA,* Bruce Chatwin (1988. $13.95. Penguin.) One of the most imaginative travel books ever written.
- *ARGENTINE TROUT FISHING,* William C. Leitch (1991. $24.95. Frank Amato Publications.) The definitive regional fly-fishing guide.
- *THE VOYAGE OF THE BEAGLE,* Charles Darwin (Multiple editions in print.) Some of the seminal observations that changed our view of the biological world over a hundred years ago.

The Central Coast

*...the fish towered overhead, framed by nothing but
the tops of the mangroves and clear blue sky*

A nice snapper taken on a fly.

I love the sight of tailing bonefish. Although cruising bones often appear as little more than subtle patterns of dots and dashes displayed against a complex visual background, their tailing counterparts look tangible and fishy even at a distance. Tropical sun has a way of making bonefish tails glisten that suggests precious metal, or mica swirling underfoot at the bottom of a trout stream. Experienced flats anglers also know that tailing bones equal feeding bones, which means a well-presented fly is more likely to result in a quick take than a frustrating refusal. And bonefish have big tails; a tailing 4-pounder can easily masquerade as a fish several sizes larger, a delicious illusion one should savor as long as possible.

Hence the excitement Lori and I felt as Charlie cut the motor and let the skiff ease onto the flat somewhere in the Hen and Chickens Cayes north of Belize City. Back in the skinny water next to the mangroves, tails waved in the

AMBERGRIS CAY

Belize City

Belize River

TURNEFFE ISLANDS

Dangriga

GLOVER'S REEF

BELIZE

Punta Gorda

CARIBBEAN SEA

sunlight as a half-dozen scattered singles rooted through the marl for their breakfast. The caye's soft-bottomed lee made wading impossible, which meant that one of us had to take a long shot from the bow. "You first," I urged Lori as I unlimbered my trusty four-piece Sage.

"They're out of my range," Lori replied.

A true gentleman might have insisted, but I've never been one to stand on ceremony. Never mind that the fish were nearly out of my range too. After an overlong absence from the flats, I *needed* a bonefish and Lori knew it.

Charlie worked the skiff as close as possible as I worked a loop of line into the still morning air. The cast proved accurate, but the bead-eyed Crazy Charlie hit the crystalline water with a faintly audible *plop* that immediately sent its intended target streaking through the sound barrier. "Need to change flies," Charlie suggested from the stern. Nothing makes easy knots difficult like the proximity of fish, and I complied with nervous fingers as he eased us toward another potential target.

This time my presentation felt as delicate and dreamy as a cast meant for a wary spring-creek brown, and the fish pounced on the fly at once. The acceleration of a bonefish's first wild run enjoys a prominent position on my personal short list of favorite experiences, and this one did not disappoint. I was rigged light, and in less time than it takes to tell, an uncomfortably limited reserve of backing remained on my reel.

Belizean waters suffer from a reputation for small bonefish, and in a sense this conventional wisdom proves accurate: There are a lot of small bonefish in Belize. But there are nice bonefish too, especially in out-of-the-way backwaters like those we were fishing. This fish would have pushed 8 pounds, and with my heavy rod lying in the bottom of the skiff, rigged for permit, it was about as much bonefish as I could handle. But the flat was free of obstructions, and after its second run the fish was soon trailing along beside the boat like a puppy on a gossamer leash.

I bent over the gunwale, anointed my

AT A GLANCE

SPECIES Bonefish, permit, tarpon, snook, jacks, barracuda, snapper

TACKLE 7–8-weight rods for bonefish, 9–10-weights for permit and snook, 10–12-weights for tarpon; floating lines; heavy-monofilament shock tippet for tarpon and snook

FLIES Basic flats and backcountry selections; include some small bonefish flies—down to hook size #10

PRIME TIME February–June

CONSERVATION ISSUES Coastline development, local overharvesting of fish stocks

PRICE RANGE $2,500–$3,500

STAGING CITY Belize City, Belize

HEADS UP Street crime has become a significant problem in parts of Belize City

MERMAIDS

Belize contains the largest population of manatees in the world outside southern Florida, and it is the only place I've ever seen one in the wild. While running from Placentia to Monkey River by skiff one day, we spotted a huge tan blob swimming along the far side of the channel and cut the motor immediately. Although manatees are widely regarded as the likely source of early Caribbean sailors' tales of mermaids, I have to report that any observer who perceived a resemblance between manatees and attractive women must have been at sea for some time.

Biologically distinct from other marine mammals, manatees share evolutionary links with the Australian dugong and the elephant. Adult manatees can weigh a ton. Unlike other marine mammals, they are strict herbivores and can consume 500 pounds of forage daily. Formerly abundant throughout the Caribbean, manatees are now an endangered species and enjoy protection as such along our own southern coast. Belizeans traditionally hunted manatees for food, and I can remember Belizean friends setting off in pursuit of manatees years ago, which just goes to show how much things have changed since I first started visiting the country. Nowadays, Belize strictly protects its manatee population. Propeller strikes from outboard motors remain a leading cause of mortality throughout the manatee's range, so exercise appropriate caution whenever boating through manatee habitat.

hands briefly in a sensuous balm of bonefish slime, and released the fish. "Thanks," I said to Lori. "I needed that."

"I know," she replied.

"This next one's yours," I said. "And this time I mean it." As she climbed onto the bow beside me, I handed her the rod and scanned the flat in front of us. Bonefish tails and nervous water covered the surface in all directions. Our first priority wasn't finding a fish but deciding which one to address.

Only in Belize.

ON GEOGRAPHIC GROUNDS ALONE, the tiny Central American republic of Belize qualifies a priori as a saltwater fly-fishing haven. Although the entire country is smaller than the state of Vermont, an incredibly complex coastline provides pristine habitat for a variety of inshore game fish. Over 400 low-lying cayes dot the water between the New World's only true barrier reef and the mainland. Two complex coral atolls—the Turneffe Islands and Glover's Reef—enclose hundreds of miles of protected shoreline. Throw in the mainland's myriad mangrove-lined creeks and brackish jungle rivers, and it's easy to realize Belize contains more interesting water than any of us could fish in a lifetime.

Needless to say, this complex marine ecosystem offers the fly-rod enthusiast an incredible array of angling possibilities. Inland lagoons and rivers along the mainland support large populations of tarpon and snook, and paddling through dense jungle surrounded by tropical birdlife and howler monkeys affords a unique wilderness angling experience. At the edge of the open Caribbean, hard sand flats offer anglers miles of wading in pursuit of permit and bones. In between, the apparently endless expanse of marl and turtle grass around the cayes provides opportunities to sight-cast to flats species from skiffs. The biggest problem for visiting anglers with a taste for backcountry adventure might be finding a way to sample all these possibilities on one trip.

As a matter of personal history, Belize will always hold a special place in my heart. More years ago than I care to remember, I caught my first bonefish there. With the perspective of passing years, it wasn't much of a fish—a typical Belizean "chicken" in the 2-pound range at best. But none of us knew much about bonefish then, and I remember the experience as well as several more conventional milestones in a young man's life. Come to think of it, I remember it better.

Back then, neither the international sportfishing community nor the nascent eco-tourist trade had truly discovered the embarrassment of natural riches along the coast of Belize. In those wild and crazy times, the airport outside Belize City remained little more than a jungle airstrip, and fellow countrymen proved few and far between. I recall spending a long night drinking Charger beer at a bar in San Pedro

Top: Young girls watch for planes landing at Belize City's airport. Above: A tiny cay off the Turneffe Islands, home to a family of four.

The guide points out a bonefish. Belize's undeveloped coast offers limited road access, making boats with guides the preferred transportation to and from productive fishing areas.

while I tried to decide what language our neighbors were speaking at the next table. Eventually, someone bought someone a round and we learned they were British Harrier pilots still assigned to protect the Queen's former colony against periodic saber rattling by the bellicose Guatemalans to the south. There we sat, true to Shaw's edict, divided by a common language.

Belize's anonymity has become a matter of history, and today rod cases routinely clutter the baggage claim area of Belize City's new airport. Although a wealth of lodges have sprung up to accommodate anglers, the waters most of them fish receive a fair amount of attention, and anglers headed to popular destinations along the coast can usually expect some company on the best flats. That's hardly meant an end to good fishing—on the course of numerous return

trips I've enjoyed memorable days all the way from the Mexican border south through the Turneffes to Placentia. But despite a continued abundance of fish, I sometimes found myself missing the deliciously lonely ambience I remembered from the old days.

Mike Heusner and Marguerite Miles—proprietors of the venerable Belize River Lodge—have come up with a unique alternative for anglers interested in true wilderness flats fishing, for their fleet of live-aboard mother ships allows anglers to fish waters inaccessible by other means. During the week Lori and I spent aboard the *Cristina* a few winters back, we fished water from Belize City south beyond Dangriga without seeing *anybody* outside our own party. Literally.

The advantages of mobility on a Belizean

fishing trip go far beyond the pleasures of soli-tude. Variety provides an important part of Belize's appeal as a saltwater fishing destination. The Bahamas produce more double-digit bones and Costa Rica offers bigger tarpon, but it's hard to name another destination that offers such consistently good fishing for both species. And the permit fishing in Belize is as good as it gets. (Of course permit fishing and permit catching are two different things, but that's another story.) Factor in opportunities to sight-cast to huge snook and enjoy a host of less glamorous flats species, from barracuda to snapper, and anglers who appreciate mixed bags would be hard pressed to imagine more exciting fishing. By customizing itineraries, fishing from a live-aboard vessel allows anglers to sample those choices from the extensive Belizean menu that most appeal to them.

THE SINUOUS CHANNEL connecting the hidden lagoon to the sea wove its way through the man-groves as quietly as a secret. Rays scuttled beneath as we eased our way along, their wings transcribing perfect sine waves in the impossibly clear water. Tropical wading birds turned grace-ful pirouettes overhead. My East Coast ornith-ology skills might have atrophied through decades of disuse, but the essential memories remained intact, like the recollection of a for-eign language unspoken for years. By the time we reached the lagoon, it was all coming back to me in a flood of feathers. Wood ibises, snowy egrets, little blue herons; somehow, I remained connected to them all.

The first tarpon caught me by surprise. Casting for snook when it struck, I was so intent on the technical demands of rolling the fly up into the mangroves that I never saw the fish until it smacked the streamer and exploded right in front of my face. Nothing on earth seems quite as brilliant as a tarpon suspended in tropical sun-light, and the sight left me stunned. I suppose it

Noted fly casting instructor Mel Kreiger takes a jack cravalle, a great fighter.

was the element of surprise that kept me from striking hard enough to drive the hook home; at least that offered a convenient excuse. When the fish and I finally parted company after four more jumps, the gentle sound of the breeze and the birds quickly erased the frenzy of the hookup as if it had never taken place.

"I need a hook file," I said to Charlie.

"What you need is to stick 'em harder," Charlie admonished correctly.

It took me several more tarpon to learn my lesson. The fish weighed only 20 or 30 pounds, but I was fishing with my light rod again, and in the lagoon's mangrove labyrinth

A rainy afternoon on the Turneffe Islands; nothing to do but tie flies.

small tarpon were about all I could hope to manage. But I had to hook them first, and despite my confidence in the rod, it took several more strikes to convince me that it could take the punishment needed to get the job done properly.

By the time we spotted another fish, the morning sun had crested the highest mangroves, bathing the lagoon in the kind of light that begs for a camera. Lori engaged the Nikon's motor drive while Charlie maneuvered the skiff into position, and when I dropped the streamer on target, the tarpon inhaled it delicately. This time, I struck like a man trying to break a perfectly good rod in two. So much for delicacy.

At the sting of the hook, the fish roared under the boat and erupted in a clatter of gill rakers. The sun lay right in our eyes, but Lori fired away with the camera as if she were trying to mow down a mortal enemy with an automatic weapon. After three more jumps, the fish ran off down the channel, giving me a chance to organize myself in the bow while Charlie poled us into position with the sun at our backs.

"Here he comes!" I yelled as the fly line started toward the surface again, and then the fish towered overhead, framed by nothing but the tops of the mangroves and clear blue sky, as if the law of gravity had just been repealed. The light and the composition seemed perfect, but instead of the click of the camera's shutter, I heard nothing behind me but a series of frustrated expletives.

"What's wrong?" I asked.

"I shot up all the film!" Lori wailed.

The tarpon's hang time was such that most of this exchange took place while the fish was still in the air. Utterly distracted, I forgot to bow to the jump, and the fish threw the hook as it crashed back into the water and disappeared. For one edgy moment, we all stood and stared at the empty spot the tarpon had left behind. I can't remember who had the good sense to laugh first, but once it started, the rest came easily. And there were lessons to go right along with our mirth. We had sought to impose our own idea of order on the lagoon and its denizens, but from the *Pequod* to the *Titanic,* adventurers at sea have learned the hard way that such conceits seldom follow easily. By those standards, a lost fish and a wasted roll of film seemed a small price to pay for the reminder that some elements of nature are better left untamed.

Besides, I maintained a lasting image of the fish even if the camera didn't, silver sides and blood red gills suspended overhead. Right along with those well-worn childhood memories of ibises and egrets, the tarpon will always be there when I need it.

WHAT TO EXPECT

ANGLING

The short but complex Belizean coastline offers fly rod anglers abundant opportunities to pursue a variety of inshore marine gamefish. Local bonefish are small but numerous and schools of dozens are common. Large tarpon move inshore when the water begins to warm in April, and they offer excellent sight-casting opportunities on the flats inside the barrier islands. The permit fishing on the ocean flats ranks with the best in the world. Snook make a great wild card. I've taken them on the flats, in mangrove channels, and in brackish river water farther inland. Throw in an assortment of jacks, snappers, and barracuda and it's easy to appreciate Belize's popularity among anglers who enjoy variety.

Permit on the line! The permit fishing in Belize is as good as it gets, though permit fishing and permit catching are two different things.

The largely undeveloped coast offers only limited road access, and visiting anglers eventually must depend on boats for transportation to and from productive fishing areas. For this reason, Belize offers limited do-it-yourself fishing opportunities. However, anglers wishing to avoid the expense of a full-service lodge can arrange meals and accommodations in San Pedro, Dangriga, or Placentia and charter local guides by the day.

Most adventure anglers head to the flats

when they need to escape the cold months of winter. Although I endorse that impulse, it's worth noting that some of Belize's best fishing takes place during late spring and early summer. However, you can find saltwater game fish somewhere in Belize year-round.

Hats, full-length pants, and long-sleeved shirts are necessary for sun protection when on the water. Avoid bright colors (which can spook fish) while wading the flats. Take a light raincoat for long boat rides. Thick-soled wading shoes are mandatory when wading because of abundant sharp coral fragments along most ocean flats. The after-hours dress code is strictly informal except in a few of Belize City's fancier hotels.

LAY OF THE LAND

Although Belize is inhabited by barely 250,000 people, its culture reflects its population's complex ethnicity and historical roots. Originally populated by Mayans from the north and Garifuna from the south, Belize's first European inhabitants were outlaw pirates. Following a period of colonial struggle, the country became a Crown Colony in 1862 and was known as British Honduras for nearly a century. Belize attained complete independence in 1981.

Belize still projects an ambience more suggestive of the British Caribbean than of Latin America. English remains the official language, although visitors will find basic Spanish useful in outlying areas. A remarkably complex cultural community, Belize crowds strong European, Ladino, Mayan, and Creole influences into a geographically small but remarkably harmonious space.

Most visitors arrive in Belize City by scheduled jet service (American, Continental, TACA) from Houston, New Orleans, or Miami. Travelers from Mexico can connect by air from Cancun, or cross the border by vehicle south of Chetumal. A number of air services in Belize City offer both scheduled and charter flights to San Pedro, Dangriga, Placentia, and other destinations along the coast. Because of the country's small size, these flights are short and reasonably priced. Anglers fishing aboard one of the Belize River Lodge's live-aboard vessels depart directly from the lodge outside Belize City. Rental cars are available in Belize City, but they are expensive, and most prime fishing destinations cannot be reached by road. Travel to and from some fishing destinations might involve long rides in open boats.

Although biting insects are rarely troublesome away from the inland jungle, malaria remains endemic in low-lying areas. Sunburn is a constant threat at this latitude, especially on the water. Although abundant, sharks rarely pose a threat to anglers or divers in Belize. The barrier reef protects inshore waters from ocean swells, and seasickness is not a common problem for most visitors. Some 20 species of poisonous snakes inhabit the jungles, including the deadly fer-de-lance, but anglers are unlikely to encounter dangerous snakes in the marine environment. Tap water is unreliable—heed advice from your hosts or drink bottled water. Streets are usually safe in smaller communities, but Belize City contains some rough neighborhoods. Use caution and common sense after dark. (See Appendix A for further information.)

Although anglers generally focus their attention on the mainland coast and numerous offshore islands, the interior contains a wealth of unique wildlife and archeological sites that might be of particular interest to nonfishing companions. Belize's barrier reef is the world's fifth longest and the most extensive in our hemisphere. The Turneffe Islands and Glover's Reef offer some of the world's most spectacular snorkeling and diving, and a midday swim along any of the area's numerous coral heads can provide a welcome break after long hours of fishing beneath the hot tropical sun. I always take basic snorkel gear when traveling to Belize.

To find ocean flats fishing for bonefish and permit in a pristine, isolated area, head for the Turneffe Islands.

CONTACTS

BELIZE RIVER LODGE

888-275-4843

www.belizeriverlodge.com

Live-aboard flats fishing at numerous locations along the Belize coast as well as excellent snook and tarpon fishing from the main lodge on the Belize River.

TURNEFFE FLATS LODGE

www.worldangler.com/turneffel.htm

Ocean flats fishing for bonefish and permit in a pristine, isolated area.

EL PESCADOR LODGE

Ambergris Caye

www.elpescador.com

Bonefish flats in this area are limited, but the flats between Ambergris Caye and the mainland offer seasonally excellent tarpon and permit fishing.

RECOMMENDED READING

- *PERMIT ON A FLY,* Jack Samson (1996. $29.95. Stackpole Books.) Finally, someone's figured out how to catch them.
- *THE MAKING OF MODERN BELIZE,* Cedric H. Grant (1976. Out of print. Cambridge University Press.) Useful general historical background.
- *JUNGLE WALK: BIRDS AND BEASTS OF BELIZE,* Katie Stevens (1989. $4.90. Angelus Press.) Brief guide to the unique local biosphere.
- *THE BAYMEN'S LEGACY,* Byron Foster (1987. $11.00. Cubola Publications.) An excellent historical perspective on what makes Belize unique.

The Lake District & Aisen

We've already taken a dozen lively rainbows— brilliant, acrobatic fish big enough to make the reels sing

The flora: brilliant foxglove blossoms, *nalca*—a spiny wild rhubarb with leaves the size of a kitchen table—and whole mountainsides covered with towering hardwoods. Overhead: nattering parrots, a stately pair of ibises, and a giant kingfisher—*martin pescador*—carrying a hapless young trout securely in its bill. And beneath our feet: the mighty Petrohue, surging from its origin in Lake Todos los Santos toward the cold Pacific barely a long day's float away.

Forget the 7x tippets—I've already recognized the Petrohue as a junk fisherman's dream. It's our first morning on the river, and Lori and I have spent two hours pitching Woolly Buggers and Cone-Head Muddlers into pockets against high log-cluttered banks while our Chilean friend Reinaldo Ovando maneuvers the raft along in a high-octane team version of Pac-Man. Despite several days of summer rains, the current runs so exquisitely clear that we can easily see our flies

Floating the mighty Petrohue River in search of its plentiful rewards: spirited rainbows and wily browns.

tumbling along a rod's length beneath the surface. We might be fishing streamers, but the visual immediacy of every strike conveys all the excitement of spring-creek dry-fly fishing.

And there have been plenty of strikes. We've already taken a dozen lively rainbows—brilliant, acrobatic fish ranging from 15 to 17 inches, big enough to make the reels sing but not quite big enough to distract our attention from the stunning scenery rolling past as we float. The trout are splendid enough, but there is still too much novelty around us to ignore.

When the goal is a big brown, that kind of distraction can prove fatal. As we round another bend, I turn briefly to admire the towering, snow-clad profile of spectacular Mount Orsono and glance back at the current just in time to see a huge golden shape appear from the depths and bear down on my fly. Utterly rattled, I strike a moment too soon, pulling the streamer deftly from the trout's eager maw. I roll another desperate cast back upstream, but it's too late and I know it. Big browns don't reward ineptitude with second chances.

Welcome to Chile.

NEW YORK-TO-LA LONG but scarcely more than a good Texas cattle ranch wide, Chile cuts across more lines of latitude—and includes more distinct ecosystems—than most countries twice its size. In fact, among South American nations only Ecuador has a smaller surface area. But good things really do come in small (and oddly shaped) packages, and Chile's fertile midsection offers adventurous anglers some of the most spectacular fishing opportunities in the world.

The history of Chile's sportfishing turns out to be as unique as its geography. Bounded by the formidable Atacama Desert to the north, the Andes to the east, and the Pacific to the west and south, Chile's native biosphere evolved in virtual isolation from the rest of the New World landmass. Despite an abundance of pristine habitat, few indigenous mammals inhabit the area, and Chile's numerous lakes and rivers originally supported no fish species of sporting interest.

AT A GLANCE

SPECIES Rainbow, brown, and brook trout; king, coho, and Atlantic salmon

TACKLE 6–7-weight rods; floating and sinking-tip lines

FLIES Basic trout selection; Woolly Buggers, Cone-Head Muddlers, Chernobyl Ants, deerhair mouse patterns, and crayfish imitations

PRIME TIME February–mid-April

CONSERVATION ISSUES Hydroelectric, timber, and mining development

PRICE RANGE $2,500–$3,500

STAGING CITY Santiago, Chile

HEADS UP UV radiation from sunlight in the Southern Hemisphere can be deceptive on cool, overcast days

The Futalafu River, some 200 miles south of Puerto Montt. Recognizing the potential of Chile's clear, food-rich rivers, early Europeans quickly introduced brown trout and other non-native species.

But anglers abhor a vacuum as surely as does nature itself. In the early 1900s, European immigrants recognized the habitat potential of Chile's clear, food-rich lakes and rivers and began to introduce their favorite game fish, beginning with stocks of brown trout from Germany in 1905 and eventually including rainbows and brook trout from North America. Some of the browns and rainbows later established anadromous life cycles. Successful transplants of coho, king, and Atlantic salmon to Chile's coastal waters added to this intriguing mixture, supplemented over the last several decades by escapees from Chile's rapidly expanding marine aquaculture industry. Today, Chilean waters contain an eclectic population of all six of these salmonid species, many of which have spent time at sea. In fact, the most intriguing aspect of any strike might be determining just what kind of fish has hit your fly.

Lori and I made our initial trip to Chile as guests of Mike Darland, a friend of my family and the driving force behind Southern Chile Expeditions. Mike is one of those visionary individuals whose ideas seem bigger than the circumstances surrounding them. In another time, he might have joined the Lewis and Clark expedition or headed to the Klondike. Denied such opportunities by time and fate, he left the Pacific Northwest for Chile, where he built a spectacular lodge on the shore of Lake Llanquihue, an hour's drive from the Lake District's regional hub, Puerto Montt. Anxious to provide visiting anglers with an even wilder experience, he then established a second outpost to the south in the Aisen District, and after two days on the Petrohue, Lori and I set off to explore new waters there.

An hour's flight down the coast and a scenic afternoon of mountain driving brought us to the tiny village of La Junta. Prior to the completion of the Camino Austral barely a decade ago, this remote section of wilderness remained all but cut off from the outside world, and even today traffic on the "highway" is as likely to consist of vaqueros on horseback as modern automobiles. My kind of place.

The following morning, Jarrett Northup spent two hours working an inflatable raft around a small mountain lake while I pitched streamers against the brushy shoreline. I'd landed a dozen scrappy rainbows and several nice brook trout by the time we reached the mouth of a tumbling feeder creek that seemed the most likely spot in the whole lake to hold a big brown. Driven by warm summer rains, the clear current had opened a sinuous path barely a yard wide through the tangle of aquatic weeds that rimmed the lakeshore, and I knew I'd only have one chance to present the fly properly.

But I got it right…sort of. As soon as the fly hit the little lick of open water, an amber missile the length of my arm burst from the weeds and inhaled it. "Hog brown!" I yelled at Jarrett as the fish headed back into the cover, from which not even my sturdy 7-weight could turn the fish. Dragging an impossible burden of salad behind, my line disappeared into the depths below, carrying all reasonable hope along with it.

For the first few minutes I spent trying to sort out the mess, the vital throb of the fish on the end of the leader served to remind us that the fat lady had yet to sing. Then unyielding resistance replaced the feel of the trout, and I knew the brown had taken the line around one of the lake's innumerable submerged logs. But I still had one old trick up my sleeve. Resting the rod across the rowing frame, I grasped the line delicately between thumb and forefinger, released all tension, and waited. Suddenly the feel of the fish returned, and I knew that against

A typical football-shaped Chilean brookie.

considerable odds the trout had freed itself from the obstruction.

This triumph of technique (or luck, or whatever) proved short-lived. As Jarrett set his back against the oars to distance us from the treacherous shoreline, the line went dead, and this time I knew we'd had it. Hank Williams said it well decades ago in reference to another kind of loss: *What can I do? You win again.*

After another week in the country, Lori and I had experienced enough wild fishing and enough wild places to sustain us through a winter's worth of cold-weather blues back home. We'd spent a day on the salt water at Puyuhaupi, an unspoiled bay so lovely that not even the absence of the salmon we sought could disappoint us. Besides, I'd caught what might well be a fly-rod world record *cabrillo,* a bizarre-looking species whose capture we celebrated by taking its subject home and eating it along with a bucket of the splendid Chilean mussels Lori dredged up along the tide line. We'd hiked up a remote spring creek and hunted big trout New Zealand style, sight-casting to fish in water so clear you had to remind yourself

THE FISH MARKET

Given the length and complexity of Chile's coastline and the inevitable proximity of its citizens to the Pacific, seafood's prominence in Chilean cuisine should come as no surprise. And it's hard to imagine a better place to explore the local possibilities at bargain-basement prices than the open-air fish market in Puerto Montt, a stop I'd recommend to all Lake District visitors.

Curiosity fueled my initial visit: The recent popularity of Chilean sea bass on American menus left me wondering about the identity of this fish and its fly-rod sporting potential. To my surprise, hardly anyone we fished with in Chile seemed to know much about sea bass, so Lori and I set off to find some answers in the most likely place I could imagine. I knew it would beat going to the library.

Did it ever. Situated on the waterfront in the middle of the local fishing fleet's home port, the market pulsed with energy. Street vendors grilled fresh fish on braziers while pleasantly bustling restaurants offered more variety at little obvious increase in formality or price. And the sprawling stalls full of fresh fish provided my first good look at what this unique corner of the South Pacific had to offer…an edible museum, for all intents and purposes.

While I've spent too much time in Alaska to be impressed by aquaculture salmon as table fare, the size of the Atlantics we saw lying on ice made me realize how much fun it would be to catch fish-farm escapees. We got to put a face—and an ugly one at that—on the *congrio* (conger eel) we'd been enjoying for dinner all week. And when we slipped into a restaurant for lunch, we enjoyed a mouthwatering assortment of local mussels, clams, shrimp, and abalone for not much more than the price of a burger and fries.

Alas, the sea bass, or *corvina* as it's locally known, turned out not to be a bass at all, or even the corbina I know. And it didn't look like a species likely to set the fly-rod community on fire with enthusiasm.

But it sure tasted good.

Float fishing the Yelcho River, which flows into Corcovado Gulf south of Puerto Montt. Steep, brushy banks surround most Chilean rivers, making them very difficult to fish from shore.

consciously not to go in over the tops of your chest waders. In fact, I'd done just about everything I'd imagined doing and then some…except put my hands however briefly around the girth of a big Chilean brown trout.

Not that I hadn't come close. I'd caught big rainbows. I'd hooked big browns and landed several in the 4- to 5-pound range, which raises the obvious question: How big is big? (Answer: Like art, you'll know it when you see it.) But as Lori, Reinaldo, and I slid the raft down the banks of the Petrohue one last time, it was hard to avoid the feeling that I stood on the verge of leaving Chile with unfinished business still on the table.

All morning long, the sun danced seductively through layers of low-lying scud, reminding us of the Mapuche meaning of the river's name: "Place of Mist." When the lights went on we stared at the snow-covered volcanoes looming all around us, and when the clouds rolled back in we concentrated on the water, taking one colorful rainbow after another as we slid downstream toward a take-out rendezvous none of us really wanted to see. Then at midday we stopped to fish a gravel bar from shore. When I heard Lori let out an unusually enthusiastic war whoop, I turned to see a fish turning in the sunlight three feet above the river, and several minutes later we stood admiring the first Atlantic salmon of the trip.

Our day could have ended then and there with no regrets, but Chile wasn't through with us yet. Light rain had started to fall as we entered the long float's final mile, but the water ran so clear I could see every detail of the gravel bottom as I flicked the streamer into one more pocket behind one more downed log, and suddenly the fish I'd sought all along appeared. I remember the dark spots along its flanks and the cotton white interior of its mouth as its jaws opened to strike, and then I felt myself fast to every ounce of trout I could handle.

As Reinaldo checked the raft against the nearest gravel bar, I bailed out and started downstream on foot to guide the fish away from a series of nasty obstructions. *This isn't like fighting a brown trout,* I thought as I palmed the reel and listened to the line hiss away across the current. *This is like fighting a steelhead.* I wanted to land that fish as badly as I'd wanted to land any fish in recent memory, if for no other reason than to complete a goal I'd deliberately set out to accomplish. Then after ten minutes up and down the bank, Reinaldo was there with the net and so was the fish, and it was over. As I said, you'll know "big" when you see it, and this time I'd looked it in the eye.

Brother, had I ever.

WHAT TO EXPECT

ANGLING

Sportfishing season runs from mid-November until early May—late spring through fall in the Southern Hemisphere. December can be a good month for big fish, although rains often produce high water conditions. The period from February through mid-April offers the most consistent fishing and provides an excellent opportunity for anglers eager for a break from cold North American winters.

Chilean waters support an interesting assortment of caddis-, stone-, and mayflies. Even though these insect species differ from the versions we know at home, Chilean trout are seldom highly selective, and generic imitations usually suffice. However, aquatic insects form a relatively minor portion of the Chilean trout's diet. Woolly Buggers are a staple pattern, serving both as nonspecific attractors and leech imitations. Freshwater crabs (*pancoras*) abound in many rivers, and crayfish imitations can be highly effective. Large beetles appear on the water during late summer and fall; Chernobyl Ants make good imitations. And Alaska-style deer-hair mouse patterns can provoke furious surface strikes during the fall.

Wind and big water make 7-weight tackle an excellent all-around choice, although dry-fly enthusiasts will want to take along a 5- or 6-weight rod as well. Intermediate-density sinking-tip lines serve well when fishing streamers in rivers, and a high-density shooting head will prove advantageous in lakes. Despite the water clarity, Chilean trout are seldom leader shy, and you'll appreciate #8- or #10-test tippet when it comes time to horse big fish away from ever-present snags and obstructions.

Although Chile makes a wonderful destination to explore on one's own, the rate-limiting step in a self-guided Chilean fishing expedition arises from the nearly universal need for a boat. Steep, brushy banks surround most Chilean rivers, making them very difficult to fish from shore. Those who elect not to fish from established lodges can hire guides of varying quality in

Above: The village of La Junta, where traffic is as likely to consist of vaqueros on horseback as autos.
Opposite: Matching the hatch on Rio Simpson, where dry flies attract browns and rainbows.

Beautiful brown trout taken from Rio Serrano near Torres del Paine National Park in southern Chile.

most towns located near good water: Inquire at local hotels and sporting-goods stores. Although anglers can buy basic fly-fishing supplies in larger towns like Puerto Montt, visitors should plan on taking ample supplies of tackle.

Plan on dressing for conditions ranging from summer in our mountain West to early fall in Alaska, including layers of light wool or Polar Fleece and high-quality rain gear. UV radiation can be deceptively intense during the southern summer, so carry adequate sunblock even on cool, cloudy days.

LAY OF THE LAND

Those who know Chile only from joyless accounts of the Pinochet regime should prepare to be pleasantly surprised. Politically stable, economically robust, and populated by some of the most gracious people on earth, today's Chile would make an attractive travel destination even if it didn't contain beautiful water full of big fish. From metropolitan Santiago—where international travelers arrive and nearly half the nation's populace resides—south to the wilds of Chilean Tierra del Fuego, this unique Latin nation offers a constantly shifting array of impressions, evoking images varying from Europe to wilderness Alaska.

International flights (United, American, Lan Chile) serve Santiago from Los Angeles, New York, and Miami. Several regional carriers (Avant, Aerosur) link Santiago to Puerto Montt and destinations farther south. Good roads connect Santiago to the Lake District and rental cars are available in Santiago and Puerto Montt. Road travel south of Puerto Montt requires a 12-hour ferry ride to Chaiten, and roads in the Aisen district are rough although scenic and safe. Even basic Spanish will prove extremely useful outside metropolitan Santiago.

Chilean cuisine reflects an adaptive blend of

local and European influences. The beef and lamb are both excellent. Because one is seldom far from Chile's 2,700-mile-long coastline, fresh seafood abounds. Chile's burgeoning wine industry has earned justified international acclaim for the quality and reasonable price of its vintages. Bottom line: If you're eating unexciting food in Chile, it's your own damn fault.

Visitors to Chile can expect a safe environment with a low incidence of crime and few specific health concerns. Weather conditions vary substantially, often during the course of a single day. Biting flies can be troublesome during January. (See Appendix A for further information.)

Ancillary activities include spectacular whitewater rafting, mountaineering, hiking, and outdoor photography.

CONTACTS

SOUTHERN CHILE ADVENTURES
Km 42 Camino Ensenada
CC 197
Puerto Varas, Region X, Chile
56-65-212030
www.southernchilexp.com

CAMPO CHILENO
Lago Pollux, Coyhaique
Book through Fishabout (see Appendix C).

RECOMMENDED READING

■ *IN PATAGONIA,* Bruce Chatwin (1988. $13.95. Penguin.) One of the best travel books of our time, and essential reading for any visitor to this unique region.

■ *HOUSE OF THE SPIRITS,* Isabel Allende (1988. $7.99. Bantam Books.) Wonderful fictional perspective on the Chilean experience.

■ *SELECTED POEMS,* Pablo Neruda (1990. $17.00. Houghton Mifflin.) Few countries Chile's size have produced two Nobel laureates in literature, an indication of the Chilean people's imaginative nature. Start with Neruda and progress to Gabriella Mistral at your leisure.

Streamside lunch of grilled Pacific salmon. King, coho, and even Atlantic salmon are found in Chilean waters.

■ *THE GRINGO'S GUIDE TO CHILEAN WINE,* Fred Purdy (1999. Bell.) A useful reference to Chile's rapidly developing wine industry.
■ *INSIGHT GUIDE: CHILE,* edited by Natalie Minnis (1999. $22.95. Langenscheidt Publishing Group.) Basic travel information.

Midway Atoll

*...we fought mahi, yellowtail, rainbow runners,
and kawakawa until our arms ached*

Picking our way through the throng of gooneys—as locals affectionately refer to the Laysan albatross—we walked out to the end of the point and stared past the breakers at the enormity of the Pacific. The sight of all that open, lonely water immediately enforced our sense of isolation. With Honolulu over 1,100 miles to the east and the intangible international date line barely 100 miles in the opposite direction, tiny Sand Island—the larger of the two chunks of dry ground lying inside Midway's barrier reef—began to feel more like a life raft than terra firma. In fact, we were about as close to the middle of nowhere as it is geographically possible to get, at least on this planet.

Undaunted, Lori picked her way down to the waterline and began to strip line from her fly reel as Ed Hughes, Howard McKinney, and I cut chum and pitched chunks of leftover fish toward the cut in the reef. A cloud of rudder fish gathered quickly

Sight-casting to a large giant trevally, ulua *to Hawaiians, and just plain trouble to fly anglers.*

MIDWAY ATOLL

SPIT ISLAND
SAND ISLAND
EASTERN ISLAND

PACIFIC OCEAN

in the slick only to scatter like mice as a long, streamlined form appeared from the blue water and tacked toward the shallows. "Can you tell what it is?" I asked above the sound of the surf and the cries of the birds.

"I'm not sure," Ed replied.

Just then a bolt of sunshine broke through the clouds, illuminating the crystalline water to reveal a dark mask painted across the fish's face. "Amberjack!" Ed shouted, but his identification proved academic. Lori already had a loop of line overhead, and when she dropped the Deceiver three feet in front of the fish, the shape accelerated and engulfed the fly.

Watching someone else sight-cast to a big fish is among the most exciting spectacles in outdoor sport. The cast and the strike seemed so per-fectly choreographed that the rest of us were screaming our fool heads off by the time Lori set the hook. As soon as she struck home, the jack swirled and retreated toward the security of the reef with her reel whining in protest. But somehow she turned the fish without snapping the tippet, and from our vantage high on the bank we could see the 4-foot-long shape begin to yield to pressure from the 12-weight.

As Lori fought the fish into the surf beneath her feet, Ed scrambled down the rocks and tried to beach it. Just then a huge, dark form appeared in the surge. I was about to bellow out a shark warning when I realized I was staring at the bulky outline of an endangered Hawaiian monk seal. "What should I do?" Lori cried when I pointed out the presence of the new arrival.

AT A GLANCE

SPECIES Bluewater—marlin (black, blue, and striped), Pacific sailfish, wahoo, yellowfin tuna, Pacific yellowtail, rainbow runner, *mahi, kawakawa,* sharks. Inshore—giant trevally, *butaguchi* (thick-lipped trevally), amberjack, *moi* (threadfin), queenfish, snapper, more sharks.

TACKLE 14-weight rods for billfish, 8-weights for *moi* from shore, 12-weights for everything else; floating lines; 15# and 20# leaders for everything except *moi* (6# or 8# will suffice). Heavy-monofilament shock tippet for all bluewater fish except wahoo and sharks; use wire leader for these species.

FLIES Basic bluewater selection, with 5/0 hooks for billfish and 2/0 or 3/0 for most other species. Take a selection of Clousers for *moi* and poppers for small trevally and amberjack in the lagoon.

PRIME TIME May–October
CONSERVATION ISSUES Protection of critical habitat for endangered species
PRICE RANGE $3,500+
STAGING CITY Honolulu, Hawaii
HEADS UP Midway has an abundant shark population

The seal posed a unique dilemma. The National Wildlife Refuge staff had documented a record 14 pups born on the atoll that season, nearly a quarter of the world's yearly crop of newborns. Visitors are asked not to approach within 100 feet of seals, and now Lori had one cruising past her at point-blank range. But the rules didn't address the issue of seals approaching visitors, and our conflict quickly resolved when the seal continued its leisurely way toward the beach behind us without any indication that it cared about our presence.

By this time, the amberjack had tapped its reserves and torn back out toward the reef. At this critical juncture in the fight, the reel suddenly fell from the rod handle. While Ed wrestled the reel back into position, Lori improvised and somehow managed to avoid losing the fish. Ten minutes later, she led the jack toward Ed's outstretched hand and he lifted it gingerly from the surf.

"Unquestionably a women's fly-rod world record," Ed observed as we exchanged high fives all around. Then we remembered the mishap with the reel. According to IGFA (International Game Fish Association) rules, his assistance disqualified the fish. Not that any of us cared; both Lori and I have always viewed the urge to weigh, measure, and compare with a certain detachment.

But it was still one hell of a way to begin a fishing trip.

THE LAST WESTWARD LANDFALL in the Hawaiian chain save for an inhospitable chunk of coral named Kure, Midway lies farther from the tourist bustle of Waikiki than miles can express. Providing critical nesting habitat for 16 species of pelagic seabirds as well as the endangered green turtle and monk seal (not to mention some 250 varieties of fish), Midway typifies both the natural bounty and extreme fragility of isolated island ecosystems. With its stunning reef and incredibly clear waters, Midway could serve as the centerpiece in a testimonial to the natural beauty of the Pacific's isolated atolls.

Leave it to our own species to screw things up. Midway was largely ignored by Polynesian seafarers because of its paucity of shelter and fresh water; its first modern visitors were plume hunters who began to devastate the island's largely defenseless bird population at the turn of the 20th century. The atoll fell under American jurisdiction by then, and when news of the carnage reached Washington, Theodore Roosevelt—still my ideal as an ecologically aware politician—dispatched a squadron of Marines to protect Midway's wildlife.

But that righteous struggle turned out to be small potatoes compared to what took place in and about Midway in June 1942. Still reeling from the debacle at Pearl Harbor, the American navy lay thinly spread about the Pacific when an intelligence coup by naval code breakers identified the point of the next Japanese attack: Midway. The carriers *Hornet, Enterprise,* and *Yorktown* arrived in time for a surprise intercept of the enemy fleet. Despite overwhelming odds and the eventual loss of the *Yorktown,* American naval airmen prevailed over the course of the two-day battle, sinking the Japanese carriers *Akagi, Kaga, Hiryu,* and *Soryu.*

Opposite: The author lands a thick-lipped trevally. Though most weigh under 10 pounds, they fight like heavyweights.
Top: Nesting booby. Midway provides nesting habitat for 16 species of pelagic seabirds.

Both sides sustained heavy casualties, and the tide of the war in the Pacific turned for good.

Those of us who travel to Midway with fly rods in our luggage should appreciate its history, first because it is *our* history and second because it provides an apt metaphor for the unique flavor of the local fishing. Angling provides its contemplative moments, but reflection on Midway usually comes courtesy of its distinctive ecology rather than its fishing. The waters look large and brooding, full of threats, ranging from coral heads to tiger sharks, to the angler's best intentions. The game fish are large, powerful, and aggressive, and they come in a variety likely to amaze even experienced saltwater fly-rod enthusiasts. Combine these elements and you should expect to take a beating.

In other words, it still can be a war out there.

THE DAY AFTER LORI landed her big AJ—and I lost several over 50 pounds to the reef from the same spot—I set off for the blue water with Ed and Howard, who badly wanted a blue marlin on a fly. Less focused in my own ambitions, I felt eager to tackle anything Midway's fertile offshore waters had to offer.

The morning began as a bird-watching trip, not inappropriately, given the atoll's importance to the area's pelagic avian species. On land, the Laysan albatross is one of the most ungainly creatures on

THE *YORKTOWN*

On May 8, 1942, the U.S. carrier *Yorktown* sustained a direct hit from a Japanese bomb during the Battle of the Coral Sea. Although the ship was able to limp back to Pearl Harbor, her crew expected her to be returned to the mainland for major repairs. But when American code breakers intercepted signals indicating an impending attack on Midway, Admiral Chester Nimitz ordered her urgent dispatch from Pearl, and on May 30 she headed back to sea to join the carriers *Enterprise* and *Hornet*.

Early on the morning of June 4, bombers from the Japanese carrier fleet struck Midway. Later that morning, SBD *Dauntless* dive bombers from the *Yorktown* participated in the attack on the Japanese fleet that eventually sunk the carriers *Kaga, Soryu,* and *Akagi*. But at noon, VAL dive bombers from the Japanese carrier *Hiryu* attacked the American fleet. Bombs and torpedoes struck the *Yorktown,* crippling her and forcing her crew to abandon ship.

Somehow the ship stayed afloat, and in the aftermath of the pitched air battle the effort to save her began. Tugs arrived to begin towing her back to Pearl Harbor. But on June 6, the Japanese submarine *I-168* torpedoed the listing *Yorktown* and her destroyer escort *Hammann,* sending both ships to a watery grave.

In May 1998, aboard the search vessel *Laney Chouest,* a team led by Robert Ballard—the undersea explorer who located both the *Bismarck* and *Titanic*—found the *Yorktown* lying intact in 17,000 feet of water some 200 miles north of Midway. A remarkable technical accomplishment, the discovery offered a long-overdue moment of closure for the sailors and airmen who survived the battle that turned the tide of the war in the Pacific.

earth, deserving its derivative nickname in every respect. But at sea, the gooney becomes another creature entirely: elegant, stately, full of grace. I was watching one ride the air current behind a wave crest, the tip of its upwind primaries delicately kissing the water, when an ominous dark shape rose and smacked it like a hungry brown trout inhaling a caddis fly. Tiger Sharks—1; Gooney Birds—0. Just another chapter in the ongoing battle of Midway.

The birds we sought weren't the ubiquitous gooneys but the terns and noddies that marked schools of bait pushed to the surface by game fish below, and after a half-hour's cruise, we found them. As Ed cut the motor and we drifted down upon the action, I looked over the transom and saw a beautiful *mahi* cruising just below the surface. As soon as my streamer hit the water, a torpedo-shaped *kawakawa* exploded from the depths and struck before I could redirect my cast. Although the fish only weighed 6 to 8 pounds, it quickly turned my 12-weight rod into a pretzel. In less time than it takes to tell, the *mahi* hit the hooked fish and knocked it off my line, and as I gathered to cast again a 6-foot Galápagos shark scooped up the remains of the little tuna and then struck my fly. Only on Midway.

Because I was fishing without wire leader, I didn't expect the shark to stay connected long. But an hour later I was still grinding away at the fish, which we eventually landed. After this rapid-sequence excursion up the food chain I wasn't sure I had another round in me. But then a flock of terns appeared on the horizon and we set off in pursuit. Over the course of the morning we fought *mahi*, yellowtail, rainbow runners, and *kawakawa* until our arms ached.

And yes, it felt like a battle out there.

THE TRUE MEASURE of any angling destination lies in how it fishes under adverse weather conditions, and Midway gave us ample opportunity to test this thesis. By mid-May North Pacific weather

A fine amberjack (kahala in Hawaiian) taken on a surf popper.

patterns have usually stabilized, but we endured a freakish run of wind and rain and still caught fish. But thanks to the cold snap, we spent several days fishing the reef without tangling with Midway's signature game fish—the giant trevally, *Caranx ignobilis* to scientists, *ulua* to Hawaiians, and just plain trouble to anglers ambitious enough to challenge them on fly tackle.

Actually, that denial isn't quite accurate. We spent one afternoon casting poppers inside the lagoon to *papio*, as immature representatives of all trevally species are known in Hawaiian waters.

And we'd taken a bunch of them on the surface. They all weighed less than 10 pounds, but they fought like heavyweights and I blew up a perfectly good rod trying to horse one away from the rocks. But they still weren't the big, scary *ulua* we had come for.

Then one afternoon as Howard fought an amberjack from the boat just outside the reef, Lori called our attention to a dark form behind the transom. "Huge GT!" Ed cried in a state of palpable excitement, and no wonder. The fish would easily have exceeded the hundred-pound mark. Although the chance of landing it on a fly rod—or anything else short of a harpoon—stood at slim to none, I had to try. The fish ignored two good shots before it vanished back into the depths, and at least in retrospect I have to wonder if it wasn't doing me a favor.

But the fish's appearance inspired us, and when we returned to the dock at midday Howard, Lori, and I rounded up some chum and headed on foot for a rocky point near the reef. Howard had just broken off another huge amberjack when I saw a foreboding shape cruising in on a wave. "GT!" I cried with the same reflexive excitement we'd heard in Ed's voice earlier.

"Come down here and take him!" Howard called back as he scrambled out of the way.

"You want to take a shot?" I asked Lori.

"No way!" she laughed, and I have to admit she probably won the IQ contest.

For several minutes, the 60-pound fish played footsie at the edge of my visibility and casting range, but it finally committed to a run past our position toward the beach. I had the fly in front of its nose when it did, but the fish refused several reasonable presentations. Then it suddenly turned and approached the streamer like a crocodile stalking a baby wildebeest, and when it struck, I struck back as hard as I knew how.

Nothing in the world of angling can prepare an angler for a big *ulua*'s first wild run. Marlin might be bigger, bonefish quicker, and tarpon more acrobatic, but in terms of sheer power sustained over distance, nothing approaches a motivated *ulua*. After my mishap in the lagoon with the *papio*, I was fishing with a 14-weight borrowed from Howard and I had the drag cranked down as hard as it would go. None-the-less, the fish covered the 200 yards to the far side of the reef in a matter of seconds, leaving me with the distinct impression that all the pressure I could muster hadn't altered its behavior in the least. I doubt I could have made such a run against that drag myself, even in a pickup truck. Mercifully, we parted company at the leader rather the backing, allowing me to retrieve my fly line and a certain measure of pride. GTs—1; Anglers—0.

Suddenly I knew how the albatross felt after its encounter with the tiger shark. The difference was, I got to re-rig and play the game again.

WHAT TO EXPECT

The United States Navy abandoned its presence on Midway in 1996, spending millions of dollars on restoration in the process. The Fish and Wildlife Service assumed administrative control when everything inside the reef became the Midway Atoll National Wildlife Refuge. Refuge

Above: The remains of the old Trans-Pacific Cable Company headquarters.

Casting to amberjack from the beach at Sand Island, home to 80 percent of the world's Laysan albatross population.

management soon recognized the high cost of providing even basic visitor services in such a remote location and subsequently entered into partnership with the private Midway Phoenix Corporation, an arrangement unique within the National Wildlife Refuge system.

Only about 200 personnel inhabit the atoll full time, and air-service capacity limits the volume of visitors de facto. Island residents consist of refuge staff, visiting biologists, Midway Phoenix management, and foreign national workers, most of whom come from Sri Lanka, Thailand, and the Philippines, providing the island with a pleasantly diverse ambience. Visitors represent an eclectic mix of birders, photographers, divers, and anglers. The atmosphere on the island feels summer-camp friendly, and crime is nonexistent. Everyone waves and smiles at everyone else... it's just that kind of place.

ANGLING

While trout streams and bonefish flats share many common characteristics the world over, fly-fishing opportunities at Midway are truly unique and visiting anglers are likely to encounter fish and fishing never seen before. Flyfishers unaccustomed to bluewater species need to prepare themselves for the incredible power of species like tuna and trevally. The need for heavy tackle and technique may be obvious for billfish, but a 50-pound *ulua* can be just as demanding. Be sure to carry a 12-weight even if you don't plan to fish for marlin and practice with it before you go in order to develop the strength and technique such heavy tackle demands. Carry backup rods and fly lines. Work on your saltwater knots and be meticulous with them as you fish. Fishing Midway waters amounts to big game hunting with a fly rod, and there won't be room for many mistakes.

Fish at Midway are rarely selective, but it helps to have flies of various weights in order to vary their rate of sink.

As we proved, it's possible to catch big fish with fly tackle on your own from Midway's shore. But much of Sand Island's coastline can be closed at any time to protect monk seals, and much of what remains accessible proves difficult to wade because of rocks and leftover rip-rap from the old navy days. If you have done what it takes to get to Midway and want to fish, it only makes sense to book with one of the guides who outfit from the island. There isn't a lot of choice, but fortunately Ed Hughes and Rick Gaffney of Midway Sport Fishing would be the guys to go to even on a crowded dock. They maintain two well-appointed Bertrams for offshore fishing and three smaller catamarans for the reef, and they know their stuff. As long as Midway's fly-fishing opportunities remain in their hands, expect matters to be cared for in style.

Although a certain amount of *yadda-yadda* back and forth between divers and anglers has begun to mar relationships between the two groups at some other saltwater destinations, isolation seems to enforce notions of human companionship, and few such conflicts exist at Midway. Furthermore, at the management level both the refuge and the Phoenix Corporation seem committed to preserving and promoting Midway's angling opportunities. Fishing inside the reef is strictly catch-and-release, with only single unbaited barbless hooks allowed. The sea's bounty might seem inexhaustible, but we all ought to know better.

Visitors should pack loose-fitting, fast-drying clothing adequate to provide protection from tropical sun. Take along wading shoes and polarized glasses.

LAY OF THE LAND

Because of its isolation and the fragility of its environment, the Fish and Wildlife Service carefully regulates travel to Midway. All access origi-nates in Honolulu, from which Aloha Air operates comfortable round-trip jet service to and from Midway once a week. Traveling from the mainland on Aloha (from Oakland) will save time and energy during transfers in Honolulu. Midway flights operate after daylight hours during peak bird season to avoid disturbing nesting activity on the island. The Midway Phoenix Corporation oversees all travel arrangements. Strict weight restrictions apply on all flights to Midway—consult your booking agent for current information and plan on packing light. Midway operates four hours later than Pacific Standard Time, so travelers from the East Coast should expect significant jet lag. Because the atoll technically lies outside the United States, visitors must carry a valid passport.

Because of its isolation, few services exist on Midway. Visitors quarter in the old naval officers' barracks, an arrangement that turns out to be far more comfortable than it sounds. Everyone on the island eats at a common cafeteria, with only a few basic food supplies available elsewhere. However, for modest additional cost, visitors can dine at the Clipper House, a splendid little French restaurant that would be a treasured find in any city in America. On Midway, it's nothing short of a miracle. And don't waste space in your suitcase; sandals and shorts meet local dress code requirements even at the Clipper House. In fact, they define the local dress code.

Few special health requirements pertain to Midway visitors. A small clinic with one physician operates on the island. Complex medical problems require emergency evacuation to Honolulu. (See Appendix A for further information.)

Midway's wildlife would be worth the trip even if there weren't any fish. During our visit, 80 percent of the world's Laysan albatross population occupied Sand Island, creating an avian population density beyond belief. Of Midway's 16 indigenous breeding bird species, only the short-tailed albatross qualifies as an endangered species, and that is about the only one we didn't see during our visit. But frequent encounters with endangered monk seals and green turtles easily compensated for that minor disappointment.

Ancillary activities include exceptional snorkeling and diving, unique bird watching, and wildlife photography.

CONTACTS

DESTINATION MIDWAY

Rick Gaffney

Phone: 808-325-5000; FAX: 808-325-7023

captrick@kona.net

www.fishdive.com

Rick oversees all angling operations on Midway Atoll. Book fishing excursions through him (or one of several agencies listed in Appendix C) and take advantage of his vast knowledge of fly fishing the Pacific.

MIDWAY PHOENIX CORPORATION

Midway Island Station #40

Honolulu, HI 96820-1860

808-599-5400

www.midwayisland.com

MIDWAY ATOLL NATIONAL WILDLIFE REFUGE

Midway Island Station #4

P.O. Box 29460

Honolulu, HI 96820-1860

ALOHA AIRLINES (U.S. MAINLAND)

800-367-5250

www.alohaairlines.com

RECOMMENDED READING

■ *HAWAII'S FISHES,* John P. Hoover (1993. $16.95. Mutual Publishing Co.) Midway boasts an extremely complex marine environment, and even veteran saltwater anglers are likely to encounter unfamiliar species. Pamphlets at refuge headquarters complement this guide.

■ *BIRD LIFE IN HAWAII, FOURTH EDITION,* Andrew Berger (1986. $4.95. Island Heritage.) This guide includes descriptions of most avian species found on Midway.

The author with a queenfish taken near Midway's barrier reef.

■ *BLUEWATER FLY FISHING,* Trey Combs (1996. $60.00. The Lyons Press.) Because offshore marine angling is so unfamiliar to most fly-fishers, they will benefit from a review of this material prior to an excursion to Midway.

■ "RETURN TO THE BATTLE OF MIDWAY," Thomas Allen. *National Geographic* 195, no. 4 (April 1999). A well-written (and nicely photographed) description of the seminal event in the atoll's history.

The Far East

"But there are no fish in this river!"

Although we appreciated the historic significance of our first trip to the Russian Far East, none of us expected to see the governor of Alaska and the television cameras waiting at the Anchorage airport.

This unlikely adventure began when our old friend Doug Borland joined a group of fellow Alaska businessmen on a pioneering trip across the Bering Sea in 1990. An enthusiastic outdoor sportsman, Doug quickly appreciated the area's untapped potential and set about making the contacts needed to open doors during the death throes of the entrenched communist regime. When he returned, he asked our long-time outdoor companion Ray Stalmaster and me if we would be willing to accompany him back the following year to help assess the possibilities of outfitting wilderness expeditions for visiting American bowhunters and anglers. Neither Ray nor I required any arm-twisting.

Armed guides float supplies—including a woodstove—down the Ulya River.

RUSSIA

After months of antici- pation, we faced a sudden setback when reactionary forces launched a military coup against the reformist Yeltsin government on the eve of our departure in 1991. As tanks rumbled ominously through the streets of Moscow, our State Department issued an offi- cial advisory against travel to Russia, an exercise in common sense we greeted with all the gravity of teenagers listening to a lecture on the dangers of underage drinking. The hell with *that,* we con- cluded after several seconds of careful considera- tion. We were packed and ready, and not even armed insurrection would keep us away from the unspoiled wilderness Doug had described.

Despite all the international tension, the whoop-de-do at the airport came as a surprise. The reporters began to arrive as we stood in line before the Aeroflot counter, practicing, as it turns out, one of the most predictable elements of Russian life: waiting. Suddenly Governor Wally (You've seen one redwood, you've seen 'em all!) Hickle him- self appeared like a deranged spirit in a business suit. Alas, the fuss was never meant for us. Prince William Sound had experienced an unprecedented pink salmon return that year, and Alaska literally had more fish lying around than it could process. Never one to decline a photo op, the governor had decided to send a planeload of frozen salmon to Khabarovsk as a gesture of international good will. "Oh, great!" I snorted as reality sank in. "Humpies from Hickle." Then we resumed our wait as Aeroflot's charming personnel gave us a preview of what lay in store.

Because of the political crisis in Russia, flight security proved intense, and the gain on the metal detectors had been set to detect the fillings in our teeth. It took hours to make our way aboard the old jetliner, a decaying wreck of an airplane whose interior looked as if it had been designed by prison guards. As we settled into our seats, a burly flight attendant promptly introduced us to a

---

AT A GLANCE

Species Pacific salmon, Dolly Varden, white- spotted char, rainbow, steelhead, grayling, taimen, lenok

Tackle 10-weight gear for taimen, 6-weights for grayling, 7–8-weights for everything else; floating lines with twist-on ribbon lead to vary rate of sink; 15# tippet for taimen, 10# for everything else

Flies Basic anadromous fish selection; take a few dry flies for grayling and large deerhair mouse patterns for taimen

Prime Time June–October

Conservation Issues Inadequate control of water-quality standards near urban centers, overharvesting of critical fish stocks by local commercial and subsistence fishermen

Price Range $2,500–$3,500+

Staging City Anchorage, Alaska for Khabarovsk; Seoul, Korea for Mongolia

Heads Up Crime is a major problem throughout post-communist Russia

second inevitable Russian institution: vodka. "Better leave some extras," I suggested against my better judgment, for the flight already promised to be a long one.

As we clinked glasses, another flight attendant elbowed her way down the aisle and deposited a familiar-looking duffel bag in the seat behind us. "No room in baggage," she explained brusquely. As I confirmed the identity of the bag, I barely contained a gasp of surprise. Anticipating possible bear problems in the bush, I had stashed a short-barreled 12-gauge pump in my luggage, and there it lay, right along with a handful of slugs. And so, after hours of grueling security, we settled in for the long flight across the Pacific, fueled by Stolichnaya, armed with deadly force, and dimly aware that we would spend the next month in a land where nothing happened according to the rules as we understood them.

Within 24 hours of our arrival in Khabarovsk, Ray and I independently concluded that the entire Cold War had been a joke. Like all Americans of our generation, we had grown up practicing school evacuations and listening to sober discussions of bomb shelter designs predicated on the fear that post-*Sputnik* Russia stood ready, willing, and able to rain nuclear death upon us at any moment. But our first good look at the nation we had been raised to fear quickly made us doubt that any Russian warheads ever would have made it off the ground. At the end of the great communist experiment, Russia looked like a

TAIMEN

One of my few regrets about my own travels in the Russian Far East is that our agenda kept us too far north to fish for taimen. But I saw plenty of pictures and listened to lots of firsthand stories about encounters with these mysterious and intimidating fish.

All four species of the genus *Hucho* are unique to Eurasia, of which only one—*Hucho taimen*—inhabits the waters of the Far East. A primitive salmonid, taimen bear a passing resemblance to Atlantic salmon, with whom they no doubt share common ancestors. Taimen have a longer, leaner outline, a proportionately larger head and adipose fin, and they grow far larger—hundred-pounders are not uncommon and specimens over 150 pounds have been recorded. And they are aggressive predators, with feeding habits that resemble crocodiles more than game fish. During pink salmon runs, taimen characteristically lie in deep pools and gorge on migrating fish—not eggs or smolt, but whole adult salmon.

Russians typically fish for taimen at night with huge homemade surface plugs meant to resemble…who knows? Running dog imperialist lackeys, I suppose. I've examined some of these lures and am not sure I'd want to swim in water containing anything big enough to strike them. Friends experienced with taimen assure me that fly-rod anglers can achieve the same effect with oversized deer-hair surface bugs—the larger the better—meant to imitate mice. They also report that a surface strike from a 50-pound taimen represents one of fly fishing's most dramatic spectacles.

Sounds like a good reason to go back one more time…

High country in the Russian Far East.

Third World country, cities devoid of functional infrastructure, landscape littered with things that didn't work. The shock of this realization surprised me as much as anything I've experienced during my travels.

But the warmth of the people we met struck us even more than the country's disarray. We quickly formed strong friendships with the two bilingual members of our Russian entourage, Andrei Belayev—a Houston-trained cardiac surgeon—and Olga Anisimova—a former cardiologist who had abandoned her laboratory for the brave new world of Russian business enterprise. With the exception of occasional KGB agents—who stood out like undercover cops at a rock concert—and downcast party hacks trying desperately to hang on to the last vestiges of their

authority, the swirl of Russians into whose company we plunged proved utterly engaging. In social circumstances—usually seated behind closed doors around someone's kitchen table—we started out like boys and girls at a sixth-grade dance, only to segue quickly into a frenzy of dismay at the stupidity of our respective governments. And all that *before* the vodka appeared (which seldom took long).

Reflecting 70 years of state-controlled economic disaster, the Russians displayed a childlike fascination with the idea of personal wealth. They assumed all Americans were rich and asked "How much money do you make?" the way new acquaintances in other countries ask "How many children do you have?" After a while I began to make up answers to this inevitable question,

Russian fly-fishing pioneer Doug Borland on the banks of the Ulya with a Russian grayling.

ranging randomly between five thousand and five million dollars per year, only to note that the look of awe greeting my response did not seem to vary with the number.

But cities are still cities, and we soon began to long for the freedom of the bush. After completing our preliminary arrangements, we finally returned to the Khabarovsk airport to begin our long journey north into God-knows-what. We found ourselves the only passengers on a gigantic Tupelov military transport, and even with all our gear stored beside us we felt lost in its vast interior. After we taxied onto the runway, the captain aborted the engine run-up, returned to the passenger cabin, and engaged Andrei in a long, worried discussion.

"What's up, Andrei?" Doug finally asked.

"The captain regretfully informs us that we are overweight for takeoff," Andrei replied.

"By how much?" I asked incredulously, for the transport obviously boasted a useful load measured in tons.

"By one bottle of American whisky," Andrei replied solemnly.

Ah. As it happened, we had one squirreled away for a special occasion in camp. I dug the bottle of Wild Turkey from my pack and presented it to the captain, who retreated to the cockpit with a boyish grin. None of us gave the bottle's contents a snowball's chance in hell of seeing the ground again, a fact upon which I chose not to dwell when we shot a shaky approach into the village of Arca several hours later.

That night, we joined forces with the rest of the crew that would accompany us on our exploratory trip into the vast taiga to the north: Andrei Shepin, an obviously capable regional biologist, and Sergei, a wiry sable trapper who looked like he ate nails for breakfast. By the time we finished an evening's worth of introductions, the American contingent agreed quietly among ourselves that MacArthur had been right. Never mind the chaos back in the city: We were damn glad we never had to fight a ground war in Asia against the likes of our new friends.

The following morning we hitched a ride to our first base camp with a trio of biologists traveling aboard one of the sturdy Sikorskys that serve as the workhorses of the Russian bush. As an experienced Alaskan pilot, I never thought I'd fall victim to queasiness in the air, but that helicopter flight pushed my tolerance to the limits. The cabin full of diesel fumes and chain-smoking Russians would have been bad enough, but the biologists' cargo took olfactory issues to another level. Their mission consisted of transplanting

One of a dozen sea-run Dollies taken from "the river with no fish."

mink to the headwaters of a distant river. When the bird lifted off the ground, we were sitting on crates full of these splendidly odiferous animals as well as a winter's supply of ripe fish heads meant to keep the mink happy while they adjusted to their new home.

Needless to say, by the time we reached the river where we planned to camp, I felt ready for a break. As the chopper thudded its way back into the sky and the great silence of the bush wrapped its arms about us, I felt the solitude of the wilderness replace the glorious confusion of the trip's beginnings. Already starting to yellow in the crisp northern air, a sea of tamarack and birch stretched away across the hills, and the river ran clear as liquid crystal along the edge of the gravel bar where we had landed. After setting up camp and securing a supply of firewood, we could resist its invitation no longer. While the Russians

relaxed in front of the fire, we dug out our tackle and headed to the water.

Hulking shapes turned slowly in the current: the familiar green and maroon flanks of dog salmon. Several casts later, my rod tip bucked and a 20-pound dog broke free from the school and thrashed across the surface with my streamer hanging from its mouth. When I finally eased the fish into the shallows, Andrei Shepin appeared at my side, studied my catch happily, and dispatched it with a blow to the head. The fish proved to be a gravid hen. Andrei quickly slit its belly open with his hunting knife, stripped out the bulging skeins of eggs, and rolled them up, along with a handful of salt, in a section of *Pravda*. "Caviar!" he cried happily as he carried his prize back toward the fire, where I finally joined him after catching and releasing a dozen more brawny salmon just for the hell of it.

My own indifference to red caviar surprises me, given my general enthusiasm for sushi, seviche, and all manner of uncooked delicacies from the sea. I generally adopt a take-it-or-leave-it stance toward salmon roe on the table, but some combination of camaraderie and hunger convinced me otherwise that night. As the long northern twilight faded from the sky, the cold clots of eggs we wolfed down on top of raw onion slices and pilot bread tasted as marvelous as any meal imaginable.

We spent the rest of the month exploring the cultural differences in our attitudes toward the grizzly bears that prowled the banks in search of their own salmon dinners. Ray, Doug, and I were hunting to be sure, but we were doing so our own way, with longbows, and we tried our best to instruct our companions in the need for patience and discipline and the philosophy that made those traits important in the field. The Russians saw things differently. Sergei and Andrei Shepin had spent their lives in conflict with the bears, and they bore the scars to prove it. As Sergei explained one night: "The bears are our enemies here on the taiga. They kill us and we kill them." Because part of our mission was to train the Russians as future bowhunting guides, we clearly had a lot of work to do, and it did not always go easily.

Between go-arounds with the bears and our own camp mates, we relaxed on the water, where the Russians found our fly tackle and our refusal to kill everything we caught as baffling as our interest in hunting bears with sticks and strings. We caught dog salmon until our arms ached, and used the opportunity to introduce our Russian friends to the basics of fly-rod technique, which they quickly came to enjoy despite their original reservations. During midday lulls, we explored side channels for brilliantly colored Dolly Varden and cast egg patterns into riffles for hard-hitting white-spotted char. We kept what we needed to feed the camp and released the rest, to the

Russians' considerable amusement, and it was hard to avoid the impression that the time we spent together on the river made everything else a bit easier.

When we finally left the bush on the first leg of our return, we hitched a ride on a helicopter transporting kids from a series of far-flung Evensk reindeer-herding camps to boarding school in town. We enjoyed a warm reception in each of the camps we visited, and I found it difficult to stay dry-eyed as crowds of tough, rifle-toting parents bade their sobbing children farewell until spring. The country and its inhabitants had stolen a piece of my heart, and for a moment I considered waving good-bye to the helicopter and finding out for myself what it would be like to spend a winter on the taiga with the herders. In the end, my better judgment prevailed. I guess.

Back in Khabarovsk at last, we learned that during our stay in the bush the forces of reform had triumphed in Moscow. The tanks encircling the airport when we arrived had disappeared. The Communist party headquarters—the city's largest building—lay shuttered and empty while the young citizens of Khabarovsk staged an impromptu rock concert on its steps. The music sounded amateurish, but under the circumstances we found it hard to complain. We had not released a single arrow at a bear during our stay, but we sensed that we had made an impression on the Russians nonetheless. Over a dinner of steamed king crab, they invited us to return as their guests the following spring, to explore the shoreline of the Sea of Okhotsk, and we accepted without hesitation.

THE FOLLOWING MAY, after flying north from Khabarovsk to the tiny village of Okhotsk, Ray, Pat Barker, Andrei Belayev, and I piled our gear into another diesel-stained helicopter and set off down the coastline toward the mouth of the Ulya River while Doug and another party made their way north. The weather looked nothing less than

Camp in the Russian tundra, a rustic set-up. Note the longbows and arrows hanging in the foreground.

suicidal, but we had flown with the same pilot the year before and I intuitively trusted his ability, honed under combat conditions in Afghanistan. After picking his way along the sea for several hours in frighteningly limited visibility, he turned inland and brought the craft to a hover above a swirling sea of snow through which it proved impossible to see anything. "We are supposed to jump out now," Andrei Belayev explained as we faced the open hatch. And we did.

As the noise of the helicopter vanished into the blizzard overhead, I began to grasp for the first time what a lonely, intimidating place Siberia can be. A late-spring snowstorm had left the gravel bars covered in six-foot drifts. But the advance team had established a camp of sorts in a stand of

barren birch trees, and as we struggled through the snow with our gear we saw the familiar figure of Andrei Shepin bounding eagerly down the bank in our direction.

We spent the rest of the morning securing our quarters and renewing old friendships, but by midafternoon I was ready to go exploring. The snow clouds had parted, and the river ran low and clear past leftover chunks of ice. After boning up on my history over the winter, I knew that the Ulya marked the route the first ethnic Russian explorers had taken to the Pacific about the same time Lewis and Clark reached the opposite shore by way of the Columbia. Now Portland straddled the banks of the Columbia, whereas the mouth of the Ulya remained as wild and desolate as when

Ray Stalmaster fights a keta (dog salmon). We caught dog salmon on the Ulya until our arms ached.

tomorrow nature of anadromous fish, the water looked too inviting to be sterile. Besides, I really wanted to go fishing.

"There are absolutely no fish in the river," Andrei Shepin assured me after a brief discussion with his cohorts, all of whom plainly considered the question ridiculous.

"Bullshit," I snorted to Ray after another longing look at the water, and with that we dug out our gear and headed for the bank.

Perched gingerly on a shelf of ice, I rigged a streamer and fired it into the current. As the fly swung across the end of the pool, something bright and heavy tagged it. Driven by curiosity, I played the fish carefully and soon eased it out of the current and onto the ice. A brilliant silver monochrome, the featureless specimen stumped me for a moment, but I finally identified it as a sea-run Dolly. And as Ray and I proved over the course of the next hour, the river was full of more.

Upon our return to camp, the Russians greeted our description of events with frank disbelief. In fact, we had to walk back down to the river and demonstrate its bounty, which they plainly viewed as some kind of Yankee miracle akin to Coca-Cola, fast cars, and money. "But there are no fish in this river!" Andrei protested as I handed him a lively 5-pound char. Evidently, when it came to American optimism, wonders were never meant to cease.

The Russians plainly lacked our enthusiasm for catch-and-release fishing, and as I remembered the grim camp supplies we had lived on the previous year, I had to admit they had a point. Under the Russians' watchful gaze, we quickly caught and killed a dozen fine char. When Ray and I finally hiked back up the bank toward camp, we entertained visions of sizzling fillets, but we should have known better. Dinner that night consisted of fish heads simmered to the consistency of jelly, or snot, depending on your point of view. Fortunately, it was early in the trip and we still had plenty of vodka to go around.

its first visitors reached it two centuries ago. But despite this delicious irony, I admit feeling more intrigued by the possibility of fish than by history.

I knew we were too early for salmon, unless the river supported an early run of kings. "Are there any fish in the river now?" I asked the crew.

"Nyet," came the emphatic reply.

"Are you sure?" I asked again. Although I appreciate full well the here-today-gone-

During our second exploratory trip, we endured difficult weather, grueling physical exertion, and limited supplies, but we all remained friends. And yes, we finally made it happen with our longbows and the bears, although that is the subject of another story. But as I reflect back on those remarkable journeys, few memories remain as acute as the river that, according to the Russians, contained no fish.

We were fortunate enough to have visited the former Soviet Union at the precise hour of its collapse. During the course of the time we spent in country, we realized that although the system might have sucked, Russia and the Russians deserved our utmost respect and admiration. So what, in the decade that has passed since, went wrong?

The answer lies on the ice-choked banks of the Ulya. When Americans encounter untested water, they assume it contains fish until proven otherwise; the Russians assume the opposite. The fabric of our daily life is woven from a thread of just such assumptions. When we flip a switch, we expect a light to go on, and when we put money in the bank, we count on it being there the following day. Russian pessimism precludes such thinking. In simplistic terms, I believe that is how a society blessed with vast natural resources and an industrious, imaginative populace allowed itself to sink into poverty and chaos.

The river taught us that much, and I remain grateful for the lesson.

WHAT TO EXPECT

Reducing an area larger than the United States to a single book chapter represents a difficult task. Although the personal observations that follow pertain to the small part of Russia I have visited, I've included a few general comments on other fishing opportunities in eastern Russia and Mongolia, some of which might be of more interest to visitors devoting their efforts exclusively to angling.

ANGLING

With the exception of the white-spotted char, all the fish we encountered during our Russian travels were species native to Alaska, emphasizing the pan-Pacific origins of these game fish. And to be honest, despite the profound cultural effect our visits had on all of us, I wouldn't travel to the Russian Far East to fish for dog salmon, Dollies, or grayling, all of which are available in abundant numbers closer to home.

This doesn't mean that Russia doesn't contain some unique fishing opportunities. Atlantic salmon fishing on the Kola Peninsula has the potential to be the best in the world—whenever the locals stop netting fish—and the same can be said for steelhead on the Kamchatka peninsula. Farther to the south of the areas we visited, Russian and Mongolian rivers contain two novel species: taimen, a fascinating primitive salmonid that reaches triple-digit weights, and lenok, an interesting game fish that looks like an improbable cross between a brown trout and a sucker. No kidding.

The limitations of these fisheries arise from the Russians' near-complete inability to manage their resources, an issue that has only been magnified during the social chaos of the last decade. In a society that values a bowl of fish soup today more than a high-paying job as a guide tomorrow, keeping nets out of salmon streams proves a difficult goal indeed. Because of the remote nature of the areas we visited, commercial harvesting had virtually no impact on the resource, although it essentially ruined some splendid Atlantic salmon fishing opportunities farther to the east, as Doug found out when he tried to organize a fishing camp on the Kola.

Nonetheless, adventurous anglers can still find opportunities to explore this fascinating area's potential. Unless you enjoy tremendous reserves of time and patience, it's extremely difficult to travel freelance off the beaten path in Russia, and working through an established American-based outfitter has a lot to recommend it.

Top: Departure for the bush by ancient helicopter.
Above: We encounter local reindeer herders on the taiga.

In terms of climate and terrain, the Russian Far East proves a remarkably user-friendly locale during summer and early fall. The weather tends to be pleasantly sunny and dry compared to Alaska, although snow is always possible. Evening temperatures can be brisk, but clothing adequate for our own mountain West in late fall will generally suffice. Nonetheless, pack one set of cold-weather gear for severe cold in case unexpected conditions arise.

A lot has changed in this vast region since we made our first exploratory visits. Today, some of the best fishing for taimen can be found in Mongolia. Although I can't offer any observations based on personal experience, I've heard enough about Mongolia from reliable friends to arouse my interest, and I've included two contacts who outfit fly-fishing expeditions there.

LAY OF THE LAND

Travelers can fly on either Alaska Air or Aeroflot from Anchorage to Khabarovsk or Provideynia. From there, Aeroflot fixed-wing aircraft or helicopters provide transportation to final destinations in remote areas. Travelers to Mongolia generally fly KAL to Seoul before connecting on to Ulan Bator.

Amenities remain virtually nonexistent, so travelers should expect to be self-sufficient from the time they get off the airplane until the time they return. Language barriers can be formidable outside larger cities.

Modern medical care is hard to come by in the bush, with difficult evacuation likely in the case of serious illness or injury. Crime against travelers represents an increasing problem in most Russian cities. Grizzly bears identical to our own abound along streams containing salmon. *Giardia* commonly contaminates surface water. Visitors to certain parts of eastern Asia should consider vaccination against Japanese equine encephalitis, a sometimes fatal mosquito-borne viral infection. Because the vaccine is difficult to

A brilliantly colored Russian Dolly Varden.

obtain in this country and there is no clear consensus regarding its use, consultation with a travel-medicine clinic might be appropriate prior to departure. (See Appendix A for further information.)

Ancillary activities include wilderness camping, river rafting, and horse trekking (especially in Mongolia).

CONTACTS

KAMCHATKA EXPEDITIONS
www.anglingdestinations.com
Steelhead and rainbow near Petropavlavsk on the wild Kamchatka Peninsula. Book through Angling Destinations.

SWEETWATER TRAVEL COMPANY
411 South Third St.
Livingston, MT 59047
406-222-0624
www.sweetwatertravel.com
Today, the best fishing for taimen and lenok–

eastern Asia's most unique game fish–takes place in Mongolia, where Sweetwater Travel bases their operations.

RECOMMENDED READING

■ *REELING IN RUSSIA,* Fen Montaigne (1998. $24.95. St. Martins Press.) More travelogue than angling guide, but still a worthwhile view of modern Russia's complexities.
■ *LET THE SEA MAKE A NOISE,* Walter A. McDougall (1993. Out of print. HarperCollins.) A wonderful panoramic view of the North Pacific's history.
■ *FLY FISHING ACROSS RUSSIA, EAST EUROPE AND FINLAND,* Chris·Hole (1997. $34.95. Stackpole Books.) One of the few texts to address the subject.

The Yucatán Peninsula

Just the spot for anglers interested in taking a fly-rod bonefish, tarpon, and permit in the same day

The bank of mangroves lining the creek mouth reached ominously back into the thick Mexican jungle. Behind me, sunlight danced across a broken flat stretching all the way to the reef and the edge of the Caribbean. This was the crossroads. Clarity and light waited on one side, shadows and a vague sense of foreboding on the other. Nominally intent on bonefish, I should have kept to the open flat, but after a moment's hesitation, I headed inland toward the heart of darkness.

The water licked its way slowly up my thighs as I entered the creek, and marl began to tug at my ankles. As soon as the shadows closed overhead, a vague disturbance appeared in the water. Although it was impossible to identify its source, I wasn't about to turn up my nose at anything with scales and a tail, not after a long day of airports, customs, and related man-made hassles. Mindful of the branches all around, I rolled a Clouser Minnow in against the mangrove shoots

Boca Paila Lodge, one of the oldest sportfishing lodges on the coast, near the mouth of Boca Paila.

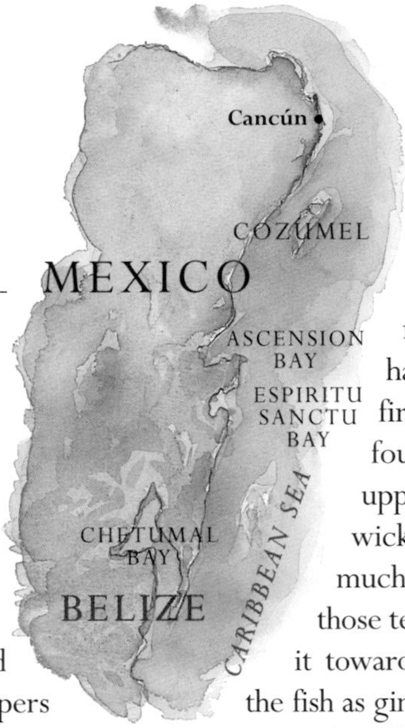

and earned a prompt and enthusiastic strike for my trouble.

The fish turned out to be a 2-pound snapper—not much by the heady standards of saltwater glamour species but all kinds of fun on the light tackle I prefer for this sort of exploratory adventure. Somehow, I kept the fish away from the brush long enough to land and release it, remembering why snappers are called snappers and giving even those little jaws all the respect they deserved.

The encounter left the fly a bedraggled mess of white bucktail and silver tinsel, but the snappers didn't care, as a half-dozen more eventually proved. The marl had deepened steadily underfoot as I worked my way up the creek, and I was about to turn back toward the open flat and its solid footing when something tagged the fly with more punch than any of the snappers had shown. While I wrestled with an undisciplined loop of slack, a small barracuda shot by toward the open sea, leaving me little choice but to follow.

Because I was fishing with monofilament leader, I shouldn't have stayed attached to the fish in the first place, but the fly had somehow found a parking place on the 'cuda's upper lip, just beyond the reach of its wicked teeth. Although the fish wasn't much bigger than a pickerel, I knew what those teeth could do, and when I finally led it toward my outstretched hand, I treated the fish as gingerly as a live bomb.

Back in the open, courtesy of the barracuda, I replaced my frayed tippet and opened my fly book. I was considering my options when the water boiled 20 yards down the beach. Reaching quickly for a small Deceiver on a light wire leader, I was soon ready for Round Three.

The predator responsible for the disturbance turned out to be a 10-pound jack crevalle. The fish pounced on the streamer aggressively, and its first run reminded me just how arbitrary the distinction between glamour species and all the rest can be. Fortunately, I had the right leader for the right fish this time, and I didn't have to rely

(Map labels: Cancún · COZUMEL · MEXICO · ASCENSION BAY · ESPIRITU SANCTU BAY · CARIBBEAN SEA · CHETUMAL BAY · BELIZE)

AT A GLANCE

Species Bonefish, tarpon, permit, jacks, barracuda, snapper, snook

Tackle 7–8-weight rods for bonefish, jacks, and snapper; 10-weights for permit, tarpon, and barracuda; floating lines; 8# tippets for bones, 12–15# for larger species; wire leader for 'cuda, heavy-monofilament shock tippet for tarpon

Flies Basic flats and backcountry selections; include crab patterns for permit, and needlefish imitations for barracuda

Prime Time March–June

Conservation Issues Coastline development, commercial netting

Price Range $1,500–$3,500

Staging City Cancun, Mexico

Heads Up Mexican traffic is justifiably notorious; drive the Yucatán's roadways with extreme caution

Releasing a bonefish at Ascension Bay, where bonefish, tarpon, and permit can be taken on the same day.

on luck as I had with the barracuda.

The ocean flat added a blue runner and several more 'cuda to the afternoon's tally before I turned and headed back toward shore and our rental car. There were also some hard strikes from unknown species and an encounter with a larger jack that ended when the fish took me around a coral head and snapped the leader. The sun had slipped toward the tops of the palms and the water had turned the color of gold. The visibility was terrible and I was pleasantly exhausted, a combination of factors that helps explain how I managed to blunder right into the bonefish.

Suddenly a tail rose in front of me, waving like a signalman's flag reminding distracted motorists to slow down at a construction site. Too

worn out to react, I just stood and stared until the fish disappeared. At the end of the long afternoon, my fleeting encounter with the bonefish reminded me how easy it can be to forget just what one has come for and how pleasant the process of forgetting can become.

AMERICANS SHARE THEIR BORDERS with only two other nations, an accident of geography that no doubt contributes to our oddly insular view of the world. To the north, most of Canada is a lot more like our own country than Canadians would probably care to admit, but heading south is another matter. Mexico offers everything a trip to another country should, including a foreign language, novel cuisine, and a rich and varied sense of history stretching back farther than most of us can readily imagine. I love Mexico, not least because it happens to be one of the best places on earth to have fun with a fly rod.

Most of the attraction our southern neighbor exerts upon anglers comes from salt water. On the Pacific side, Baja and the Sea of Cortéz offer a wide array of bluewater opportunities for heavy hitters such as *mahi,* roosterfish, yellowtail, and billfish. Although I haven't fished the Pacific coast of Mexico since I was a kid, I still have fond memories of encounters with big game I enjoyed there years ago.

Because of a personal fascination with flats fishing, most of my experience in Mexico has come on the Caribbean. From Cozumel south to the border of Belize, the reefs, bays, and lagoons that define the coast of the Yucatán peninsula provide inshore fly-fishing opportunities as varied as any in the world. For years, Ascension Bay has enjoyed a reputation as the Grand Slam capital of the world, and with good reason. Anglers interested in the *betcha can't top this* feat of taking a fly-rod bonefish, tarpon, and permit in the same day would be hard put to imagine a better spot to turn the trick.

Attractive beachfront seldom remains pristine for long, and the Yucatán's southern coast has seen a surge of development over the last decade, which is both good news and bad news for anglers. On the positive side, more good water has become accessible and the economic potential of sportfishing has led the government to begin limiting commercial netting. Fortunately, the Mexican government has wisely included much of the Yucatán's premier backcountry fishing in the Sian Ka'an Biosphere preserve, which should insulate vast reaches of coastline from development. On the other hand, more visitors means a certain loss of innocence, which might be the price the world pays for putting up with people like us.

Of course, ours is hardly the first culture to transform the landscape of southern Mexico.

Top: Prime permit from Ascension Bay. Above: The boat dock at Boca Paila Lodge.

Between 300 and 1000 A.D., indigenous Mayan peoples developed one of the world's great early civilizations in the Yucatán. Mayan mathematicians were among the first in the world to master the concept of zero. Their astronomers

A selection of permit flies displayed on a conch shell.

accurately calculated the duration of other planets' orbits about the sun. Architecturally splendid cities rose from the jungle. But well before the eventual European conquest in the 16th century, the foundations of Mayan civilization began to disintegrate. Although the Maya of the Yucatán apparently maintained some of their former glory longer than their counterparts farther south, by the time the Spaniard de Montejo conquered the area in 1546, the Mayan culture he overran remained but a shadow of its former self.

What happened to the Maya? Contemporary scholars have invoked all Four Horsemen of the Apocalypse to explain their collapse: war with neighboring cultures, famine due to overpopulation or crop failure, epidemic disease, the cultural toll of cannibalism and human sacrifice. Explanations remain as obscure as the jungles that contain them. But

when you've found your way to one of the ruins that lie hidden along the coast, it's impossible not to wonder. For someday when the vines have reclaimed the high-rise hotels proliferating like mushrooms along the coast south of Cancún, someone will no doubt ask the same questions about us.

In the meantime, we might as well go fishing.

DESPITE RECENT ATTENTION as a permit hot spot, the Yucatán built its reputation as a saltwater fly-rod destination on bonefish. Although undeniably abundant, Mexican bones run on the small side. After a morning spent catching typical Yucatán two-pounders in the waters near Boca Paila a few years back, I decided I wanted to try for something heftier. As I wasn't in the mood for frustration at the hands of the permit, I rigged a wire leader and tube fly and told our guide I wanted to drift across some deeper water and sight-cast to some of the big barracuda we'd seen while running between bonefish flats.

This suggestion produced a remarkable antipathy in the skiff's stern. Our guide that day was a taciturn but competent local named Enrique. I never did understand his distaste for barracuda, but he immediately made it clear that he somehow considered them beneath his dignity. After several minutes of cajoling in my less than fluent Spanish, I finally convinced him that I meant to do this with his approval or without, and we ran about to the upwind edge of a long flat where we had seen 'cuda lurking the day before.

Barracuda might be one of the natural

Flats fishing from a guided boat, a good way to cover more water.

world's most perfectly designed killing machines, and their form complements their function. Despite their differences, bones, tarpon, and permit all look like game fish. Barracuda, on the other hand, look reptilian, like something returned from the primordial past intent on mayhem. When I saw the first long, dark shadow lurking just beneath the surface, I felt a moment of ambivalence as I asked Enrique to pole us into a position that would allow a straight downwind cast.

Despite their aggressive nature, 'cuda can act with remarkable diffidence toward flies. I've dragged needlefish imitations past their snouts dozens of times, only to have them turn and disappear sullenly into deep water, but not this time. As soon as my tube fly entered its field of vision,

the fish accelerated and pounced furiously. When I drove the hook home, it tail-walked away across the surface with enough acrobatic vigor to make me wonder why this species doesn't enjoy more respect from fly-rod anglers everywhere.

Just like their freshwater analogs in the pike family, barracuda offer more flash than substance on the end of a fly line. The strike and first wild run can be electrifying, but barracuda are sprinters with limited reserves over the long haul. After a few minutes of fury, the fish conceded and returned gently to the skiff, where I admired the terrible outline of its teeth while Enrique made unhappy faces in the stern.

Distasteful as Enrique evidently found the 'cuda, the fish served as a perfect reminder of everything I love about fishing the Yucatán. Few coastlines on earth offer the opportunity to do so many things with a fly rod at such a relaxed pace. Throw in warm weather, cold beer, and good company and the Yucatán practically screams *Road Trip!*, especially when the snow is flying at home. Close enough to be practical and cheap enough to be affordable, the Yucatán still offers everything a trip to an exotic destination should, with or without a flats Grand Slam.

WHAT TO EXPECT

ANGLING

From Cozumel south to the Belizean border, the Yucatán peninsula offers visitors a long, spectacular shoreline. On the outside, a broken barrier reef provides protection from the Caribbean, and hard sand beaches offer anglers an opportunity to wade and fish from shore.

Inland, a complex series of bays and lagoons open up into the mangrove jungle behind the beach, providing rich fish habitat. In the bays, the bottom often consists of soft marl and most fishing takes place from skiffs, although sandy ocean flats allow wading in some areas.

Known primarily as a tourist destination, the waters around Cancún and Cozumel support large populations of fish, including tarpon, barracuda, and jacks. Because there aren't a lot of flats on the northern end of the Yucatán coast, this area doesn't receive much attention from visiting fly-rod anglers, although friends who have fished the area assure me game fish abound there. The Yucatán's reputation as an angling destination derives from the shallow flats farther south, primarily in the waters near Boca Paila and Ascension Bay. Farther from civilization yet,

THE REAL JAWS

The largest of the world's 20-odd species of barracuda, the Caribbean's great barracuda (*Sphyraena barracuda*) consistently arouses more trepidation from divers and less respect from anglers than it deserves.

'Cuda certainly present a formidable appearance. Although 100-pound specimens have been taken offshore, any 'cuda over 40 pounds is a large one in shallow water, where fly-rod anglers are likely to encounter them. That's still a lot of fish, especially when equipped with long rows of prominent, daggerlike teeth. Those who have lost hooked fish to barracuda will testify to the brutal efficiency of the 'cuda's dental work, which can slice through a large game fish with effortless surgical precision. To compound matters, the 'cuda's undershot jaw and prominent eye create a particularly malign countenance.

In fact, barracuda rarely attack humans,

particularly given the frequency with which swimmers and divers encounter these common, inquisitive fish. But attacks do occur, usually in cloudy water or when a fish has lunged at a shiny object worn by a swimmer. Avoid wearing jewelry while swimming, or dangling hands and feet overboard in waters barracuda frequent.

Anglers must treat barracuda with respect. Boated barracuda aren't nearly as dangerous as sharks, but it's still wise to be cautious when working near their mouths. Remove flies only with long pliers or hemostats while the fish is under control. My own closest call came as I bent down to release a bonefish I had just landed on a shallow flat. Appearing from nowhere, a large 'cuda slashed through the spent bone, leaving me holding nothing but the head. The neatly transected fish very easily could have been my own wrist.

A small snook, another of the many flats species that can be taken along the Yucatan coast.

Espiritu Sanctu and Chetumal Bays afford true wilderness flats fishing. Accommodations and services in these remote areas remain limited, although I expect the reputation of these areas to develop quickly in the years ahead.

Yucatán waters contain vast numbers of bonefish, and large schools of feeding bones appear frequently inshore. That's the good news; the bad news is that most Yucatán bones weigh less than three pounds, and anglers specifically intent on large bonefish are likely to be disappointed. On the other hand, the permit fishing ranks among the best anywhere both in terms of size and number. Lodges operating in Ascension Bay have declared their waters the Permit Capital of the World, and it's a hard claim to argue. And as described earlier, the Yucatán offers a tremendous variety of saltwater species. Even when the bonefish are small and the permit uncooperative, the Yucatán always seems to offer the fly-rod angler some new challenge.

Spring and early summer provide the most consistent fishing opportunities. Although the fish are there year-round, cold fronts can compromise fishing in winter. However, winter weather is generally less problematic than in flats locations farther north, so those who really need their flats fishing during the cold winter months might consider the Yucatán as an alternative to locations in Florida or the Bahamas.

LAY OF THE LAND

Visitors with time can reach the Yucatán by private vehicle. Be sure to obtain adequate Mexican automobile insurance and exercise due caution regarding bad driving conditions and petty crime on the roads. Drivers should expect to encounter military roadblocks, especially during periods of political unrest. Most air travelers connect through Cancún, served by regularly scheduled flights from a number of departure cities in the southern United States. Most lodges routinely arrange

Boated barracuda aren't as dangerous as sharks, but be cautious when working near their mouths.

transportation by vehicle and/or boat from Cancún. Visitors touring the area on their own can rent vehicles in Cancún and travel south by road to Punta Allan or Chetumal. Expect poor road conditions south of Playa Carmen.

Although most fishing lodges in the area employ English-speaking guides, even a basic knowledge of Spanish can be very helpful when traveling the Yucatán off the beaten path. The tourist scene in Cancún and Cozumel can get old

in a hurry, but away from these population centers I've found Yucatán residents unfailingly helpful and gracious.

It's always wise to avoid drinking tap water outside larger hotels or established lodges. Travelers' diarrhea is common. Biting insects can be troublesome inland away from coastal breezes, especially during the summer. Petty crime is a common problem near tourist destinations. Drug traffic remains active on the Yucatán: Avoid suspicious activity. Snakes are rare in the marine environment and sharks, although common, rarely cause problems in this area. Malaria occurs occasionally in southern Mexico. Consult the Centers for Disease Control (CDC) for current advisories. (See Appendix A for further information.)

The water along the Yucatán's outer reefs offers world-class diving. South of Cozumel, these opportunities remain largely unexplored. Mayan ruins dot the entire peninsula. Not even the commercialized ambience of developed sites at Chichen Izta and Tulum can compromise the grandeur of what the Maya left behind, and experts estimate that only a small fraction of the area's archeological sites have been discovered. While fishing, I've visited overgrown ruins in the backcountry that haven't seen outsiders in years. Those with the urge to explore should be limited only by their imaginations.

CONTACTS

BOCA PAILA LODGE

www.bocapaila-lodge.com
One of the oldest sportfishing lodges on the coast, situated in a scenic location near the mouth of Boca Paila. Good permit fishing and lots of small bonefish in a pleasant setting.

ASCENSION BAY LODGE

Located on the southern end of Ascension Bay, this remote, air-accessible lodge enjoys a well-earned reputation as one of the world's best permit fishing spots.

The faint glow of sunset colors moonrise over Ascension Bay as another day of fishing ends.

RECOMMENDED READING

■ *A FOREST OF KINGS: THE UNTOLD STORY OF THE ANCIENT MAYA,* Linda Schele and David Freidel (1992. $19.00. Quill.) It would be a shame to visit the Yucatán without some appreciation of its rich pre-Colombian history.

■ *A FIELD GUIDE TO MEXICAN BIRDS,* Roger Tory Peterson (1999. $21.00. Houghton Mifflin.) Biocomplexity increases dramatically in the tropics. This installment in the popular Peterson Field Guides series will help visitors sort out the birds.

■ *FLY-FISHING THE FLATS,* Barry and Cathy Beck (1999. $39.95. Stackpole Books.) A clear, concise volume especially useful for freshwater anglers making their first trip to the flats.

Kodiak & the Southeast

This is a marine wilderness that speaks in superlatives...
And the fish fit right in.

A fresh male silver salmon recently returned from the sea to spawn.

I'm not ashamed to admit that Shelikof Strait intimidates me. Stretching between the Alaska mainland and the north shore of Kodiak Island, this 40-mile-wide reach of angry sea does more than its share to make the Kodiak coast guard station the nation's busiest. My trepidation derives from an element of personal history as well. Years ago while fishing commercially for halibut, our boat lost power in Shelikof Strait. Although nothing untoward came of this mishap, I

have never seen the sea look so big or a boat so small. Sometimes I wonder if I should ever go back.

But as they say, *Nothing ventured...* By the light of the long June dawn, the sea looked flat as a millpond outside my friend Bob May's front door. With a favorable marine forecast crackling over the radio, we decided to ignore the salmon teeming just around the corner in the Litnik River and head to sea in search of something new and exotic. By the time the light had risen enough to

coax some color from the landscape, we were under way in Bob's sturdy skiff: Bob and his wife, Denise; Lori and I; and one of the May's seaworthy Chesapeake Bay retrievers thrown in for good measure.

We were after black sea bass, an intriguing fish that deserves more attention from fly-rod enthusiasts than it commonly receives. Actually, this species (*Sebastodes melanops*) is not a bass at all but a member of the rockfish family, distinguished from its bottom-dwelling cousins by its pelagic lifestyle and feeding habits. Because sea bass frequently chase bait near the surface, they are one of the few Pacific rockfish that offer reasonable opportunities for the fly rod.

But first we had to find them. As we left the security of protected water and rounded the corner into the strait, broad swells rose to meet us and the sea took on a menacing Devil's Triangle quality that I did my best to ignore. Bob headed for a likely looking kelp bed while Lori and I

rigged our gear with more help than we really needed from the dog. We soon had a teaser spoon trailing the downrigger 20 feet below the boat, and I settled back to glass the coastline for bears while everyone else studied the depth finder for provocative blips.

Fifteen minutes later, something snapped the line from the downrigger, and Lori soon had the spoon—and several aggressive sea bass—at the surface behind the transom. For one wonderful moment I found myself thinking about teasing sailfish into fly-rod range off the coast of Central America, and the memory felt so incongruous with our surroundings that I stood and stared until a blast of chilly breeze brought me back to my senses. Finally I took the only logical course of action, which was to dive for my fly rod.

As soon as it hit the water, the gaudy streamer earned a reception appropriate to a piece of chum

AT A GLANCE

SPECIES Pacific salmon (king, red, pink, silver, chum), steelhead, cutthroat, Dolly Varden, halibut, rockfish

TACKLE 5–6-weight rods for cutthroat, 7–9-weights for steelhead and salmon in fresh water, 10–12-weights for halibut and king salmon in salt; floating or sink-tip lines for fresh water, fast-sinking shooting heads for halibut and rockfish; 10–12# tippet for steelhead and salmon in fresh water, 15# for saltwater species

FLIES Basic anadromous selection for fresh water; weighted, bright baitfish imitations on 2/0–3/0 hooks for salt water

PRIME TIME April–October

CONSERVATION ISSUES Inshore habitat degradation by logging, high seas interception of migratory fish, oil spills and other forms of marine contamination

PRICE RANGE $1,500–$3,500

STAGING CITY Anchorage, Alaska for Kodiak; Seattle, Washington for the southeast coast

HEADS UP Alaska's strong tides can take visitors by surprise

thrown to a school of feeding sharks. Before I could strip my line, a bass smacked the fly and headed for the bottom. Those who have met sea bass while trolling for salmon with conventional tackle might not think much of their sporting qualities, but they give a vigorous account on the end of a fly line. My first fish took me well into my backing before I finally brought it to the net.

We had proved it could be done, and now it was someone else's turn. Lori headed to the stern armed with her fly rod while I conceived the brilliant notion of coaxing fish to the surface by hooking one on a jig and seeing what followed it to the boat. But there were problems. Because of a cut sustained the day before, I had a bandage right where the line from the spinning reel needed to leave my forefinger during a cast. Furthermore, I had not picked up a spinning rod in years. The result was no doubt inevitable. On my first cast, the boat pitched, the line caught my bandaged finger, and the metal jig crashed straight into Lori's head.

Talk about an argument for barbless hooks. At least her sunglasses prevented a stupid mistake from turning into a tragedy. But she still had one-third of a treble hook imbedded in her forehead, and as I was both perpetrator and ship's doctor, the problem was mine to solve. Bob quickly produced an array of cutting tools, but I decided this would be an opportune time to demonstrate the right way to remove a fish hook from the human body, an operation with which I've had more than my share of experience. With a loop of stout leader around the hook's bend and downward

pressure on the shank, I prepared to snap the hook free while Lori made a face. "I'm not going to hurt you," I assured her.

"I don't care about *that*," she replied. "Just get this damn thing out of my face so I can go fishing!" What a woman.

With the hook free at last, Lori climbed back into casting position in the stern. By this time, we could see fish on the depth finder 25 feet below. Declining my offer of another attempted assist with the jig, she reached for the rod we had set up with a high-density shooting head and a lead-eyed streamer. Though undeniably ugly, the fly earned a brisk strike as soon as the line straightened beneath the boat. Denise quickly hooked a second fish, at which point lines began to cross as chaos reared its ugly head. Somehow, we sorted out the mess without consequences and landed both bass.

And so it went for nearly an hour, until I landed a bass that might well have been a fly-rod world record if there is such a thing for this species. Because we had no means of weighing the fish aboard the boat, I can only say that I have looked at a lot of black sea bass over the years without seeing one anywhere near that size, taken on any kind of tackle. By the time the fish lay in the net, the wind was freshening from the north as the sea began to flex its muscles beneath the hull. Bob wisely decided it was time to run for home, and no one argued despite the pace of the fishing.

And what of the potential world record? That night it became a bowl of seviche, remembered as I would like to be when it becomes my turn to contribute to the food chain. So much

Opposite: One of thousands of meandering rivers typical of the Alaskan wilderness. Above: Rainbow from a lake. Freshwater lake and stream fishing opportunities abound not far from the coast.

Top: Gus (left) meets a silver salmon. Above: The author's wife, Lori, takes a black sea bass near Kodiak Island.

images of each other, a shocking violation of protocol in a phylum noted for its orderly attention to biological structure. And there is also the matter of size. Halibut reach Godzilla-like proportions in Alaska waters, where 100-pound fish are common and 400-hundred-pounders appear every year. The thought of fish like that on the end of a fly line should be enough to rattle anyone's nerves.

Although the fish themselves are intimidating enough, their habits make them an even more daunting challenge for the fly-rod angler. Generally regarded as bottom feeders, halibut often frequent depths measured in hundreds of feet, which puts them beyond the reach of fly tackle. Furthermore, the strong tides that tear along the coast of Alaska often make it difficult to get a hook down to halibut depth with anything less than a cannonball lead sinker. Obviously, anglers who want to catch halibut on flies need to learn a few tricks of the trade.

Despite their general preference for deep water, halibut move into relative shallows to spawn in late May, and they often reappear to feed on salmon carcasses near river mouths during late summer. Furthermore, during favorable tide conditions halibut will rise to feed middepth in the water column, which means flies can be effective even some distance from the bottom.

The art of getting flies to halibut always begins with an understanding of local tides. Flats enthusiasts accustomed to tidal fluctuations measured in inches will have to reprogram their computers before tackling Alaska waters, where 20-foot tides regularly scour the coast. Complex shorelines keep tidal currents in constant motion, and when the tide is running hard, halibut conserve energy by staying glued to the bottom. The key to success at this difficult game is to fish hard for a half hour on either side of every tide change.

No matter what the manufacturers of specialized tackle would have us believe, most saltwater

for world records…and the notion that salmon are the only fish in Alaska's salt waters that deserve attention on a fly.

THE BASS PROVIDED A fascinating diversion, but we had come for big game. In the cold water surrounding Kodiak Island, that means halibut, perhaps as unlikely a quarry for the fly-rod angler as the world's oceans will ever provide.

The species' eccentricity begins with its anatomy. The halibut and its immediate relatives are the only vertebrates that lack a longitudinal axis of symmetry. Stated simply, there is no way to cut a halibut into two pieces that form mirror

fly fishing can be done with freshwater equipment, at least in a pinch. Halibut fishing is different. Because it can be so difficult to get down to the fish, a high-density sinking shooting head is mandatory. Lead eyes and short leaders help keep flies working near the bottom. Leader shyness isn't a problem, but leaders should contain a section substantially lighter than the backing, a precaution that might save a fly line if you snag a piece of kelp or hook a hopelessly large fish. If all this sounds a bit overwhelming, remember that no one ever confused halibut with spring-creek browns.

By the time we reached sheltered water just before slack tide, Bob and I found ourselves beset by a serious case of the lazies. Because we needed a small halibut for our evening meal, we settled back inside the cabin while Lori and Denise prospected for fish with conventional tackle from the stern. On our first drift across the sunken ridge known as Halibut #4 to Bob's GPS, something tagged Lori's herring. Several minutes later, a 20-pound halibut came over the side to end our dinner concerns.

The fish quickly barfed up a clot of fresh candlefish that bore an uncanny resemblance to the white streamer on the end of the 10-weight stowed atop the wheelhouse. A quick glance at the depth finder showed that Lori had taken the fish in 65 feet of water—well within reach of our fly tackle. With no further ado, I grabbed my rod, scampered to the bow, and gauged the drift. After a few quick strips, I sent the shooting head arcing upstream into the waning tidal current.

The fly never reached the bottom. The fish struck so subtly that it took me a moment to realize what had happened. As soon as I set the hook, the rod tip practically buckled. One of the true pleasures of fishing Alaska's coastal waters arises from the uncertainty of every strike, as you consider the question asked by anglers from Jonah to Santiago: *Just how big is this damn thing, anyway?*

This time, the answer turned out to be: *Not very*...15 pounds or so. Enthusiasts of un-

The author with two halibut, perhaps as unlikely a quarry for the fly-rod angler as the world's oceans will ever provide.

conventional species often overstate the fighting qualities of whatever fish has just captured their imagination, a tendency I deliberately try to avoid. The halibut fought hard for a minute or two, but once I had the fish headed to the surface the contest was over. After all, you don't do this because halibut fight like tarpon. You do this because...well, because they are there.

I wound up taking several more halibut on successive drifts across the bank before the tide picked up. None weighed more than 20 pounds, but every strike felt like some kind of miracle. And each time the line hesitated and I set the hook I asked myself *How big?* and wondered if I had made contact with something larger than any of us.

And who knows? Perhaps I had.

THE SHEER ENORMITY of the Alaska coastline can challenge the imagination. Two of America's three largest islands—Kodiak and Prince of Wales—lie nestled in the vast crescent of volcanoes and glaciers that stretches from the panhandle to the Alaska Peninsula. This is big land and big water, a marine wilderness that speaks in superlatives, from the giant conifers of the panhandle's temperate rain forest to the oversized bears that lumber along Kodiak's deserted shores. And the fish fit right in. I've discussed sea bass and halibut because these species don't get much attention in the fly-fishing literature, but anadromous fish attract most of the attention along Alaska's coastline, and none deserves its reputation more than the steelhead.

Deep in the rain-soaked heart of southeast Alaska's panhandle, I am standing beside a tiny stream that does not officially support a steelhead run. I have just invested an hour of slip-and-slide hiking upstream from the beach in an effort to prove officialdom wrong. In a just world, the thrill of this discovery would serve as its own

SEAFOOD PLATTER

To experienced visitors with a taste for seafood, Alaska's southern coast resembles one vast sushi bar. Those with well-developed hunter-gatherer instincts might find themselves spending more time pursuing invertebrates than game fish.

Three popular species of crab inhabit the Gulf of Alaska. Because of their deepwater habitat preferences and the inshore harvest restrictions mandated by declining stocks, most visitors won't see king crabs outside restaurants in larger towns. Tanner (also known as queen, or snow, crabs) and Dungeness crabs are plentiful near shore where they can be taken by hand. Crabbing gear is available at many lodges. Season, sex, and size restrictions apply, so consult current regulations.

Shrimp abound in Alaska waters, where they form an important link in the food chain. Although many species are smaller than shrimp from warmer waters, their taste is unrivaled, and many regard the Alaska side-stripe as the finest-tasting shrimp in the world.

Several species of clams occur on Alaska beaches, including the prized razor clam and giant geoduck. For everyday cuisine, most Alaskans prefer the butter clam, a silver-dollar-size bivalve found at shallow depths along most gravelly beaches. Delicious steamed, fried, or in chowder, butter clams can easily be dug on almost any low tide, making them the local seafood enthusiast's equivalent of the slam-dunk. Alaska clams have caused outbreaks of PSP (paralytic shellfish poisoning). Exercise caution and heed local knowledge.

Finally, don't overlook the unappealing sea cucumber. Despite their appearance, sea cucumbers are highly prized by the Japanese, who know North Pacific seafood better than anyone. Generally brown or orange and varying between one and two feet in length, sea cucumbers can be gathered with nets or gaffs along rocky outcroppings during low minus tides. Prepare them by cutting off each end of the hollow tube, slitting them open, and filleting out the longitudinal strips of muscle that line the interior. It's a lot of work for not much meat, but fry them in butter and the results will provide a memorable culinary experience.

Floatplanes and the bush pilots who fly them are synonymous with Alaskan fishing

reward, but I have a different kind of compensation in mind. I want contact, a close encounter of the third kind. Although it is not my intention to kill, I at least need to reach out and touch one of the huge shapes I've spotted finning their way along the gravel bottom.

A stone's throw away across the tumbling run, a water-worn cliff rises toward the brooding sky. To cast from those rocks would require technical climbing gear. This side of the stream isn't much friendlier, as the crowded brush behind me promises to swallow any attempt at presentation. The log remains the only possible option.

Even in repose, the log stands so tall that I have to toss my gear up first before I can scramble up behind. From this elevated position, I can see fish outlined clearly against the pale gravel below. The geometry of current, depth, and drift seems impossible at first, but after a couple of failed attempts I manage to roll the fly right up where it

belongs. By the time I catch up to the current with a furious series of mends, my line isn't doing what the water is telling it to, and when I haul back on the rod, the stream comes alive just for me.

The good news is that I've hooked what a growing number of knowledgeable anglers regard as the country's premier fly-rod game fish. The bad news is that the log that allowed me to make the cast in the first place now threatens to prevent me from landing the fish. The steelhead could tear downstream, which would leave me with trouble enough on light tackle. But it chooses to run upstream instead, and because I started out casting from the downstream side of the log, this decision means that several tons of dead Douglas fir now separates me from the fish.

The further details of this absurd situation scarcely matter. It is enough to know that the fish took a whole lot of line under the log before snapping the leader and leaving me to sort out the

Silvers, the author's favorite quarry of all the Pacific salmon, show up in late August and September.

mess left behind. What does matter is that I hardly regard the loss of the fish as, well...a loss. On the Kenai River I've seen grown anglers sit down and sob after losing big kings next to the boat. I'm not being critical; I've been close to the same response myself a time or two. But the special thing about wild Alaska steelhead is that touching one—even with nothing more than a small fly on the end of a light line—can sometimes be enough. For here in this wild country, the fish become a means rather than an end. We come

seeking the promises they fulfill. Who could ask for anything more?

WHAT TO EXPECT

ANGLING

From the tip of the panhandle near Ketchikan north through Prince William Sound and on to the Kodiak archipelago and the shore of the Alaska Peninsula, Alaska's southern coast forms a vast maritime wilderness containing some of the country's most spectacular scenery and wildlife.

From the original Aleut, Haida, and Tlingit to the era of the Russian fur trade, this area enjoys a unique cultural heritage every bit as fascinating as its natural history.

Although game fish can be found in Alaska's coastal waters during any month of the year, darkness and inclement weather discourage all but the hardiest anglers during the winter. Fishing starts to become productive in March, when steelhead return to southeastern Alaska streams. These runs continue through May. King salmon show up in salt water around the same time. Red salmon return in June and July, pinks and dogs in August, and silvers—my favorite flyrod quarry of all the Pacific salmon—in late August and

A heavy August run of salmon in a clear-water spawning stream in the southeast.

September. Timing of salmon runs varies by species and locale. Some steelhead streams support both spring and fall runs. Contact local sources for specifics. Summer months provide the best fishing for halibut and sea bass. Spring is prime time for sea-run Dollies and cutthroats.

The panhandle's inside passage and parts of Prince William Sound offer relatively protected water, but boating can be dangerous anywhere along the coast, and visitors should exercise due caution. Strong tides can produce rough seas quickly. Monitor weather information, heed local advice and knowledge, and err on the conservative side. Visitors lacking experience with small craft in rough water should not operate their own boats. Expect strong currents at sea, plan ahead to avoid getting cut off by incoming tides, and don't think you're going to swim your way out of trouble (I've done it, but it wasn't fun).

Although summer weather can be pleasant along the coast, anticipate wind and rain, and dress accordingly. Carry appropriate survival gear and the means to combat hypothermia. High-quality rain gear is mandatory throughout the area. Dress in layers, including Polar Fleece and wool. Calf-high rubber boots will keep feet dry aboard boats. Pack plenty of extra socks, as wet feet are likely.

Coastal Alaska is serious bear country, supporting large populations of both black and brown bears. Anglers should anticipate the presence of bears along streams whenever salmon are present. In southeast Alaska, the larger and more aggressive brown bears are found only on the mainland and the so-called ABC islands: Admiralty, Baranoff, and Chichigoff. They are ubiquitous throughout the Kodiak archipelago, where there are no black bears.

Some coastal streams on Kodiak offer relatively easy wading and casting, but in most of south-coastal Alaska, brush and steep terrain can make foot access challenging. I generally prefer ankle-fit hip waders to chest waders when exploring because of the frequent need to cover lots of difficult ground. Watch out for devil's club when hiking—this plant's tiny thorns cause irritating inflammation that lasts for days. I often wear light leather gloves when hiking to keep the thorns out of my hands.

Anglers who wish to explore the area's possibilities on their own can find fishing opportunities from the road on Kodiak and Prince of Wales Islands. Vehicle rentals are available in both locations, and both can be reached by ferry via the Alaska Marine Highway. The Forest Service maintains a number of cabins in remote locations throughout the area, many of which offer excellent wilderness fishing at nominal cost. Reservations must be made in advance, and popular fishing spots often book quickly, so plan ahead.

LAY OF THE LAND

A number of major air carriers provide scheduled service to Anchorage. Travelers to Kodiak can connect from there on Alaska Air or its subsidiary, ERA. Access to southeast Alaska generally originates from Seattle, with scheduled flights on Alaska Air to Ketchikan, Sitka, or Juneau. Visitors can also travel by vehicle to these same points via the Alaska Marine Highway, departing by ferry from Prince Rupert. Because of the area's limited road system, travel to final destinations usually depends on charter service by boat or air.

Expect bear encounters along salmon streams during the summer. *Giardia* organisms are common in backcountry water sources. Although insects are generally less troublesome than in Alaska's interior, they can be a problem during summer months. (See Appendix A for further information.)

Ancillary activities include sea kayaking, climbing, hiking, wildlife viewing (everything from whales to bears), and wonderful outdoor photography.

CONTACTS

WHALE PASS LODGE
Bob and Denise May
P.O. Box 32
Port Lyons, AK 99550
800-4-KODIAK
www.whalepasslodge.com
This small, remote facility near the north end of Kodiak offers seasonally excellent fishing for steelhead and all Pacific salmon species as well as superb opportunities to take halibut and sea bass on a fly.

McFARLAND'S FLOATEL
Jim and Jeannie McFarland
P.O. Box 19149
Thorne Bay, AK 99919
888-828-3335
floatel@thornebay.com
Pleasant cabin accommodations, and vehicle and skiff rental near Thorne Bay on Prince of Wales Island. Reached by convenient floatplane service direct from Ketchikan, this scenically located do-it-yourself facility offers unguided fishing for steelhead and salmon in local streams as well as salmon and halibut in salt water.

SEAHAWK AIR
Box 3561
Kodiak, AK 99615
907-486-8282
An experienced air charter providing service throughout the Kodiak archipelago, Seahawk can arrange unguided fly-out fishing trips for those interested in exploring on their own.

ADF&G DIVISION OF SPORT FISHING
1255 W. 8th St.
Juneau, AK 99802-5526
907-465-4180
www.state.ak.us/local.akpages/FISH,GAME/sportf/sf_home.htm
The State of Alaska offers a number of area-specific sportfishing guides who provide a wealth of local information.

TONGASS NATIONAL FOREST
Federal Building
Ketchikan, AK 99901
907-225-3101
For information about Forest Service cabins in southeast Alaska.

Heading to the floatplane for the return to reality.

LUKIN AIR

P.O. Box 1058, 4871 Tongass Hwy.
Ward Cove, AK 99928
907-247-5360
Charter air service to Forest Service cabins and
other remote sites in the Ketchikan area.

RECOMMENDED READING

- *ADVANCED FLY FISHING FOR STEELHEAD,*
Deke Meyer (1992. $29.95. Frank Amato
Publications.) Don't let the title fool you: great
advice for steelheaders of all experience levels.
- *STEELHEAD FLY FISHING AND FLIES,* Trey
Combs (1976. $19.95. Frank Amato
Publications.) An excellent companion volume
to the above title.
- *BREAKFAST AT TROUT'S PLACE,* Ken Marsh
(1999. $16.00. Johnson Books.) One of the best
personal reflections on the Alaska outdoor expe-
rience ever. No kidding.
- *WHITEFISH CAN'T JUMP,* E. Donnall Thomas
Jr. (1999. $12.95. McGraw-Hill.) What the hell;
I wrote it. And it does contain some useful infor-
mation on all five Pacific salmon species.

- *BEAR ATTACKS,* Stephen Herrero (1988.
$16.95. The Lyons Press.) The definitive guide to
the ultimate worst-case scenario.
- *FLY PATTERNS OF ALASKA,* edited by Dirk V.
Derksen (1993. $19.95. Frank Amato
Publications.) Drawn from a wealth of experi-
ence, notes and tying tips for every fly you could
ever need in the north.
- *LET THE SEA MAKE A NOISE,* Walter A.
McDougall (1993. Out of print. Harper Collins.)
An excellent overview of Alaska's early history,
especially the influence of Russian exploration.
- *ALASKA* magazine. 619 E. Ship Creek Ave.,
Anchorage, AK 99501; 800-288-5892. An excel-
lent regional publication, more useful for back-
ground information than technical outdoor
specifics.
- *FLYFISHING ALASKA,* Anthony J. Route (1995.
$17.95. Johnson Books.) Good overview of
Alaska's complex fisheries.

The Everglades &
Coastal Backcountry

…as the Whistler hit the water, the rod tip bucked and the fish exploded in our faces

The landscape: a vast mosaic of shallow brackish-water bays and channels separated by tangled warrens of mangroves. The inhabitants: a brilliantly colored aviary of wading birds, brooding alligators hauled out in the sun, endless schools of who-knows-what bulging just beneath the surface. The ambience: splendid, delicious loneliness, a quality made all the more remarkable by proximity to south Florida's urban sprawl. Although little more than an hour's drive away, Miami's busyness might as well belong to another planet.

We are canoeing through the No-Motor Zone inside Everglades National Park, land of the Seminoles and the Florida panther. In fact, calling this the *land* of anything is a bit misleading. Water dominates the terrain; we said good-bye to dry land long, damp miles ago. Accustomed to concise demarcations between earth and sea, it's hard to appreciate just how effectively the Everglades

Chickee platform and shelter on Rogers River in Chokoloskee National Park, base camp for snook fishing.

FLORIDA

blurs the distinction until you've been there. These backwaters look like a great place to get lost (no difficult task, as it turns out) or to hide from anything and anybody. They also look like a great place to fish.

Emerging from a jungle channel festooned with death's-head spiderwebs, I stand and test my balance in the bow while Lori and friend Adam Redford ease us along a brush-choked line of mangroves. Adam has chosen this flat because the terrain protects it from the morning's prevailing wind and tide, affording some measure of water clarity. Nonetheless, the flat's warm broth and mud bottom form an indistinct horizon, and it takes a sounding from my rod tip to confirm that we're gliding through water less than a foot deep. Vast schools of mullet create a distracting background of wakes and splashes, and when Adam whispers "Fish!" it takes my rusty eyes a moment to determine the source of his excitement. Then a sustained pulse of energy appears in the middle of

the mullet and their chatter. With the tropical sun perfectly positioned over my shoulder, I finally identify the broad shoulders and amber flash of a large redfish.

Accustomed to sight-casting to aggressive reds on the coast of Texas, I calculate a short lead, drop the Clouser Minnow just in front of the fish's snout, and watch in dismay as my quarry spooks in terror. The water is so broad and shallow, we can watch the wake recede for half a mile. "Lead 'em farther," Adam councils from the stern. "On these shallow flats, the fish are vulnerable and they know it. They're so spooky you have to treat them like Keys bonefish."

A hundred yards farther down the line, I spot an opportunity for redemption. But as the line curls overhead, I notice something unusual about the stocky form cruising along beside us. It isn't a redfish at all, but a closely related black

AT A GLANCE

SPECIES Tarpon, snook, bonefish, permit, redfish, sea trout, jacks, ladyfish

TACKLE 12-weight rods for large tarpon, 10-weights for small tarpon and permit, 8–9-weights for everything else; floating lines; heavy-monofilament shock tippet for tarpon and jacks

FLIES Basic backcountry and flats selections; include weedless "spoonflies" for fishing in thick grass

PRIME TIME March–June

CONSERVATION ISSUES Industrial pollution, declining water tables, and changes in salinity caused by inland development

PRICE RANGE Less than $1,500

STAGING CITY Miami, Florida for Everglades; Jacksonville, Florida for Amelia Island

HEADS UP Backcountry Florida is a great place to get lost; concentrate on staying oriented and pack plenty of extra drinking water

drum, a species notoriously difficult to take on a fly. But when the streamer hits the water, the fish swirls and pounces. After all the time I've spent casting flies unsuccessfully to migrating black drum in other waters, the strike seems almost too easy to believe. Weighing only a couple of pounds, the fish isn't large by the standards of the porkers Adam sometimes catches here, but it's a black drum on a fly and I'll take it.

With the fish brought to hand and released, it's time to stretch, change leaders and flies, and ease on around the corner to see what surprise the Everglades can serve up next.

THE APPEAL OF SOUTH FLORIDA'S backcountry as a saltwater fly-fishing destination derives from two principal sources: the area's exotic natural beauty and the staggering variety of game fish its waters contain. Perfectly designed for anglers with an inquisitive instinct, the Everglades' unique marine environment offers so many opportunities to savor the spice of life on the end of a fly line that it can be difficult to predict what might come boiling up next on any given cast.

Asked to identify one conventionally glamorous quarry from south Florida's inshore waters, most experienced hands would name the legendary Silver King. In fact, the Everglades' brackish outer reaches form one vast rearing pond for young tarpon. Tarpon enthusiasts used to stalking triple-digit bruisers in the Keys may be forgiven a certain disregard for the young of the species, but a 20-pounder hooked in close quarters on a 7-weight rod can cause just as much excitement as a far larger fish played on heavy tackle in open water. Believe me.

We were working our way down a narrow, tree-lined creek when we saw the tarpon surface beside the bank. The overhanging foliage didn't offer room for anything but a tight-looped roll cast, but as soon as the Whistler hit the water, the rod tip bucked and the fish exploded in our faces. The confinement of the narrow channel made it feel as if the fight were taking place in our living room. Narrowly missing an opportunity to throw a perfect half hitch around the bow of the canoe, the leaping fish tore away against the tidal current, leaving me to sort out the mess left behind. Employing far more luck than skill, I finally managed to get rod, fish, and line free on the same side of the canoe. Just then the tarpon raced back down the channel in the opposite direction, obligating me to repeat the process. I've certainly landed larger tarpon, but I can't remember one that provided quite the same level of frenzy.

Saltwater anglers accustomed to gin-clear flats take note: The visibility in the Everglades' waters requires a bit of adaptation. The constant action of wind and tide against soft bottoms means some degree of turbidity just about everywhere. Employing knowledge derived from years of experience in the area, Adam found relatively clear water in a number of sheltered inland lees, but it still proved too dingy to let us see the outlines of fish below the surface. I soon learned to depend on a number of ancillary cues, including wakes, flashes, nervous water, muds, and gurgles.

Gurgles? Well, yes. We were closing the distance toward a large jack crevalle's fast-moving wake when I heard something that sounded like a toilet flushing deep in the mangroves. "Snook!" I

Opposite: Sight-casting for tarpon in the Florida Keys. Above: A selection of flies for snook and tarpon.

Sea of grass. The Everglades' unique environment offers so many opportunities that it can be difficult to predict what might come boiling up next on any given cast.

guessed aloud from the bow, and when Adam voiced his agreement I rolled a cast as far back into the overhanging branches as I dared. At the first twitch of the fly, a golden flash erupted from the mangroves and inhaled it. The fact that I eventually landed the fish derived entirely from a tactical error on the snook's part. After an initial surge back toward the tangle of brush, the fish changed course and raced off across the open flat behind us in a hissing arc of fly line, where it eventually spent itself against the drag. I'd told Adam at the beginning of the day that I really wanted to land one big snook and suddenly I'd done it. Lucky me.

Early that afternoon, we pulled up beside a stately picket line of roseate spoonbills to cast to a channel teeming with baby tarpon. My first strike felt nothing like a tarpon, and after several minutes of sullen shaking at the bottom of the channel I finally coaxed a bright sea trout to the side of the canoe. "You know," Adam remarked as we admired the fish and released it. "You've got three-fourths of the Backcountry Slam. And the trout is the hardest part."

Ah yes; the Slam. I've always held a skeptical opinion of artificial measures of accomplishment that only detract from proper appreciation of the important things outdoors. Now, utterly by accident, I found myself on the threshold of one: snook, tarpon, sea trout, and redfish—all in one day. I remembered my blown shot at the big red earlier that morning and thought about all the redfish I've caught in my life and laughed. "Do you want to go campaign for a redfish?" Adam asked.

"Let's fish our way home and take what comes," I replied without a second thought. Half a dozen snook and baby tarpon later, we cut across one last flat toward the tidal creek that led toward home. Suddenly a familiar broad outline appeared in the water ahead and I snapped off a hurried cast. The big red turned and made a pass at the fly but missed. Then the canoe's momentum carried us helplessly into the fish's danger zone and spooked it, leaving me to trace my last best shot at the Backcountry Slam in the outline of its retreating wake.

An unusually high tide had sent the current pouring in against us, and we had to pull for all we were worth to make it back to the tethered skiff before dark. Halfway down the last channel, a huge form erupted in the water next to the bank and made the canoe rock as it passed beneath the keel. "Gator?" Lori wondered aloud.

Speeding through the Everglades. Most backcountry fishing takes place from a boat, because muddy bottoms make wading difficult.

"Big shark," Adam replied. The creature's wake followed us ominously against the current for a quarter of a mile, never varying more than a paddle's length from the side of the canoe. We finally reached the boundary of the No-Motor Zone and the welcome sight of Adam's skiff. As we stowed our gear aboard and lifted the canoe onto its carrying rack, I considered all that we had seen and done since we arrived at first light: alligators, sharks, and birds; the spectacular smorgasbord of fish; the Grand Slam that came so close to realization.

But who needed it? The day had been grand enough.

IN THE WAKE OF the notorious Value Jet plunge into the Everglades, television cameras lingered relentlessly on the crash site's allegedly menacing population of gators and snakes, as if anyone who has just fallen 10,000 feet from the sky could possibly care what lies below. Despite the obvious sensationalism, the media had a point. True wilderness lies just beneath the approach paths to Miami International Airport and the people of America deserved to know about it.

When Ponce de León arrived on Florida's shore, barely 20,000 Calusas and Tequestas inhabited the area. Today, 15 million *Homo sapiens* crowd one of the continent's most fragile ecosystems, an abrupt juxtaposition of people and wild places that comes with trouble written all over it. In the face of a classic case of Nature-Meets-Development conflict, the fate of south Florida's backcountry wilderness looms as one of the great environmental battles of the new century.

Meanwhile, committed outdoor enthusiasts owe it to themselves to visit: to look and listen, to appreciate, to bear witness. Just don't forget to take a fly rod.

I HAVE NOTHING BUT PLEASANT MEMORIES of fishing in Florida when I was a kid. Back then—pre-Cape Kennedy, Disney World, Orlando Magic, etc.—the place felt like one extended small town, with just enough tropical flora and fauna to suggest the exotic. The fishing always had a languid Huck Finn quality to its pace, like a summer vacation that didn't want to end. The fish we caught didn't amount to much, as we were relative novices, but they didn't have to. And that was what really counted.

After my family moved west, I pretty much forgot about Florida as an angling destination. My occasional appearances there were confined to unpleasant stops in crowded airports on my beleaguered way elsewhere. Needless to say, this kind of exposure did little to inspire me regarding Florida's outdoor recreational potential. Little did I know.

In fact, saltwater fly fishing owes a huge historical debt to Florida's waters. There, pioneers like Joe Brooks and Stu Apte first proved that traditional fly-rod methods developed for trout could be modified to meet the challenge of large, powerful marine game fish. Most of those early efforts focused on tarpon and bonefish, and during the outdoor recreational boom that followed the end of the Second World War, the clear-water flats of the Florida Keys became one of the world's most renowned destinations for serious fly-rod anglers intent on those species.

Recently, continued innovations in tackle and technique coupled with the inevitable urge to expand angling horizons have led to the development of exciting new fly-rod opportunities in Florida, from snook in the Everglades to tarpon beneath the bridges of Biscayne Bay. Although the appeal of the traditional flats species remains, a new generation of anglers has learned to take a variety of species, including snook, drum, and sea trout, from backcountry Florida waters on fly-rod tackle. And because this smorgasbord of hard fighters inhabits a wide range of marine habitats, the traveling angler can now enjoy saltwater fly fishing near virtually every major airport in Florida. In fact, the adventurous angler with the urge to explore can find something interesting to catch on fly tackle just about anywhere Florida meets the sea.

AMELIA ISLAND, FLORIDA: Airliners on approach to Jacksonville crowd the sky while endless acres of spartina grass glow beneath the oblique rays of the setting sun. Egrets dot the landscape like sculpted ivory sentries. A spoonbill muddles through the shallows beside the skiff, an outrageous morsel of color that practically demands the eye's attention. But we have not come as bird watchers, not tonight. We are waiting for the tide to offer us a unique opportunity, and as all who have waited for tides know full well, there is nothing we can do to hurry its advance.

Back atop the polling platform in the skiff's stern Russell Tharin studies the grass flats with a seasoned eye. A fifth-generation Floridian, Russell defies more stereotypes of a fishing guide than he fulfills, but because those are ones we can do without, Lori and I have enjoyed his company from the moment we set foot aboard the skiff. And this much is certain: Russell knows his water and he knows his fish. And so we fiddle with our

Above: Everglades swamp off the Tamiami Trail Highway.

Small Florida tarpon are fun to catch because they jump a lot and don't take an hour to land.

knots and tell stories and wait until Russell finally declares it time to go hunting.

Redfish prowl the river mouths near Jacksonville, and there are three ways to catch them on a fly. At low tide, you can ease along the oyster bars and cast in front of the wakes left by cruising redfish. When the offshore winds die down and leave the ocean clear, you can chase them in the surf on the outer beaches. And when the high tide approaches 10 feet, you can wade the flooded grass flats to stalk feeding redfish, which is why we are waiting patiently for the highest flood of the month to push its way into the spartina.

"It's time!" Russell finally declares from the stern like a happy prophet, and we're off. With measured strokes of the push pole, he eases the skiff slowly up a narrow channel while Lori and I study the water on either side. It's actually a bit of a stretch to say that we are studying the water, for the grass stands so tall and thick I can hardly see the surface beneath it. "We ain't fishing," Russell reminds us from his perch. "We're hunting, using our eyes and ears."

Our *ears?* Once again, exactly. Something splashes out in the grass and Lori elbows me emphatically. "That's it!" Russell cries. "That's just what we're listening for!" The grass opens briefly before us, allowing a glimpse of a wake in the calf-deep water.

The skiff grounds gently on the soft bottom, leaving us well out of casting range. I ease over the gunwale and set off through the grass, which provides surprisingly solid footing. Moving forward cautiously, I watch the rose-colored tail appear and disappear like a mirage. Ten full minutes pass before I can close the gap.

Finally I begin to work line overhead, searching for a clear lane through the grass to the fish. None appears, and as Russell shouts encouragement from the skiff, I let fly anyway. Coils of floating line festoon the grass like misplaced tinsel on a Christmas tree, leaving my fly dangling nearly a foot above the fish's head.

"Strip!" Russell cries, and I comply, although it is hard to imagine anything productive coming from the effort.

In order to understand what happens next, it's necessary to know what's on the end of my leader. Russell has lent me a Spoon Fly, a golden glob of epoxy molded onto a hook fitted with an industrial-strength weedguard. This is just the sort of offering that can inspire all sorts of impassioned debate about the proper limits of fly tackle, but I soon have more important issues to ponder. As I twitch the line, the fly (such as it is) scuttles through the grass and slaps the water, and the fish turns and pounces.

There is something primordial about the enthusiasm of its pursuit, and although it's hard to imagine the hook remaining free in all that grass, I offer another encouraging twitch. To my amazement, the resistance that greets me feels soft and vital, and as I strip-set the hook, the drum tears off through the cover with my line hissing frantically along behind.

Ten minutes later, I am standing in the

GATOR COUNTRY

By the 1960s, habitat destruction and uncontrolled poaching for meat and hides had reduced Florida's alligator population to critical levels. Legislation at both the state and federal levels, including listing of the alligator under the Endangered Species Act, led to a dramatic rebound in gator populations throughout much of their historic range. Anglers visiting Florida's backcountry can reasonably expect to see alligators while fishing, and the opportunity to observe these spectacular reptiles in their native habitat can provide more enduring memories than the fish.

The largest American alligator ever documented measured over 19 feet long. Such specimens are highly unusual. Today, any gator over 11 feet in length is a big one, and few exceed 13 feet. Of the world's 22 species of crocodilians, only two account for their reputation as ferocious human killers: the Indo-Pacific saltwater crocodile and the Nile crocodile of Africa. Although the rest are relatively benign, Florida alligators occasionally attack pets and rarely people. Gators habituated to human presence and accustomed to food handouts are especially unpredictable, which is why feeding alligators is strictly illegal in Florida.

Large male alligators wander considerably during the breeding season, but females tend to remain near established "gator holes," small ponds dug out by generations of alligators and frequently surrounded by dense layers of vegetation. These ponds in turn serve as water reservoirs during periods of drought, sustaining populations of wading birds and fish. Consequently, alligators play an important role in the continuity of the fragile backcountry ecosystem despite their formidable and occasionally intimidating appearance.

Florida offers unique flats fishing for those willing to sacrifice numbers for a shot at a few really big bonefish or tarpon.

middle of what Montanans politely call a goat rope: awash in mud and brackish water, surrounded by spirals of line enclosing clumps of grass in lazy half hitches, and, amazingly, in sole temporary possession of a 10-pound redfish with a thumbnail-size Spoon Fly hanging delicately from its lower lip. Lori and Russell cheer wildly from the skiff at this improbable accomplishment. No wonder; fish like this demand some kind of applause.

WHAT TO EXPECT

ANGLING

Florida's coastal waters served as the birthplace of modern saltwater fly fishing. A generation ago, that meant fishing the Keys for tarpon, bonefish,

and permit. Although I have done most of my own fishing for flats species elsewhere, Florida still offers unique flats fishing, especially for those willing to sacrifice some numbers for a shot at a few really big bonefish or tarpon. I find the backcountry so appealing, however, that I'd rather spend my time searching out-of-the-way waters for less glamorous species purely as a matter of personal preference.

You can find game fish of some kind in Florida's inshore waters at any time of year. However, unpredictable cold fronts can dampen fishing during the winter months, and hot weather and biting insects can make backcountry exploration uncomfortable in summer. Consequently,

A five-pound snook taken from Rogers River in the Everglades.

spring and early summer are the most popular seasons among visiting anglers, but if circumstances take you to Florida at other times, don't hesitate to take along a fly rod and see what you can hustle up.

Flats-wading enthusiasts should be forewarned: Most backcountry fishing takes place over soft, muddy bottoms that make wading difficult or impossible. Some beaches and bars allow anglers to wade productively. However, visitors should plan on spending most of their time fishing from a boat.

Backcountry species are seldom picky eaters, and being able to get the fly to the fish generally counts more than fly selection. Distance casting isn't as important as it is in clear flats waters, but it still helps to be able to throw a fly line, and freshwater anglers should

practice their double hauls prior to departure. Accuracy can be quite important, and anglers might have to deal with lots of brush and obstructions when they cast.

LAY OF THE LAND

In contrast to many remote saltwater locales, there aren't really any lodges operating in these areas. Anglers just stay at motels and fish by the day.

The sun doesn't pose as serious a threat as it does at more tropical latitudes, but unconditioned visitors from the north can still burn during a long day on the water. Inland, biting insects can prove troublesome, especially during warm summer months. Florida supports a significant population of poisonous snakes. Alligators inhabit brackish as well as fresh water. Although they are seldom a threat to human visitors, large gators should be treated with respect. (See Appendix A for further information.)

Florida's coastline supports a unique bounty of wildlife, and binoculars and a birding book should go along on any fishing trip. In addition to a spectacular array of wading birds, watch for endangered species such as the manatee and American crocodile. And if you are operating your own power craft, be sure to heed all local rules and regulations designed to avoid propeller injuries to manatees.

Ancillary activities include backcountry canoeing, swimming and snorkeling, superb bird-watching opportunities, and wildlife viewing.

CONTACTS

ADAM REDFORD
8701 SW 148th St.
Miami, FL 33176
305-255-7618
adamredford@prodigy.net
www.captadamredford.com/charters
Specializes in backcountry snook and tarpon by canoe in the Everglades' No-Motor Zone.

RUSSELL THARIN
P.O. Box 8042
Amelia Island, FL 32003
904-261-2202
Redfish and sea trout in the Jacksonville area.

JIM DUPREE
105 NW 25th St.
Gainesville, FL 32607
352-371-6153
Guides for tarpon and redfish on the Gulf Coast and manufactures a killer version of the spoonfly.

EVERGLADES NATIONAL PARK
40001 State Rd. 9336
Homestead, FL 33034-6733
305-242-7700
www.nps.gov/ever
General information about access, facilities, and fishing in park waters.

RECOMMENDED READING

■ *THE EVERGLADES, RIVER OF GRASS,* Marjory Stoneman Douglas (1997. $18.95. Pineapple Press.) Excellent study of Everglades' natural history by one of wild Florida's most determined defenders.

■ *THE EVERGLADES HANDBOOK,* Thomas E. Lodge (1996. $41.95. St. Lucie Press.) Useful background information on this unique and vulnerable ecosystem.

■ *KILLING MISTER WATSON,* Peter Matthiessen (1991. $14.00. Vintage Books.) When a great novelist turns his attention to an out-of-the-way area you plan to fish, you better read the damn book.

■ *BACKCOUNTRY FLY FISHING IN SALT WATER,* Doug Swisher and Carl Richards (2000. $19.95. The Lyons Press.) Great resource material for freshwater anglers making the transition to this unique aspect of saltwater fly fishing.

South Island

...for memorable fish taken in a spectacular setting, few destinations on earth can rival it

Experienced international travelers soon learn to respect jet lag's impact, in which regard the best thing to be said about the air route from Los Angeles to Auckland is that flights to southern Africa are worse. Measured in hours, the long haul across the Pacific takes nearly as long, but the flight crosses fewer time zones and flying west is always easier on the limbic system than flying east. It's still a hell of a long way though, and the deviltry of the international date line always adds its own measure of temporal disorientation. Little wonder Lori and I spilled out of the 747 and stumbled toward customs in a state of rummy confusion.

"Anything to declare?" the agent inquired pleasantly.

"Not a thing," I mumbled back.

"Here to do some fishing?" he asked, leaving me to puzzle over the accuracy of his intuition, for we weren't carrying anything obvious to betray

"The valley reminded me of Montana, but in the distance we could hear the Pacific surf crashing."

NEW ZEALAND
SOUTH ISLAND

our intentions. "And did you bring your own boots?" he continued after my sleepy assent. When I confessed that I had, he explained that I would have to surrender them briefly for sterilization. "Whirling disease, you know," he went on apologetically as I rummaged through my duffel. After decades' worth of rude treatment from customs agents around the world, the whole exchange felt so benign I probably would have let him sterilize me had he asked. By the time it occurred to me to ask him how he knew we were anglers, the press of the crowd had carried us onward into the terminal.

"Anything I can do to help you?" a gray-haired lady with a becoming smile asked as we groped our way through the haze of confusion toward the domestic departure terminal. Accustomed to cult solicitations, political crackpots, and predatory hustlers of all persuasions in airports elsewhere, my defenses went up at once. "A cup of coffee, perhaps?" she continued, pointing toward a table behind her where an entire contingent of similarly appointed gray-haired ladies stood beaming. I felt

as if we had blundered into a church social by accident. Warming to her manner in spite of myself, I accepted a cup.

"And what is your job here?" I finally asked.

"Nothing really," she replied cheerfully. "We're just here to greet new arrivals."

Someone needed to pinch me. We had just arrived in New Zealand, home of big fish and the most disarmingly pleasant people in the world.

Several days later, Lori and I helped our host Doug Sheldon launch his jet boat into the lower Waitaki River just upstream from the South Island's eastern shore. The Waitaki, like many of the streams that drain New Zealand's southern Alps, contains some of the world's most stunning turquoise blue water. The current's unnaturally vivid hue made us want to stop and gawk every time we crossed the river on the drive from Doug's farm down to the sea. The Waitaki valley's pastoral terrain reminded me of our own Montana home, but downstream in the distance we could hear the sound of the Pacific surf crashing over the bar at the river mouth as a riot of marine birdlife keened eagerly overhead.

AT A GLANCE

SPECIES Brown and rainbow trout, king salmon

TACKLE 5–6-weights for trout in smaller waters, 7–8-weights for salmon and trout in lakes and rivers

FLIES Basic trout selection. North American patterns generally work well in New Zealand. Contact area fly shops for local favorites. Basic anadromous fish selection for quinnat.

PRIME TIME November–December, February–March

CONSERVATION ISSUES Vulnerability of fish stocks to alien diseases

PRICE RANGE $1,500–$3,500

STAGING CITY Auckland, New Zealand

HEADS UP Drivers need to remember to stay on the left-hand side of the road

Stalking trout on a small tributary of the Waitaki.

We had driven to the mouth of the Waitaki that morning in search of quinnat, a deviation from the usual Kiwi angling agenda that warrants a bit of explanation. Although Lori and I were working on a couple of assignments that didn't leave a lot of time for fishing, we never planned to visit New Zealand without taking our fly rods along. But trout—the traditional angling pièce de résistance on the South Island—didn't excite me that much. Because we live in the middle of what I chauvinistically regard as the best trout fishing in the world (see Chapter 2), I've never felt the need to travel halfway around the world to do what I can do at home. But when I heard about the quinnat, my interest was aroused at once. I never did receive a scholarly explanation of the name's origins, but New Zealand's quinnat turns out to be an old personal favorite: *Oncorhynchus tshawytscha,* the king salmon. As an old Alaska hand I've caught my share of kings, but the thought of doing so half a world away from their traditional haunts intrigued me.

When we declared our intention to fish for quinnat with fly tackle, our hosts politely informed us that it couldn't be done, an opinion that only confirmed my own resolve. In turbid glacial water, fly tackle can indeed put the angler at considerable disadvantage in the pursuit of kings. But fishing clear current, I've always felt that a well-presented fly will draw strikes as effectively as conventional tackle. Our hosts listened with polite nods, but I quickly realized that words alone would create few believers. In fact, Kiwi anglers traditionally fish for quinnat with predatory intensity for the most elementary reason of all: They want to kill them and eat them. I wasn't putting on airs—I just wanted to demonstrate that one could kill and eat with finesse if one chose.

It was a splendid cloudless day in March, traditionally the peak month of the Waitaki's salmon run, and a pleasant throng of anglers stood about the launch site. All too often I've watched similar crowded boat-ramp scenes degenerate into horn-honking, fist-waving chaos, but this was New Zealand, where everyone seemed content to defer to everyone else. My fly rod drew some polite inquiries, giving me another opportunity to explain my mission to those who wished to listen, as almost everyone did. Then we eased out into the blue current, where Doug goosed the jet boat onto the step, and we ran down to the mouth of the great Waitaki with the crisp autumn air whistling past.

NEW ZEALAND'S INLAND GAME FISH are all transplants, strangers in a strange land—a trait they share with a remarkable percentage of the country's flora and fauna. Like most of the Pacific's isolated archipelagoes, prehistoric New Zealand supported little biodiversity, and what species inhabited the islands were poorly suited to compete with outsiders. The South Island's only indigenous mammals were two species of bats, and because the area supported no predators, much of the local birdlife never bothered to learn to fly. All that changed with the arrival of you know who: *Homo sapiens,* originally in the form of the Maoris, who came from the north by seagoing canoe sometime around 600 A.D.

These early settlers found the islands populated by huge, flightless moas, largely defenseless thousand-pound packages of chicken-on-the-hoof. For centuries, Maori culture thrived on these easy pickings, and archaeological evidence suggests almost no evidence of warlike behavior on the part of the islands' early human inhabitants. Finally the inevitable took place, as it must in any unstable relationship between predator and prey. The Maoris killed the last of the moas, and faced suddenly with the need to compete in order to survive, they promptly set about mastering the art of war.

KIWIS

Flightless birds tend to evolve in isolated island ecosystems devoid of land-based predators, and New Zealand is no exception. None has captured the popular imagination quite like the diminutive kiwi, as evidenced by New Zealanders' cheerful adoption of the bird as their national namesake.

Unable to tolerate alien predators introduced by colonists, many of New Zealand's indigenous avian species went the way of the moa. Fortunately, three species of kiwi survive, all now strictly protected: the brown, great spotted, and little spotted. Ranging between 16 and 20 inches in length, kiwis have no tail, and their rudimentary wings lie concealed beneath their plumage. Largely nocturnal, they have poor eyesight and depend upon their sense of smell as they forage for food, which consists largely of earthworms. Their nostrils lie far out on the end of their elongated bills, a unique morphologic adaptation to their habits.

Due to the kiwi's reclusive nature, visitors are unlikely to stumble upon one in the wild. If you don't feel your trip will be complete without seeing a kiwi, take the easy way out and visit the Kiwi and Birdlife Park in Queenstown or the Willowbank Wildlife Park in Christchurch.

When Captain James Cook arrived in the islands aboard the *Endeavor* in 1769, he found a bellicose local population that eventually gave the British military the stiffest sustained resistance it ever encountered from an indigenous population. But the British—no slouches at warlike behavior themselves—eventually prevailed, more as the result of introducing gunpowder, alcohol, and disease than through strategic brilliance. As colonialists set about converting New Zealand's stunning terrain into their own vision of pastoral productivity, they began to fill its apparent ecological vacuum with their own favorite wildlife: red stag and fallow deer, pheasants and mallards, and, eventually, trout.

Rainbow trout eggs arrived from our own country in 1883—perhaps this contribution explains the nearly universal friendliness Kiwis demonstrate toward Yankees today. Originally released in the North Island's Lake Taupo, these stocks formed the genetic basis for the entire country's eventual population of rainbows. Brown trout arrived first on the South Island, where they still predominate in inland waters. And as much as contemporary anglers take the presence of these admirable species for granted, it's worth remembering that they're aliens in the last analysis—just like us.

For the introduction of any foreign species to an isolated ecosystem always comes at a price. Echoing a biologic theme I've seen replayed from Hawaii to Tierra del Fuego, New Zealand's poorly adaptive indigenous species have taken a tremendous hit from these new arrivals, no matter how well intended their original introduction. Australian opossums have decimated local populations of ground-nesting birds. Hares continue to consume just about everything that grows. Gorse has taken over hillsides, choking out whatever native plants preceded it. Even the noble red stag has stretched its welcome by munching its way through most of the South Island's delicate indigenous flora.

And what of the imported salmonid fishes? I suppose they stand as an example of our own biologic hubris, illustrating the odd notion that we somehow get to pick and choose which species share our space. As a scientist, I recognize the absurdity in that principle; as a conservationist, I recognize the sadness. But as an angler…hell, I'm going fishing.

BACK AT THE MOUTH of the Waitaki, I've spent hours casting my arm into a state of numbness without producing a single testimonial to the cause of catching quinnat on the fly. This failure isn't really the fault of my stubborn equipment choice, as even Doug guardedly admits. The river mouth stands pleasantly congested with local anglers tossing conventional salmon hardware into the current, and none of them are catching anything either. Despite the lack of action, the Kiwis' universal sense of civility prevails, in distinct contrast to the manners I've observed on comparably crowded Alaska salmon streams. Everyone seems to be more or less cheering everyone else on, and the inquiries my fly tackle arouse all sound unfailingly enthusiastic. But the universal rule of angling for anadromous fish prevails: You can't catch them

Above: A local landowner. Anglers can obtain access to many waters across private property simply by asking.
Opposite: The eastern slope of the Southern Alps is quite dry, the landscape tussocky.

when they're not there. Finally, we pull up stakes and set off upstream to explore new water.

By early afternoon, I've reluctantly accepted the fact that my next king salmon is not going to come from New Zealand. Abandoning my sinking

A South Island backcountry hut built specifically for hikers and anglers.

line, I rig up for trout. "The bloody hell's that?" Doug inquires as I remove my selection from the fly book.

"A Woolly Bugger," I explain.

"Never seen such a thing."

"Trust me."

Although South Island locals might regard the quinnat as a meat fishery, a residual British decorum applies toward the pursuit of trout on a fly, and the Woolly Bugger plainly isn't what Doug had in mind. But in contrast to the British, who seldom miss an opportunity to display their disdain toward American provincial crudeness, the Kiwis remain too accommodating to let their reservations show. So while Doug and Lori busy themselves preparing lunch, I set off in hip waders, working my way along the shallow bars that crisscross the mighty Waitaki like latticework and make its water far more accessible to the wading angler than it first appears.

I'll admit that my Woolly Bugger won't win many charm school awards, but I have the feeling it's just what I need to coax a big Waitaki rainbow up from the depths, and sure enough. On my third cast, as the line straightens downstream, leaving the fly plainly visible in the dancing water, a long, dark shape appears from below and smacks it. The fish is so big that for a moment I believe I've finally turned the trick on a quinnat, but the first jump dispels my illusions. The fish is a rainbow as long as my arm, and even with my 7-weight I'm hard pressed to turn it when it heads downstream toward the distant sea.

Ten minutes pass before the fish eases its way into the shallows beneath my feet. I'm not carrying a scale—I never do—but I'm sure this fish weighs somewhere between seven and eight pounds. Balanced on my outstretched hand, it stares down at the ugly black glob of feathers stuck to its lower lip as if to admit it should have known better. But *no harm, no foul;* I back the hook out and watch the hulking 'bow drift back into the current and disappear with a quick flick of its tail. The species was our gift to New Zealand, and now this specimen has briefly been New Zealand's gift to me. In a society where courtesy reigns as the order of the day, it all feels fitting somehow, the perfect metaphor for an enlightening day.

Driving back to Doug's house that night for dinner, we encounter a simple structure that neatly illustrates the difference between Kiwi culture and our own: a one-lane bridge spanning a tributary of the Waitaki. There isn't much remarkable about the bridge itself, which looks quite ordinary except for its narrow width. But there are no traffic signs indicating right-of-way. Just as we ease onto the bridge, a farm truck approaches from the other side. Doug immediately stops and begins to back down as the driver of the other vehicle does the same. Each gestures toward the other with a friendly wave. After a full minute of this Alphonse and Gaston routine, we finally proceed, eventually passing the farm truck with another series of friendly waves.

In fact, one-lane bridges are the rule in rural New Zealand, and it never occurs to anyone that the order in which vehicles pass across them could be the subject of dispute. Imagine what might happen if two lines of New York cab drivers approached such a bottleneck from opposite directions at the same time: gunfire, bloodshed, chaos. A single bridge like that in southern California could destroy the entire population of LA within a week. But in New Zealand? No worries.

I have to admit that by the end of our stay I almost started to long for a little conflict, which probably indicates just how deeply Americanized I remain even after decades in the backwaters of Alaska and Montana. For better or worse, the entire South Island began to feel like someone's grandmother's house, at which point I realized it really was time to go home. But New Zealand had already joined a short list of destinations to which I eagerly anticipate returning. And of course I'll take my tackle.

Someone has to show the Kiwis it's possible to take king salmon on a fly.

A fishing lodge just outside Mount Aspiring National Park near the Southern Alps. Overleaf: Only the South Island's landscape exceeds its angling possibilities.

WHAT TO EXPECT
ANGLING
In contrast to the country's smaller but far more densely populated North Island (which offers some of the best rainbow fishing in the world), the South Island contains spectacular mountain scenery and relatively few people. Although South Island waters also hold huge rainbows, brown trout predominate in most streams. King salmon

return only to the South Island, which also contains a few localized populations of brook trout and landlocked Atlantic salmon.

The South Island contains myriad lakes and rivers, most of which hold fish. Nestled against the stunning Southern Alps, Queenstown provides access to the waters of the Southern Lakes district including the tributaries of Lake Wakatipu. Farther south, Invercargill serves as the hub of the Southland district including the famous Mataura River system. The renowned Clutha and Pomahaka river systems lie between Invercargill

and Dunedin to the north along the island's eastern coast. The Waitaki lies still farther north.

Because of New Zealand's strong angling traditions, flies and tackle are readily available in most communities, in distinct contrast to many overseas fishing destinations. Local fly shops can be an invaluable source of information and materials, and breaking your only rod isn't necessarily the trip-ending disaster it might be elsewhere.

Along the area's numerous river valleys, large farms and ranches dominate South Island terrain, which I find highly reminiscent of Montana. Courteous visiting anglers can still obtain access to many waters across private property simply by asking. Coupled with the area's ready accommodations and ease of access by vehicle, the South Island is well suited to angling exploration on one's own, although those operating on time constraints will no doubt get more fishing done by working with guides and a booking agency. Many of the booking services listed in Appendix C offer packages to New Zealand.

Because New Zealand lies south of the equator, its seasons are the opposite of our own, making it an attractive angling destination during cold winter months at home.

Because of its proximity to the sea, temperatures are generally moderate. Plan on dressing as you would for a visit to our own mountain West in late summer or early fall. The South Island's undeveloped west coast is quite wet, and visitors to this area should bring quality rain gear. Hip boots will suffice on many waters, but anglers planning to fish large rivers or lakeshores should bring chest waders.

In general, New Zealand trout fishing emphasizes quality rather than quantity. South Island waters seldom afford the opportunity to catch lots of trout, and the fishing can be challenging. But for the seasoned angler willing to sacrifice immediate gratification for the possibility of a few memorable fish taken in a spectacular setting, few destinations on earth can rival this one.

LAY OF THE LAND

International flights arrive in Auckland, allowing visitors a ready opportunity to explore the North Island and its own unique fishing. New Zealand customs allows the import of flies containing natural fur and feathers, but raw tying materials cannot be brought into the country unless they are declared and sterilized. Anglers also must declare waders on arrival. Visitors continuing on to the South Island can take regularly scheduled airline flights to Christchurch or travel by rental vehicle via ferry from Wellington to Picton. Rental vehicles offer an economical, convenient means of touring the South Island.

Even smaller South Island communities offer a wide range of accommodations, including hotels, motels, lodges, and homestays, roughly the equivalent of the North American bed-and-breakfast. Many locals rent their own South Island holiday homes by the week or month at very reasonable rates, and visitors planning an extended stay in the area might explore this option. (Consult *Beaches and Holiday Homes to Rent,* available from 210 Hereford St., Christchurch, New Zealand; 03-379-1280).

New Zealand is one of the world's safest countries, and excellent medical care is readily available. Street crime is rare outside Auckland. Although tap water is invariably safe, unimproved backcountry water sources can transmit giardiasis. (See Appendix A for further information.)

Ancillary activities include excellent hiking and trekking, climbing, canoeing, and rafting.

CONTACTS
CHAPPIE CHAPMAN'S FLY-FISHING ADVENTURES
31 Charlcott St., Bishopdale, Christchurch, NZ
011-643-3595
fishinchappie@xtra.co.nz
www.chappie.co.nz

First brown trout, then rainbows were introduced to South Island rivers from abroad; browns like this one still predominate in inland waters.

A Christchurch-based outfitter with access to many prime waters near the South Island's largest community.

KIWI SAFARIS

Mike Freeman
P.O. Box 27-079
Christchurch, NZ
FAX: 64-3-382-1752
mike.freeman.kiwi.safaris.NZ@xtra.co.nz
www.datalink.co.nz/hosts/kiwisafarisconz/
Customized South Island expeditions designed to match the individual angler's interests.

NEW ZEALAND FISH AND GAME COUNCIL

P.O. Box 13-141
Wellington 4, NZ
04-499-4767
Ask for the official *Sport Fishing Guide* for rules, regulations, and specific destination information.

NEW ZEALAND PROFESSIONAL FISHING GUIDES

P.O. Box 16
Motu, Gisborne, NZ
06-863-5822

WESTERN RIVERS LODGE

Raft trips and helicopter fly-outs.
Book through Frontiers (see Appendix C).

RECOMMENDED READING

■ *BLACK GNAT,* John England (1990. The Caxton Press.) Personal reflections on New Zealand fly fishing.

■ *TROUT FISHING IN NEW ZEALAND,* Rex Forrester (Out of print. Madronna Publishers.) The dead fish pictures seem dated, but the book still contains useful information.

■ *COMMON BIRDS IN NEW ZEALAND* (2 VOLS.), Geoff Moon (1995. NZ $14.95 each. Reed.) The birdlife isn't all that diverse, but it is almost totally unfamiliar. This book will get you started. Currently available only in New Zealand.

■ *FROMMER'S NEW ZEALAND,* Adrienne Rewi (2000. $21.99. Hungry Minds.) Basic how-to-get-around information, clearly presented.

Pacific & Caribbean Coasts

There's no place like Costa Rica for anglers intent on the challenge of big game

The pace of chasing sailfish reminds me of flying airplanes or hunting dangerous game: long hours of tedium punctuated at unpredictable intervals by outbursts of chaos, confusion, and panic.

Calm May weather lay spread across the sea like a comforter. Lori, fellow Montanan Jim DeBernardinas, and I were fishing Drake Bay, known primarily as a remote wilderness ecotourist destination. The Aguila de Osa Inn, our base of operations, sits nestled above the shoreline adjacent to Corcovado National Park, one of Costa Rica's most stunning natural preserves. This unspoiled coast greets the eye as spectacularly as any piece of waterfront I've ever visited. Pristine beaches stud the shore between outcroppings of weathered rock. Just inland, raw jungle teems with exotic wildlife. In short, Drake Bay easily passes my personal acid test for exotic fishing destinations: I could have a great time there even if I didn't love to fish.

Fortunately, skipper Bradd Johnson and mate

Sailfish on! For the saltwater angler after big game, there is nothing like the Pacific coast of Costa Rica.

Jenner Morales weren't about to let it come to that. They operate several well-equipped offshore boats that make sampling the area's marine resources a pleasure. Although most visiting anglers concentrate on sailfish, enough marlin roam the nearby continental shelf to add extra excitement every time a fin breaks water behind the boat. The rocky sections of the coastline might be the best place in the world to catch roosterfish on a fly. And abundant yellowfin tuna provide opportunities to test tackle and enjoy fresh sashimi.

That morning, Lori stood in the batter's box when the first sail of the day broke water behind the hookless teasers Jenner had carefully deployed in our wake. As Bradd threw the boat into neutral and Jim and I scrambled to clear the deck, Lori began to work out line while Jenner skillfully coaxed the fish into range. Her cast proved accurate and the fish pounced eagerly on the fly, but it raked the leader with its bill as it turned and broke off during the first manic run.

"What did I do wrong?" Lori asked unhappily. The answer was *"Nothing,"* and after a brief pep talk to this effect, Lori was back in the stern with a new fly, a new leader, and a restored attitude. She didn't have to wait long for redemption. Within 20 minutes, Jenner had another hot fish teased in behind the transom, where it

---

AT A GLANCE

Species Pacific—sailfish, marlin (black and blue), roosterfish, yellowfin, snook, snapper; Atlantic—tarpon, snook, jacks, snapper, barracuda, *mojarra, machaca, guapote*

Tackle 12–14-weight rods and reels with floating or sink-tip lines for billfish and fast-sink lines for tarpon at sea, 9–10-weights with floating lines for roosterfish and snook, 6–8-weights with floating lines for jungle species; 15–20# leader with 80# monofilament shock tippet for all offshore species, 10–12# tippet for jungle species

Flies Basic bluewater and backcountry selections with 4/0–5/0 hooks for billfish and 3/0–4/0 hooks for tarpon and snook. Some tarpon flies should have lead eyes for a faster rate of sink offshore. Floating bass poppers sizes 6–8 for jungle species.

Prime Time January–May (Pacific billfish); February–June and September–December (tarpon); September–January (snook). Most other species are available year-round.

Conservation Issues Overharvesting of Pacific billfish by commercial longliners

Price Range $2,500–$3,500

Staging City San José, Costa Rica

Heads Up Sharks abound along both coasts and are especially troublesome in the murky waters near Caribbean river mouths

The Rio Colorado, on the Caribbean coast, produces some of the world's largest snook.

slashed the surface with its bill as if it were challenging us to a duel.

Once again, the cast and the hookup went smoothly, but this time there were no mishaps. After its first spectacular run, the fish sounded and sulked, obligating the 12-weight rod to the workout of its life. Finally, the fly line appeared behind the transom and then the leader, and finally the fish lay alongside the boat. Because Lori has to stand on her toes to break 5 feet in height, it occurred to me that we might have witnessed a unique outdoor accomplishment.

After all, it isn't every day someone catches a fish bigger than they are, especially on a fly.

SMALLER THAN WEST VIRGINIA, the tiny Central American nation of Costa Rica offers visitors a happy conjunction of circumstances out of all proportion to its size. Here the great New World landmass constricts to a wasp waist, and descending into the capital city of San José on a clear day you can look both the Atlantic and the Pacific in the eye at the same time. In a troubled region historically racked by war and turmoil, the people of Costa Rica remain so thoughtfully laid back that they don't even bother to maintain an army. In fact, Costa Rica might well be one of the world's most pleasant places to visit even if you don't carry luggage stuffed with fly tackle.

Ah, but if you do. For the saltwater fly-fishing enthusiast, there's no place quite like Costa Rica, especially for anglers intent on the challenge of big game. And if you're having trouble deciding which ocean to fish, Costa Rica's unique geography offers an elegant solution to the conflict:

Fish them both.

ALTHOUGH THE MORNING SUN had just started to penetrate the jungle canopy, Lori and I were already well into our own rendition of *The African Queen*. All I needed to complete my retake of the Bogart role was a case of cheap gin and a few good leeches. On the channel's banks, spider monkeys turned delicate arabesques in the trees. Stately and graceful, they looked as if they were performing for an audience. Then a troop of howlers appeared. Burly as outlaw bikers, they looked like the guys the landlord used to send around to remind me I was late with the rent, and the jungle shook with the low bass rumble of their cries.

We had flown to the Silver King Lodge at the mouth of the Rio Colorado on Costa Rica's Caribbean coast in search of tarpon, but capricious weather—the potential bane of nearly every worthwhile fly-fishing destination—greeted us immediately upon arrival and kept us off the ocean. Fortunately, the Rio Colorado offers better alternatives to bad weather than the usual options of worn-out paperbacks and early retirement to the bar.

We began the morning canoeing along a tortuous little creek that connects a hidden brackish lagoon to the mighty Rio Colorado. The walls of the jungle closed around us as we made our way inland until I felt myself separate from the distant world of the familiar like an astronaut pushing away from a portal at the beginning of a space walk. Suddenly, the appropriate cultural references felt less like Bogart and Hepburn than Conrad. Finally, we broke out of the trees and entered the lagoon. Richly steeped in organic matter, the water looked black as polished ebony. After the long passage through the jungle our emergence felt liberating, not because there was room to see but because there was finally room to cast a fly.

Lori graciously volunteered for duty in the canoe's stern while I rigged a 7-weight rod with a yellow popping bug. As we started down the shoreline, the feel of the canoe gliding through the dark water reminded me oddly of the Canadian north woods. Then the howlers cut loose with a chorus of moans high in the canopy to remind us we weren't in Kansas anymore.

As I cast from the bow, the little popper gurgled across the surface of the lagoon, only to disappear to a delicate rise that could have been made by a spring-creek brown trout. The fish proved to be a *mojarra,* one of several collectively named local species of panfish that look like bluegills raised on steroids. The lagoon was teeming with them, and we worked our way down the shoreline to a steady rhythm of strikes punctuated by howls from our simian audience.

Suddenly a flash of silver appeared beneath the popper, and the violent strike that followed announced that I had hooked something larger and more aggressive. The snook turned out to be the first of several we coaxed from the little lagoon that morning. We didn't catch one over 10 pounds, but the Rio Colorado produces some of

"...we had come for the giant tarpon that prowl the Barra del Colorado..."

the world's largest snook, and the mere thought of an encounter with one of the local 40-pounders was enough to keep us careful with our leaders and knots.

Our interlude in the jungle provided three days of fishing unlike anything we had experienced before, thanks to the area's natural history as well as the fish. Toucans and parrots coursed overhead. More than 850 species of birds inhabit Costa Rica, far more than in all of North America. Sloths and iguanas peered from the trees as we paddled silently past. One morning we watched a tapir swim the channel in front of us. And even though we never saw or heard a jaguar, we found it impossible not to imagine their presence in the jungle's richly textured shadows.

Despite its geographic proximity to the Pacific, Costa Rica's Caribbean coast feels like a different world. Thick accents flavor the local Spanish, making it a joy to listen to and a challenge to understand. Inland, the terrain lies low and wet. Offshore, turbid river water clouds the sea. But we had not come in search of postcard scenery. We were there to enjoy the wildness of the place, its rich natural history, and, of course, the fish.

We spent two more days exploring jungle waters for snook, *mojarra,* and two other interesting local game fish: *machaca,* an acrobatic fighter that strikes surface poppers with abandon, and *guapote,* a broad-shouldered relative of the peacock bass. And we caught plenty of fish. But we had come for the giant tarpon that prowl the *Barra del Colorado,* and as soon as the weather began to cooperate, we accepted the invitation and headed to sea.

Even though the winds had fallen off, the river mouth still looked like a war zone, as is usually the case when two large, opposing bodies of water advance across the same space from different directions at the same time. Add wind and tide, stir gently, and voilà...chaos. During the long, brutal civil war upstream in nearby Nicaragua, both sides used the Rio Colorado as a dumping ground for dead bodies. As we headed out across the bar in the little skiff with guide Marvin Douns, I tried not to think about all the local sharks and saltwater crocodiles that had acquired a taste for human flesh.

The first time my streamer hesitated out in the chop, I set my hook and felt a gratifying, solid wall of resistance. The fish kicked and ran but never surfaced, suggesting that it was something other than a tarpon. When I finally worked it to the boat, the fish turned out to be a nice jack crevalle, one of a number of predatory species, including snook, barracuda, cubera snapper, and—attention shoppers!—one of the world's greatest concentrations of bull sharks, that feed in the river mouth.

The encounter with the jack evidently lulled me into complacency, for my response to the next strike proved a bit too reserved. At least that's what Marvin thought, and he wasted no time urging me to *stick him, stick him, stick him again!* And I did, but the fish threw the hook anyway, although not until I'd enjoyed a good look at more tarpon than I had ever seen before in one place at one time.

BEAUTIFUL BUT DEADLY

Poison dart frogs (genus *Dendrobates*) are among the world's most vividly colored vertebrates. Dozens of species inhabit the jungles of Costa Rica, sporting a spectrum of brilliant colors, including crimson, gold, green, and blue. *Dendrobates* secrete a complex mixture of alkaloid toxins through their skin, minute quantities of which can prove fatal on contact even to large mammals, including humans.

As the common name of these amphibians suggests, indigenous Central American hunters  recognized the potency of these toxins and used them to poison the tips of their blowgun darts. The process involves no elaborate preparation. Frog toxins are so powerful that merely rubbing a dart across a frog's skin will convert it into a lethal projectile. Indigenous hunters who still practice these traditional skills handle the frogs with the utmost care.

So if you encounter a brilliantly colored little frog deep in the jungles of Costa Rica, look but don't touch.

The next time the streamer met resistance, I decided to try to break my new rod on the strike just for the hell of it. I whacked the fish so hard that not even Marvin could ask for more. Despite all this effort—and a freshly honed hook—the fish came unbuttoned on its third jump, leaving me staring across the empty reaches of the sea once again.

And so it went. Fish threw hooks. They jumped and sounded and wrapped lines around boat and motor. They turned and ran for the open ocean, showing nothing but disdain for our pathetic efforts to restrain them. And when Lori finally managed to land a "little" 80-pounder, we each felt like Ahab at the end of another fish story dedicated to the proposition that people are still small change in the larger order of things.

And we wouldn't have missed it for the world.

IN COSTA RICA, a lovely colloquialism—*pura vida*—punctuates conversation at every opportunity. Literally translated as "pure life," the phrase is used to suggest a shared sense of the human experience, and it can imply everything from ecstasy to resignation.

I think the Costa Ricans are onto something. Although many of the game fish we encountered there were more than a little intimidating, I left the country feeling revitalized, as if the sailfish and tarpon had somehow charged me like a run-down battery. It does us good to be reminded that nature is still tougher than we are, an elementary truth often less than apparent in the modern world of shopping malls and cyberspace. And if that means taking a beating at the hands of a few fish, well …

Pura vida.

WHAT TO EXPECT
ANGLING

Angling opportunities differ substantially between Costa Rica's two coastlines. While the

Top: The machaca, *a local game fish, strikes surface poppers with abandon on the jungle river waters near the Caribbean coast. Above: Just inland from the Pacific Coast's sand beaches, rainforests teem with exotic wildlife.*

Pacific side offers the opportunity to cast to roosterfish, snapper, and snook near the shore, this is principally a bluewater destination. Anglers intent on the area's unique billfish opportunities should expect one to two-hour runs offshore, modest ocean swells, and extended periods out of sight of land. Those unfamiliar with billfish teasing techniques should be sure to run through the drill with the crew before the first sail appears behind the teasers. Be sure to practice casting bulky billfish flies before leaving home. And unless you're really obsessed with catching as many billfish as possible, don't forget to spend some time prospecting for roosterfish near shore. The experience will allow the visiting angler to enjoy one of the most beautiful coastlines in the world.

The Caribbean coast, in contrast, consists mostly of low-lying jungle and a marine environment punctuated by the influx of large river systems, resulting in turbid inshore water. Anglers accustomed to sight-casting to tarpon on the flats in Florida or Belize will have to adjust both their expectations and technique for the pursuit of the Costa Rican version of these great fish. Off the mouth of the Rio Colorado, skiffs usually anchor up while anglers cast blindly or in the general direction of rolling fish. Unlike most fly rod tarpon fishing, sinking fly lines are useful in this situation.

While tarpon draw most of the attention in this fishery, Costa Rica's Caribbean coast supports a variety of important game fish. Anglers interested in bluewater fishing can head offshore for *mahi,* wahoo, tuna and sails. Large snook abound both in the surf and the rivers. From November through January, huge runs of *calba* ("fat snook") enter the Rio Colorado from the sea, allowing anglers the opportunity to catch dozens of these 5-10 pound snook per day. And by all means plan to spend a day canoeing the jungle lagoons fishing for *mojarra, machaca,* and *guapote.* While small compared to the tarpon, these species provide fascinating action on fly rod poppers in a unique setting.

Anglers unfamiliar with the demands of fly rod big game fishing need to prepare prior to departure for either coast. 12-weight tackle is a minimum for Costa Rican tarpon or billfish and you won't feel over-gunned with 14-weight gear. Practice casting with unfamiliar heavy tackle prior to departure. Reels should contain 300 yards of backing. Prepare plenty of leaders topped off with 60# shock tippet and be meticulous with your knots. These are big game fish and they allow little room for error.

LAY OF THE LAND

Boasting a long history of democracy, stability, and general common sense, Costa Rica remains one of Latin America's most enjoyable destinations. City streets are generally safe and *ticos* (as the people of Costa Rica refer to themselves) invariably friendly, although the burgeoning tourism trade will no doubt test their patience with visitors in the future.

The Costa Rican government demonstrates a highly enlightened attitude toward the country's natural resources, and nearly a quarter of Costa Rica currently lies within the boundaries of national parks and reserves. Although the country enjoys an abundance of jungle hardwoods, government policy has kept logging to a minimum. In fact, national law forbids the export of timber unless it has been turned into a finished product, in order to maximize the local economic benefit from every felled tree. (Note to our own Forest Service: Why wouldn't that policy work at home?)

Although still a bargain compared to destinations in Europe and North America, Costa Rica's relatively prosperous economy makes it a bit more expensive to visit than other countries in Central America. Businesses in most major cities accept credit cards, travelers' checks, and American dollars. You can exchange dollars for *colones,* the national currency, at banks and major hotels and airports. Street money-changers might offer somewhat more favorable rates, although the practice is illegal.

Costa Rican travel generally begins in San José, served by regular scheduled jet service (United, American, Continental) from Los Angeles, Houston, or Miami. Because of the country's small size, rental cars offer a scenic way to reach coastal destinations for those with a bit of time to spare. However, many prime fishing locations are accessible only by air: Refer to charter services listed under Contacts.

Costa Rica is a safe destination with little

political unrest and a low incidence of violent crime. Malaria is uncommon, but the Centers for Disease Control (CDC) recommends prophylaxis for visitors to low-lying areas. Tap water is generally safe to drink in San José and in reputable fishing lodges. Exercise appropriate precautions with water from other sources. Costa Rica operates on Central Standard Time, so jet lag should not trouble North American visitors. (See Appendix A for further information.)

Ancillary activities include canoeing and river rafting inland, sea kayaking (especially on the Pacific coast), jungle trekking, wildlife viewing, and photography.

CONTACTS

AGUILA DE OSA INN
Bradd Johnson
506-232-7722
www.aguiladeosa.com
Excellent accommodations in a remote setting north of Corcovado National Park. Outstanding fishing for billfish, roosterfish, yellowfin, and large Pacific snook.

SILVER KING LODGE
Ray Barry or Shawn Feliciano
800-VIP-FISH
slvrkng@sol.rasca.co.cr
www.silverkinglodge.com
The premier fishing camp at the mouth of the Rio Colorado offers superb fishing for big tarpon and snook in both fresh and salt water as well as inland fishing for *mojarra, machaca,* and *guapote.*

ALAS ANPHIBIAS
800-308-3394
Provides amphibious floatplane transportation from the airport at San José to marine destinations on both coasts.

AERO COSTA SOL
9506-440-1444
Provides twin-engine charters from San José to airport destinations around the country.

Top: Rocky sections of the Pacific Coast are among the best places on earth to catch roosterfish on a fly. Above: Eye to eye with a Pacific sailfish.

RECOMMENDED READING

■ *COSTA RICA,* Rob Rachowiecki (2000. $19.95. Lonely Planet.) A general guide to the basics of getting around.

■ *BLUEWATER FLY FISHING,* Trey Combs (1996. $60.00. The Lyons Press.) Excellent background material for anglers headed offshore, especially those unfamiliar with fly-rod big game.

■ *COSTA RICA OUTDOORS,* This regional periodical provides useful area-specific information. Contact their North American office: P.O. Box 3770, Seal Beach, CA 90740-7770.

The Labrador Peninsula

*I had come home at last,
home to brook trout country*

The flight north provided a splendid a transition between civilization and wilderness. I did my medical internship in Montreal years ago, but lack of time and money kept me from appreciating the enormity of the city until I saw it from the air that August afternoon. Surrounded by farmland, Quebec City looked pastoral in comparison. By the time we reached Sept Isles on the Gulf of St. Lawrence, the impression was of an outpost hanging on between sea and forest. On the final leg of the flight to Labrador City, caribou trails began to appear in the tundra below as miles of splendid nothing slid beneath our wings. Earth yielded to water: apparently endless ribbons of rivers and lakes created by great glacial gouges eons ago, all practically crying "Come down here and fish me!"

Early that evening, host Robin Reeve and I climbed into a DeHavilland Beaver—the great

An angler and his guide head out for an evening of brook trout fishing on Lake Minipi.

workhorse of the north—for the final leg of the journey to Robin's Three Rivers Lodge. The water looked even more inviting from the low altitude the Beaver allowed, and it was impossible not to imagine trout holding in the rapids between the lakes. Suddenly the caribou trails had caribou standing in them: velvet-racked bulls intently migrating from some obscure point A to an equally obscure point B for reasons known only to the caribou. By the time we made a glassy-water landing on the lake and taxied to the dock in front of the lodge, the sense of a long journey's end felt complete. I had come home at last, home to brook trout country.

Prior to the introduction of the brown trout to the New World in 1883, American fly fishing *meant* brook trout fishing and our forebears' methods and techniques reflected the character of their quarry: long on charm, short on guile. The vintage books in my parents' angling library included virtually no discussion of the insects familiar to modern fly-rod anglers, but they contained glorious color plates of hundreds of wet-fly patterns tied from exotic natural materials and boasting romantic, utterly meaningless names. Then along came those wary, sophisticated browns, followed by Theodore Gordon, the development of the modern dry fly, patterns that actually imitated insects on the water…in short, progress, I guess.

Nearly five decades after my own childhood introduction to *Salvelinus fontinalis* in New England and Upstate New York, I found myself longing to go back, not despite all I had seen and done around the angling world but because of it. I wanted to revisit the brook trout for the same reason anglers weaned on high-modulus graphite suddenly develop a passion for bamboo. *Simplify!* Thoreau once urged, from the middle of prime brook trout country no less. *Simplify!*

AT A GLANCE

SPECIES Brook trout, Atlantic salmon, lake trout, arctic char, northern pike

TACKLE 5–6-weight rods for brook trout, 7–8-weights for other species; floating and sink-tip lines for most fishing; fast-sinking shooting heads useful for lake trout; wire tippet for pike

FLIES Basic trout and anadromous fish selections; include deer-hair mouse patterns for large brookies on the surface, large streamers for lake trout, and surface poppers for pike

PRIME TIME Late June–August

CONSERVATION ISSUES Hydroelectric power development, native sovereignty, commercial Atlantic salmon harvest

PRICE RANGE $1,500–$3,500

STAGING CITY Montreal, Quebec

HEADS UP Prepare to cope with the Mosquitoes from Hell!

Endless ribbons of rivers and lakes all practically crying "Come down here and fish me!"

Of course, Alaska and Montana—the two angling havens I've called home for the last 30 years—hold brook trout, not by natural design but because anglers who missed brookies chose to introduce them to new environs. But fishing for brook trout as I remembered required measures of ambience that didn't travel as well as the fish: morning mist on glassy lakes that erased the distinction between land and water, current that flowed black and tan without ever looking dirty, the eerie quaver of a loon's cry. Without those determinants of mood the artificial western version of the brook trout felt immaterial. I needed to experience the real thing again, and when Robin's invitation arrived I pounced upon it like a hungry predator.

Labrador. If I meant to travel all the way across the continent to rediscover my brook trout roots, I might as well do it right.

EARLY THE FOLLOWING MORNING, Robin, John Webber, and I set off to the south and east by canoe. Azure skies studded with benign puffs of cumulus clouds sprawled overhead. Despite the latitude, the sunlight felt pleasantly warm. The loons were there and so was the dark water, but the morning still suggested something missing. *Bugs!* I finally thought to myself. *Was it really possible to fish Canadian brook trout water without being tormented by insects?*

"It's been an unusually dry summer," Robin explained in response to my query, and John pointed out the customary waterline on the rocks along the shore—fully two feet above the lake's surface—to confirm this assessment. "Not many bugs and not many blueberries."

"A fair trade," I observed despite a lifelong affinity for fresh blueberry pancakes. Then the walls of rocky terrain began to narrow and we felt the first suggestion of current against the bow of the canoe. A dozen caribou clamored down through the boulders on our left and plunged into the water. Finally the canoe ground to a halt against the shore, and we assembled our gear and began to hike across the broken tundra.

A mile upstream, we picked our way down through the boulders toward the sound of dancing rapids. In Labrador, the distinction between lakes and rivers feels somewhat arbitrary as still water collects itself, tumbles briefly, and spreads out into yet another lake en route to the distant sea. But brook trout gather in those narrows as surely as the water itself; and the current tumbling through the worn rocks looked as appealing as an engraved invitation.

As John and Robin picked their way downstream, I scrambled atop a huge boulder that commanded the nearest run like Gibraltar at the mouth of the Mediterranean. There would be no standard-issue Bead-Heads or Woolly Buggers, at least not yet. This was classic water and I meant to fish it classically, with a wet fly...remember those? I removed an old Montreal from the fly book, a faded pattern on a well-worn hook dug up from deep in the guts of my gear closet just for this occasion. The pattern didn't look like anything at all in the modern sense, but that was precisely the point. This wasn't about matching hatches. It was about being there.

I crimped down the barb—an unknown gesture back when I tied the fly decades earlier—and flicked it into the foam behind the first rock upstream. Before I could review the neglected mechanics of the classic wet-fly swing, the rod tip bucked and I struck back against something soft and heavy. *First cast,* I chuckled to myself as the fish roared about the tumbling pool. Did I deserve this? Absolutely not.

I'd picked up a dozen nice fish by the time I worked my way up to the flat water that marked the next lake's outlet, but none over three pounds. Does size matter? That day it did, not because I needed to register some arbitrary measure of accomplishment but because I wanted to recapture my personal image of a brook trout: football shaped, brooding, and brilliant. When Robin and John rejoined me at last, we hiked on up the lake to the little cove where another canoe lay stashed and proceeded onward across the second lake toward the next section of moving water.

This series of rapids ran shorter and less strenuously than the first. While Robin stayed by the canoe to work the lake's inlet, John and I bulled our way through the alders toward a deep pool in the middle of an inviting run. Rich in tannin, the current glowed like amber beneath the midday sun. *And still no bugs,* I thought to myself as I climbed the boulders into casting position. *Have you been living right or what?*

The fly—I'd switched to an Egg-Sucking Leech by this time—dropped into the water as I absently stripped out a length of line, and to my amazement I watched a long, foreboding shadow materialize briefly as the dark feathers fluttered through the eddy beneath my feet. Suddenly aroused, I cast into the surge, and as the fly arced across the current the fish returned and struck. This was the fish I had come for, and I wanted to land it in a way I could not remember wanting to land a fish for some time.

And land it I did. As the trout—Five pounds? Who knows?—lay panting in John's net, I bent over for one definitive look before releasing it. What a splendid riot of color: green vermiform dorsal markings, orange fins unlike anything else in nature, brilliant speckled sides awash in scarlet undertones. There are fish you chase because they're big and others that you chase because they're strong, but this one was about beauty, pure and simple.

Beauty, and the capacity of one good fish to transport an enthralled observer back to the species that started it all. *Brook trout. Rosebud.* It was that kind of connection.

A 9¹/2-pound arctic char. While less coveted than the Atlantic salmon, it is just as strong.

THE LABRADOR PENINSULA represents one of the world's last great wilderness domains, a fact made all the more surprising by the area's geographic proximity to North America's eastern population centers. Stretching northward over a thousand nearly roadless miles from the mouth of the St. Lawrence to Ungava Bay and the Hudson Strait, this vast expanse of tundra and water seems determined to defy the forces of civilization to the south. So far,

SALTERS

Sea-run rainbows enjoy a cult following among West Coast steelheaders, and anadromous browns are famous as sea trout in the British Isles and as *plateados* in Tierra del Fuego. Although few anglers realize it, brook trout come in a seagoing version as well. Historically known as silver trout on Long Island and salters on Cape Cod, anadromous brook trout have largely disappeared from their original southern range in the United States, primarily due to loss of freshwater spawning habitat. But brook trout still return to the sea in some drainages along the Labrador peninsula.

In *Trout Maverick,* Leonard Wright Jr. describes his fortuitous discovery of a large population of brook trout in salt water near the mouth of Labrador's Eagle River. Wright plainly didn't quite know what to make of his unusual find, and I'm sure I would have felt equally amazed. But I've had plenty of experience with sea-run representatives of two other North American members of the genus *Salvelinus:* the Dolly Varden and the arctic char. Because both of these closely related game fish thrive at sea, there's no reason the familiar brookie shouldn't too.

Isolated by geography, Labrador represents the salter's last stronghold. Perhaps someday it will join the steelhead and the sea-run brown on the fishing world's list of exotic glamour species.

so good…although the area's abundance of mineral resources and hydroelectric power potential remain a highly inviting target for development.

Although the wandering line dividing the peninsula between the provinces of Newfoundland and Quebec looks like the work of a drunken surveyor, the boundary enjoys a firm basis in principle: On the Newfoundland side, rivers flow east to the Atlantic, whereas in Quebec they flow west to Hudson Bay. Social demarcations seem nearly as abrupt. To the west, the fleur-de-lis still flies as if Montcalm had never lost the battle of Quebec, and visitors who want to get anything done had better be willing to trot out their high school French. On the Newfoundland side, the hearty accents of the Devon fishermen who first settled the coast still prevail, and even inland one never feels far removed from the sea.

And it seldom takes Labrador long to enforce an important lesson: Wilderness is usually wilderness for a reason. Winter—a season willing to arrive in September and hang around until May—can challenge anyone's survival skills. During the brief summer—the months of interest to anglers—bugs can be ferocious. Endless miles of water largely preclude travel by road, and visitors unenthusiastic about floatplanes and canoes are better off staying home. Bears raid camps, and icy waters can turn the simplest boating mishap into an emergency.

But those are the elements that lend wild places their fundamental appeal. And anglers have the most compelling reason of all to brave what Labrador has to throw at them: fish.

ANOTHER TIME, ANOTHER LAKE, and the brook trout's compelling beauty lies momentarily forgotten. For according to the eternal algebra of esthetics, every beauty implies the presence of a beast, and tonight it's my job to make contact.

Black and smooth, the water seems to stretch away forever toward the setting sun. The

Sunset on Lake Minipi, reached by floatplane out of Goose Bay.

evening lies so still I can practically feel the tamaracks transpiring. Although I've been out here in the backcountry for days, I can still hear the eerie hum that always rises in my ears when I've been away from the wilds too long: the sound of silence, true silence, something most members of our species will never know.

The canoe beneath my legs feels perfectly suited to the venue. A single effortless stroke from the paddle sends the little craft gliding 20 yards across the gathering shadows. With miles of unspoiled shoreline stretching away ahead, there seems little to choose from and little to compel a choice. Finally I let the canoe's momentum die beneath me one long cast removed from a rocky

Catching brookies is about beauty, pure and simple.

point and reach for the fly rod.

Forget those classic wet flies. Tonight I'm rigged with a deer-hair popper the size of my thumb, a grotesque Cubist imitation of a frog. As if to emphasize my departure from the elegance of the brook trout tradition, the leader concludes with a foot of wire, the kind of stuff a contract killer might use to garrote an enemy. Grateful for the lack of breeze, I work a loop of line overhead and deposit this unlikely offering next to the rocky shoreline. The gurgling noise the bug creates as I strip it across the surface sounds loud enough to rouse the dead.

At this latitude, summer twilight seems to last forever. Good thing…alone in the canoe, I have to interrupt the rhythm of casting every few minutes to paddle a little farther down the shoreline. Although this is hardly an efficient way to cover water, an appreciation of the solitude seems even more important than catching fish, and tonight I'll take the trade.

When the beast finally stirs at last, it seems inappropriate to call its response to the popper a strike. Trout *strike* dry flies, but this is an attack, something a hungry alligator might do to an unsuspecting duck. Shattering the lake's quiet surface, the fish boils and slashes and I set the hook angrily: two quick punches traded in a barroom brawl. As I set my back against the rod, I'm already asking myself the inevitable question— *How big is this thing?*—because in this country you never really know, not at first.

There's no point going on about the fight because it really isn't that big a deal. Pike are assassins, not warriors, and after the initial excitement the encounter quickly devolves into work.

In a matter of minutes, the fish lies quietly at the surface next to the canoe, with just enough light left in the western sky to allow me to stare and try to answer Samuel Morse's question: *What hath God wrought?*

And the beast it is, as malign in appearance as the brook trout is beautiful. The fish weighs perhaps 10 pounds, but it seems bigger somehow…big enough, say, to snap my hand off if I were to give it the chance. But I've torn up enough fingers on northerns not to let it come to that, and with a click of steel on steel and a quick twist of the hemostat, the fish and I part company. Then it's time for each of us to return, to camp in my case and the bottom of the lake in the pike's.

Tomorrow, perhaps, the brook trout will look a bit more beautiful than usual.

WHAT TO EXPECT

ANGLING

Labrador's terrain consists of low rolling hills with scattered conifers yielding to open tundra at higher latitudes. Hiking generally proves easy and enjoyable, with some thick brush along watercourses. A high percentage of Labrador's surface area consists of water, making canoes and floatplanes the most practical means of transportation in the bush. Most streams offer relatively easy wading under average water conditions, but larger rivers contain strong currents and powerful rapids, so exercise due caution.

Wilderness brook trout generally feed in nonselective fashion. The ability to cover water efficiently usually matters more than the details of the pattern, as our wet-fly-fishing predecessors

proved a century ago. Despite their cold temperatures, however, Labrador streams support significant insect populations, and anglers should be prepared for brief but intense periods of surface

Heading across a remote lake on a long Labrador summer evening in search of more brookies.

activity as trout rise to caddis and stone flies, for which generic imitations usually suffice.

Any northern landmass surrounded by salt water represents potential anadromous fish habitat and Labrador delivers handsomely. The East Coast's undisputed glamour species, Atlantic salmon, ascend many Labrador rivers. Their pursuit lies beyond the scope of this discussion, and I would simply refer interested readers to the Recommended Reading list. At the same time, I'd like to offer a tip of the hat to the sea-run arctic char, a species just as strong (if somewhat less acrobatic) and even more beautiful. Nowadays, the opportunity to fish for Atlantic salmon often depends on money, whereas the opportunity to fish for char depends on how badly you want to get to the wild places they inhabit. My kind of fish.

With latitudes comparable to those of southern Alaska, Labrador has long evenings during the brief summer fishing season that afford

The malign-looking northern pike is a sprinter; it strikes with lightning speed, but quickly subsides.

even the most ambitious anglers plenty of time on the water. On clear nights, visitors can enjoy the aurora between late-evening meals and bedtime.

Labrador's weather is predictable only in its unpredictability. During the summer fishing season, I've experienced everything from balmy days that had me down to shirt sleeves, to horizontal rain cold enough to challenge woolens. Fluctuations between these extremes can take place rapidly. Dress in layers, and never leave base camp without the means to endure deteriorating weather. Because of its wide comfort range and water resistance, Polar Fleece makes a good basic choice for clothing material.

LAY OF THE LAND

Most air travel to Labrador originates in Montreal, with scheduled airline flights north from there to Labrador City, Goose Bay, and similar jump-off points. Float-equipped aircraft usually provide transportation to final destinations in the bush. The Trans-Labrador Highway allows access to southern Labrador by vehicle, with fishing water reached by boat or canoe from the road. With prior arrangement, air charters can transport canoes lashed to aircraft floats for adventurous travelers interested in setting up their own remote canoe trips.

Mosquitoes and blackflies have probably soured more visitors on wilderness experiences in Labrador than all other causes combined. Dry weather and early frosts can produce pleasant surprises, but anglers should go prepared for everything the class Insecta can throw at them. Head nets and bug suits weigh very little and represent a small investment for the comfort they can provide. It is impossible to bring too much insect repellant on a fishing trip to Labrador. Campers should be sure tents are mosquito proof and bring duct tape to repair minor tears in netting. Water temperatures are cold even in the middle of the summer, and even minor boating mishaps can be potentially life threatening. (See Appendix A for further information.)

Wolves and black bears are common enough to offer the realistic possibility of a sighting. In the right place at the right time, anglers might get to observe the Ungava caribou herd's annual migration. Despite its relative proximity to the bright lights and big cities of our own eastern seaboard, the Labrador peninsula represents true wilderness.

Take along one presentable set of clothes if you plan to overnight in Montreal—the cuisine is too good to miss.

Ancillary activities include superb wilderness canoeing and camping, wildlife viewing (large numbers of caribou pass through this area midsummer), and photography.

Supply plane on the Eagle River at Rifflin' Hitch Lodge, an Atlantic salmon camp.

CONTACTS

THREE RIVERS LODGE

www.trophylabrador.com

Tremendous angling for big brookies, lake trout, and pike in a pristine wilderness setting.

ASHUANIPI AVIATION

P.O. Box 219

Labrador City, NFLD, Canada A2V 2K5

Floatplane charter flights throughout central Labrador.

NEWFOUNDLAND DEPARTMENT OF TOURISM

800-563-6353

www.gov.nf.ca/tourism

QUEBEC DEPARTMENT OF TOURISM

800-363-7777

RECOMMENDED READING

■ *VIRGIN WATER,* Leighton Brewer (1941. Out of print. Coward-McCann.) A classic account of brook trout in the good old days.

■ *THE ATLANTIC SALMON HANDBOOK,* Peter Bodo (1997. $25.00. The Lyons Press.) A wonderful resource book for anglers unfamiliar with one of angling's true glamour species.

■ *BROOK TROUT,* Nick Karas (1997. $35.00. The Lyons Press.) A wealth of knowledge on eastern Canada's definitive game fish.

■ *PIKE ON THE FLY,* Barry Reynolds and John Berryman (1993. $16.95. Johnson Books.) The definitive work on an underappreciated fly-rod quarry.

The Gulf Coast

*Redfish tails were sprouting from the glassy surface
like mushrooms on a moist lawn*

T hanks to a frontal system out in the Gulf of Mexico, the treetops were dancing to a brisk southeast wind as we pulled away from the dock. Gray sky met gray water somewhere ahead, but the precise location of the horizon remained a matter of conjecture. Seated in front of the boat's console, Lori and I instinctively drew closer to preserve some measure of warmth as salt spray blew across the bow. Had anyone asked, I would have been forced to make a series of admissions: I had no idea where we were going and no idea how to coax fish from the bay on a morning like this.

But our friend Dick Negley did. Half an hour out of Port Mansfield, Dick banked the skiff hard, cut the power, and let the boat settle into a vast sea of skinny water. They do things big in Texas, and the size of their saltwater flats is no exception. "You might head off that way," Dick suggested quietly as he gestured toward the distant merger of

On the push-pole as an angler gears up, just after sunrise on a redfish flat.

TEXAS

Houston

Galveston

GULF OF MEXICO

Corpus Cristi

Port Mansfield

PADRE ISLAND

LAGUNA MADRE

bay and sky. After too many days in too many airports, the idea of heading anywhere quiet and uncluttered sounded just fine. Lori grabbed her rod and eased over one side of the boat while I did the same on the other. Soon we were 50 yards apart, moving through the calf-deep water, as removed from the world onshore as if we were the last people on earth.

Because of the mud the boat kicked up in its wake I expected the footing to be unpleasant, but the bottom proved surprisingly firm. The water felt warm and comforting against my legs, and by some miraculous accident of physics, its surface lay smooth as a mirror despite the wind out in the gulf.

After a brief period of acclimation, I began to feel less like a tourist. My eyes wandered easily across the polished surface of the flat, search-

ing for anything that might betray the presence of fish. Then off ahead in the amorphous sweep of gray, a brief disturbance appeared. The visual relationship between figure and background felt so disconnected that I had no concept of range. At first, I thought the object might be a feather floating on the water, but then it rose and fell in a manner impossible for anything inanimate.

I was moving upwind to investigate when a second tail appeared, and this time there could be no doubt about its identity. A black spot occupied its center as rose-pink colors glowed briefly in the dim morning sun. I shot a quick loop of line into the air and let the wind carry it forward. The fly plopped into the water a little closer to the fish's business end than I intended, but it didn't matter. The water bulged, my line hand

Overleaf: Sunset on a redfish flat on the Laguna Madre off the southern Gulf Coast.

AT A GLANCE

SPECIES Redfish, speckled trout, sand trout, flounder; seasonally, black drum

TACKLE 7–8-weight rods for redfish and speckled trout, 9–10-weights for black drum, 5–6-weights for sand trout; floating lines for all species except black drum, which run deep and require sinking heads; high-quality polarized sunglasses are a must

FLIES Basic backcountry selection; bass poppers sizes 6–8 for redfish and trout on the flats, large wool-head mullet patterns for sea trout, heavily weighted Clousers for black drum

PRIME TIME Most species found year-round; weather patterns are most favorable for flats fishing from May–October; black drum run during March and April

CONSERVATION ISSUES Inshore water-quality degradation by agricultural runoff and commercial shrimp farming

PRICE RANGE Less than $1,500

STAGING CITY San Antonio or Corpus Christi, Texas

HEADS UP Stingrays abound in the gulf's warm inshore waters; wade with care

Black drum run through the channels from the gulf in the spring.

and the fish proved more powerful than enduring. Matters soon turned in my favor despite my equipment shortcomings.

By the time I landed the fish, Lori was casting furiously at one of her own. Suddenly, I realized that something remarkable had taken place in the water all around us. Redfish tails were sprouting from the glassy surface like mushrooms on a moist lawn. There were so many tailing fish in sight that I literally couldn't decide which way to turn. All the conflicts we face in life should prove so pleasant.

No matter; we still had hours' worth of favorable tide ahead of us to work things out.

OUR INITIAL VISIT to the state's Gulf Coast took place in April. Spring might not be the optimal time to fish south Texas salt water, more because of the threat of unstable weather than any shortage of fish. But that time slot happened to fit our complicated travel schedule, and we always seem to do our warmwater flats fishing when we need a break from winter weather rather than when the fishing is necessarily at its best. It had been a long, brutal winter back home in Montana, with the Freemen on one side of us and the Unabomber on the other. We felt we deserved a break, and the Laguna Madre provided one.

Running all the way from the mouth of the Rio Grande north to Corpus Christi, the Laguna Madre forms a vast inshore fish factory shielded from the Gulf of Mexico by Padre Island. The Laguna contains a vast array of shallows, with countless miles of flats broken by a mosaic of islands that offer lees somewhere in almost any wind.

All thoughtful outdoors enthusiasts love conservation success stories, and only a few years ago few fisheries needed one more. Blame Paul Prudhomme. When the garrulous New Orleans chef introduced the world to blackened redfish, demand for this once little-known regional specialty soared and redfish stocks suffered all along

felt the solid shock of contact, and I was fast to my first south Texas redfish.

I was fishing with a beat-up old reel with far too many miles on its chassis. As the fish ran, the spool wobbled and the drag went on strike, leaving me overwhelmed down in my backing. But the Laguna Madre contains friendly, snag-free waters,

Ed Gray, founder of Gray's Sporting Journal, *with guide and snowy egrets on a redfish flat.*

the Gulf Coast. How unfair to anglers! Fish fillets smothered in garlic and pepper and seared in a white-hot skillet might as well be hake or something equally uninteresting on the end of a fly line. Fortunately, thanks to intense lobbying by concerned anglers, Texas banned commercial inshore netting, and redfish populations rose like water during spring runoff.

The red drum was not the only game fish in the Laguna Madre to benefit from the commercial netting ban. These protected waters also teem with speckled sea trout, and spring happens to be an excellent time to catch big ones. During our initial stay in Port Mansfield, we visited extensively with Dick's friend Jim Dailey, a former marine biologist for the Texas Parks and Wildlife Department and self-confessed sea trout fool. Jim regularly takes big specks on his oversized mullet patterns, and he has no doubt that the waters of the Laguna Madre hold world-record sea trout.

THE AFTERNOON AFTER OUR first workout on the flats, a freshening breeze and falling tide concentrated the bait in deeper water, and we decided to run the channels until we spotted birds working over feeding fish. We had to do a little looking, but suddenly a flock of gulls appeared above the waves

Sight-casting to redfish. Anglers accustomed to gin-clear bonefish flats will find sight-fishing Texas inshore waters a bit frustrating. Fortunately, feeding redfish are easy to see when tailing.

in an obvious state of excitement. As we cautiously maneuvered upwind of the activity, Lori and I hopped from the boat in waist-deep water and advanced cautiously toward the wheeling maelstrom of birds.

As soon as we reached casting range, we pitched our weighted Clousers under the gulls, earning immediate, emphatic strikes. Lori's fish threw her hook somehow, but I soon stood admiring a shimmering 4-pound trout. Even as I released the fish, I began to work my way into

position for another shot beneath the birds. That cast produced a quick strike too, the second of many and enough to establish my confidence in our new technique.

We chased birds and fished beneath them until dark, and I learned a trick or two in the process. Keeping the gulls happy proved critical, which meant side-arming casts low against the water to prevent spooking the birds. The fish ran in mixed schools, with redfish feeding deeper than the trout. Allowing the fly to sink before retrieving let us catch some nice reds along with the specks before we finally conceded the day to the sunset and ran for home.

That night as we sat around Dick's kitchen trying to catch our collective breath, we noticed activity beneath the lights on the boat slip. While the rest of us gawked, Lori wisely rigged up a 5-weight rod. Her silver Clouser Minnow turned out to be a drop-dead imitation of the bait swarming beneath the lights, and her initial cast resulted in a quick strike. The fish was a sand trout that came to hand vomiting clots of minnows it had been unable to digest during the feeding frenzy. These fish weren't much over a foot long, but on light tackle they didn't have to be.

Cloudy weather kept us from catching a lot

STINGRAYS

Every year anglers and swimmers sustain about 2,000 injuries from stingrays in American waters. Wading the shallows of the Texas Gulf Coast affords anglers an excellent opportunity to join this unfortunate company.

Members of the family Dasyatidae, stingrays are primitive cartilaginous fishes distantly related to sharks. Seven species of stingrays inhabit waters along our Atlantic coast, of which the southern stingray accounts for the majority of injuries to humans. Described by Aristotle more than 2,000 years ago, their unique defensive envenomation apparatus has earned stingrays a long history of animosity. Devilfish indeed.

In fact, stingrays are not the least bit aggressive unless provoked, a character trait that paradoxically explains most "attacks" on humans. When not actively feeding, stingrays often lie quietly on sandy or muddy bottoms with only their protruding eyes exposed. Because of their flat profile and docile disposition, they're easy to step on, and that's when the trouble begins.

Pinned down by a wader's foot, a stingray will strike reflexively, creating a deep puncture wound with the sharp, barbed envenomation apparatus at the base of its tail. Driven with remarkable force, a ray's stinger can penetrate clothing, wading boots, and even the sides of wooden boats. Stingers frequently break off on impact, creating an ugly, contaminated wound. The stinger comes coated with an elaborate mixture of toxins capable of producing intense pain and, rarely, cardiovascular collapse and death.

First aid in the field consists of washing the wound with the cleanest fluid available and removing any obvious stinger fragments. When feasible, the injured part (almost always a foot) should be immersed in water as hot as the victim can tolerate. All stingray strikes should be evaluated medically, as antibiotics are usually appropriate and surgery can be required to remove deeply imbedded stinger fragments.

The best way to prevent stingray injuries is to shuffle your feet while wading. This tactic will alert the ray to your approach and diminish the chance of pinning it beneath your foot.

So tread lightly out there.

of trout up on the flats that trip. Because they seldom tail, trout are harder to see than redfish, making bright sun and good visibility necessary when sight-casting to them. But we saw enough big trout while we were running in the skiff to

The guide points out redfish tailing well ahead of the boat's path.

arouse my interest. Two years later, I finally had an opportunity to sample what Texas sea trout had to offer at their best.

On a torrid July morning during a return trip to the area, I was wading the shoulder of the dredge cuts along the Inland Waterway just south of Port Mansfield. Herons lined the shore in front of me as a skimmer traced a delicate V across the surface with its oversized mandible. I had just worked a school of tailing reds unsuccessfully, switching to a surface popper when my streamer fouled repeatedly in the abundant grass. But the next time I spotted a fish, something looked different, and as I maneuvered into casting position I finally realized that the long, dark outline beneath the surface belonged to a trout.

The fish was cruising slowly back toward the channel, and with no time to switch to a more conventional pattern, I let the popper fly.

The fish thrashed and struck and began to plow its way back toward the security of deeper water. Sea trout don't pack a tremendous punch on the end of a line, but they make up for a lot of their sluggishness with their physical appearance. In contrast to the brawny red's carplike features, specks look sleek and silvery, and after I landed the fish I spent an extra minute or two admiring my catch before releasing it to fight again.

WE LEFT THE DOCK before dawn in order to get a jump on the breeze that usually rises from the gulf by midmorning, even during the calm months of summer. The early sun remains a tenuous presence behind a soft layer of fog. A pair of snowy egrets guards the entrance to the flat as a flock of roseate spoonbills glides low over the water behind us, the warm blush of color in their plumage suggesting the hue of redfish yet to come.

Dick cuts the motor and the skiff slides easily to a stop. The noise fades and dies and then we are alone with the birds. Lori and I exchange knowing glances as we hop over the side, afoot once again in the middle of all the wonderful loneliness.

"Got a tailing fish over here," Dick calls when I'm a hundred yards from the boat.

"Go ahead and take him," I call back, for I suddenly have reds of my own breaking the surface right in front of me. Once again, we seem to have wandered into the middle of acres of tailing redfish. Lori is working her line intently overhead while I study my own possibilities, trying to judge size and movement patterns before making a commitment. Finally, I cast; the fish disappears, and I can see its frightened wake retreating quickly toward deeper water. I have spooked the first fish of the day, although it scarcely seems to matter.

And that is just the kind of unforced pace I have come to love about the Laguna Madre. Despite challenging light conditions, there are so many reds tailing in front of us that I can spook a good fish and laugh about it. I double-haul, plop the fly down on top of another feeding fish, and savor the sudden boil that marks the take. To all those conservation-minded outdoors enthusiasts whose political determination allowed this miracle to happen: Take a bow.

WHAT TO EXPECT

ANGLING

Trout and redfish now abound in bays and lagoons all the way along the Texas Gulf Coast, with popular fishing locations stretching from Port Elizabeth north to Aransas Pass. I've done most of my fishing out of Port Mansfield, a bare-bones waterfront town south of Corpus Christi. Services are limited, but the town contains a large marina, and a number of experienced guides base their operations there. I have visited the Laguna Madre on numerous occasions between March and August and enjoyed good fishing on every trip. Most locals prefer the summer months, and excellent fishing takes place during the fall as well. Huge black drum run through the channels from the gulf in the spring. Although difficult to take on flies, these powerful, challenging fish offer a potential bonus at that time of year.

Anglers accustomed to wading gin-clear bonefish flats might initially find sight-fishing in Texas inshore waters a bit frustrating. Wind, tide, and soft bottoms often mean turbid water and limited visibility. Fortunately, feeding redfish are easy to see when tailing. The area's complex shoreline almost always makes it possible to find flat water somewhere, which makes spotting tails

Since Texas banned commercial inshore netting, redfish populations have steadily increased.

or the wakes left by cruising fish possible even in cloudy water. On bright days, it's possible to see both reds and trout beneath the surface. If sight-casting conditions deteriorate completely, try to locate fish under feeding birds.

Although it's possible to fish on your own from shore, the best fishing requires access by boat. Rentals are available in most coastal

"Allowing the fly to sink before retrieving let us catch some nice reds. . .before we finally conceded the day to the sunset and ran for home."

communities, but visitors must exercise caution to avoid running aground in the area's countless and largely uncharted shallows. Most locals use specially designed shallow-draft boats to negotiate the bay's tricky tidal flats. The Intracoastal Canal provides a well-marked channel through the Laguna. Stray out of bounds at your own risk.

Long-sleeved, fast-drying clothing proves comfortable while wading the flats. Take along a windbreaker or light Polar Fleece jacket for long runs by boat. During the spring, many locals—who seem to have less tolerance for cold than I do—wear lightweight chest waders, but I've always felt comfortable wading wet.

Despite the conservation success generated by Texas' netting ban, the future of this unique fishery remains far from certain. (Do conservation battles ever really end?) Inshore gamefish species remain highly susceptible to changes in water quality: salinity, temperature, and oxygen content. Inland agricultural practices and organic discharge from commercial shrimp farms remain a potential threat to the Laguna Madre.

LAY OF THE LAND

Most visiting anglers arrive by air in San Antonio or Corpus Christi and take rental vehicles from there to their final destination along the coast.

Full-service guest facilities are limited at many Gulf Coast fishing communities. Local-property rental pools can provide very reasonably priced accommodations especially during the spring off-season (which happens to be one of my favorite times to visit).

Visitors must respect the south Texas sun, even under overcast skies, when a long day on the water can produce unexpected burns. Always carry enough clothing to cover yourself head to toe and bring plenty of sunscreen. Don't forget to take along plenty of fresh drinking water, as sustained physical activity like flats wading coupled with high temperatures and humidity can easily lead to dehydration. Beware of stingrays while wading. (See Appendix A for further information.)

The Laguna Madre sustains a huge population of birdlife, including a tremendous variety of wading birds and one of the country's largest populations of roseate spoonbills. The spring bird migration can be spectacular, and enthusiasts should be sure to carry field glasses, a birding book, and a camera.

Ancillary activities include world-class bird watching (mentioned above), sea kayaking, and surfing on the outside of Padre Island.

CONTACTS

PORT MANSFIELD CHAMBER OF COMMERCE
P.O. Box 75
Port Mansfield, TX 78598
210-944-2354
Listing of local guides, facilities, and rental properties.

TROY MONJARAS
210-944-2879
Inshore flats-fishing guide services from Port Mansfield.

TEXAS PARKS AND WILDLIFE
800-792-1112
www.tpwd.state.tx.us/fish

BAYSHORE BOAT RENTAL (PORT MANSFIELD)
210-944-2355

THE BROWN TIDE COALITION
15315 San Pedro
San Antonio, TX 78232
210-494-5237
A local conservation group dedicated to preserving the water quality of Texas's inshore marine waters.

RECOMMENDED READING

■ *FLY FISHING THE TEXAS COAST,* Phil H. Shook and Chuck Scates (1999. $19.95. Pruett Publishing Co.) A concise and useful regional guide.

■ *BIRDS OF TEXAS,* Roger Tory Peterson (1998. $23.00. Houghton Mifflin.) Because of the area's proximity to the Central American tropics, south Texas birdlife is unique. This volume from the classic Peterson Field Guide series will help observers through the confusion.

■ *ISAAC'S STORM,* Erik Larson (2000. $13.00. Vintage Books.) A vivid—and tragic—reconstruction of life on the Texas Gulf Coast in the early days, focused on the hurricane that destroyed Galveston.

■ *LONE STAR,* T. R. Fehrenbach (2000. $22.00. Da Capo Press.) Excellent Texas history background reading.

■ *FLYFISHING FOR REDFISH,* John Kumiski (1997. $19.95. Argonaut Publishing Co.) A useful source of practical information about an increasingly popular game fish.

Andros Island

When the urge for an over-the-top bonefish seizes me,
I pack my bags and head to Andros

As my old friend Nelson cut the motor and let the current ease the skiff up onto the flat, only a few things seemed to matter: the absence of snow, the warmth of the morning sun, the saline smell of the Caribbean. The air felt like amniotic fluid against my skin, and after a long, brutal winter back on the high plains the very idea of venturing into the elements without protective layers of wool seemed positively decadent. The fish could wait, I thought. For the moment, it was enough to dangle my legs over the gunwale and let the effortless feel of the place sink in.

Finally I roused myself, climbed to attention on the forward deck, and fumbled with my gear. Because we were staying with legendary Bahamian bonefish guide Charlie Smith at the time, it seemed only appropriate to tie on a Crazy Charlie, a pattern that subsequent decades of experience have convinced me might be the most

Bonefish guide known as "Bonefish Shakey" casts to one of his namesakes.

BAHAMAS

Nassau

GREAT BAHAMA BANK

ATLANTIC

ANDROS ISLAND

• Moxey Town

MIDDLE BIGHT

SOUTHERN BIGHT

effective prototype bonefish pattern ever invented. By the time I finished the knot and polished off my spray-drenched polarized glasses, I could begin to feel the lure of bonefish in the shimmering mosaic of sand and water ahead. But I had been gone from the flats too long, and I knew I'd have to endure a morning's worth of amateurish mistakes before my eyes found their way again.

For the ability to spot bonefish against complex visual backgrounds represents one of those quirky skills that can neither be acquired nor maintained without practice. Sometimes, mercifully, bonefish can be as apparent as the zits on your face staring back at you from the mirror when you were a teenager. But more often than not, they appear as little more than subtle aberrations in the pattern of light and shadow that the flats project onto the human retina. The ability to identify fish in this endless sweep of visual confusion resembles muscle tone or facility in a foreign language: You use it or lose it.

Because I knew I had lost it, the sudden appearance of a form in motion right at the edge of the shallows took me something by surprise. Reflexively, I gathered a loop of line and began to work it into the wind. "I dunno, mon," Nelson cautioned from the stern, and after a second look at the fish I aborted the cast. It was just too big to be a bonefish.

AT A GLANCE

SPECIES Inshore—bonefish, tarpon, permit, snapper, barracuda, jacks; blue water—billfish, tuna, wahoo, dolphin

TACKLE 8–9-weight rods for bonefish and permit; 10-weights for tarpon, 'cuda, and permit; 12-weights for blue water. Bonefish taper, floating lines for all flats fishing. 10# tippet for bones, heavy-monofilament shock tippet for tarpon, wire for 'cuda.

FLIES Basic flats selection; include Crazy Charlies and Gotchas in a variety of colors, and weighted Clousers for big bones in deeper water. Crab patterns for permit, needlefish imitations for 'cuda, poppers or large streamers for jacks; include basic blue-water selection if you plan to fish offshore.

PRIME TIME October, November, and March–June offer the most consistent flats fishing. January–March can be great months for big bones, which seem more tolerant of cool water temperatures than smaller fish. Late spring and summer are peak for permit and tarpon.

CONSERVATION ISSUES Coastal development and increasing demands on freshwater supplies

PRICE RANGE $1,500–$3,500

STAGING CITY Fort Lauderdale, Florida or Nassau, Bahamas

HEADS UP Although serious shark attacks are highly unusual in Bahamian waters, small inshore sharks sometimes behave aggressively toward wading anglers

"Lemon shark," I suggested even though I hadn't seen the characteristic undulating motion of a shark's tail. But then the fish glided gently past the bow, and the sun over my shoulder afforded a definitive, jaw-dropping look at the biggest bonefish I'd ever seen. Collecting myself at last, I rolled a sloppy cast in the general direction of the disappearing fish but to no avail, and then there was nothing to do but glance back at the stern for some form of confirmation.

"Sorry, mon," Nelson apologized sheepishly. "Never see one that big before."

Well, that made two of us.

ALTHOUGH THE BAHAMAS' ready juxtaposition of flats habitat and blue water offers anglers a variety of saltwater opportunities ranging from barracuda to billfish, the islands' reputation among fly-rod enthusiasts has always focused on bonefish. Based on personal experience, I'm happy to report that reputation justified on the basis of two factors, the first of which is big bones.

No doubt about it: On a good day on the Yucatán or in Belize you'll probably see (and catch) more fish than on a comparable outing in the Bahamas. But once you've mastered the basic elements of spotting and casting to fish, 2-pound bonefish, like Chinese food, tend to leave you hungry for something more substantial. And at some point in every angler's development (which some might not fish long enough to reach), testing the limit of the size envelope becomes more rewarding than catching another dozen fish like the last one. Even splendid flats destinations like Christmas Island (see Chapter 1) and Los Roques (see Chapter 3), which offer plenty of drag-challenging 6- to 8-pound bonefish, seem to come with a built-in upper size limit. Sometimes I need to step onto a flat and know I might see the biggest bonefish of my life. Why? Because, to paraphrase Mallory on Everest, it's there. Somewhere.

The two best places in the world to find giant bonefish are the Florida Keys and Andros Island. Although I have nothing against the Keys, I've always personally regarded bonefishing as a get-out-of-town affair, something I can't do right unless I have my passport stamped. So when the urge for an over-the-top bonefish seizes me, I pack my bags and head to Andros.

In addition to the allure of truly big fish, the Bahamas offers an ambience I find impossible to resist. I know; hard-core anglers aren't supposed to care about anything but fish. But I can enjoy great fishing in my own backyard (either of them). The role of traveling angler means new experiences as well as new fish, in which regard there's no place quite like the Bahamas, for reasons ranging from the unique lilt of Bahamian English to the incessant beat of music from the radio and the buttery aroma of conch fritters. Subjective, I know, but those are the kind of intangibles that make big fish seem even bigger.

A RECENT RETURN TRIP to Andros provided a sterling opportunity to make amends for my blown shot at that first huge fish years ago. Lori and I were fishing out of the new Mangrove Key Club on the south shore of Andros' Middle Bight, and coincidentally our guide was Nelson's nephew Nick Leadon. (On Andros, the last names Leadon, Moxey, and Smith are practically synonymous with bonefish.) After an hour's run from the

Opposite: Releasing a 6-pound bonefish on the west side of North Andros.

lodge through the bight to Andros's storied and largely unexplored west side, Nick eased the skiff onto a huge, empty flat and began to pole. Despite high wind and intermittently cloudy skies, we soon began to encounter more big bones than I'd ever seen in one place at one time.

Over the course of the most remarkable morning of flats fishing I've ever experienced, Lori and I lost four monsters in addition to hooking and landing a number of fish in the 6- to 8-pound range, and our excuses were legion. Wind threw fly line around rod butts. I watched helplessly as a 12-pounder lost a race against its little brother to my fly. And when a knot I'd tied blew up while Lori was fast to a comparable fish, I despaired briefly for the future of my marriage.

But in the end there was nothing to do but salute the vast flat for what it had shown us and promise to return the following day.

I'm hardly the world's most punctual person, but I always find ways to keep that kind of appointment. After Lori missed a shot at a large single, Nick spotted a school of fish working toward us downwind. I usually don't expect to see big bones in groups, but the rules are different in remote Andros waters. As the distance between our skiff and the fish closed, slowly I could see that all of them were large fish. This time, no excuses were necessary, and after surviving a sizzling run that tested my gear to its limits, we eventually wound up admiring a beautiful 11-pound Andros bone.

HAIL THE QUEEN

I doubt that any mollusk has exerted as much influence on local culture as the queen conch (*Strombus gigas*) has in the Caribbean. Indigenous peoples fashioned buttons and jewelry from conch shell and used conch shell trumpets in religious ceremonies. When the absence of rock in low-lying areas made masonry construction difficult, locals substituted conch shells, which can still be seen protruding from the foundations of many Bahamian homes. And then there is the matter of conch on the table.

Bahamians prepare conch (pronounced "conk" throughout the islands) in a number of distinctive ways. Diced raw and served marinated in peppers and lime, it makes a distinctive form of seviche. Fried crisp, cracked conch reminds me of West Coast razor clams. And many of the best meals I've enjoyed in the Bahamas began with conch fritter appetizers. With its pleasantly chewy texture and distinctive nutlike taste, I've found conch delicious in all its various incarnations and look forward to eating it as eagerly as I look forward to the fish. Almost.

Over the course of the next hour, we managed to lose two more fish in the same size category. Then we saw a huge single tacking slowly toward us into the current. I felt happy with my cast, but the fish followed the Gotcha right to the boat. When it finally took the fly, I had nothing left to strike back with. "Tell me honestly," I said to Nick as we watched the spooked fish retreat across the flat. "How big?"

"Fifteen, easy."

That was exactly the weight I'd guessed myself, and the memory of that monster zeroing in on my fly promises to haunt me until I find a way to go back yet again and catch him.

ALL THE WAY ACROSS the remote South Bight, we're fishing out of the Rahming family's Bonefish Bay resort in Kemp's Bay, about as far from anywhere as you can get in the Bahamas by road. The Rahmings are an old Andros family whose many enterprises include Rahming Marine, makers of some of the Bahamas' most widely used flats skiffs. Their Kemp's Bay facility offers visiting anglers access to the remote waters off the south tip of Andros and, by way of Deep Creek and Little Creek, the southern end of the island's west side.

With calm seas and clear skies waiting for us at the dock, we readily accept the Reverend Captain Felix Smith's invitation to head south. As the hamlet of Mars Bay, the last settlement on the island's road system, slides by to starboard, we enter a tropical wilderness of unsurpassed beauty that makes Nassau's hustle and bustle nothing but a distant memory. I'm not sure I've ever seen water look so many shades of blue. After running for an hour through a vast labyrinth of flats and cays, I stop trying to stay oriented and settle back to enjoy the view.

Finally we come to a stop at the upwind edge of a long hard-sand flat. The tide is just starting to build, and as we ready our gear we can see waves of tailing bonefish flooding onto the flat right along

Andros provides the lure of both giant bonefish and a laid-back culture and atmosphere.

with the water. Within 50 yards of the beached skiff, we manage a double hookup and I then watch Lori land six more fish without taking more than a dozen steps or waiting more than a minute between releasing one and hooking the next.

As a matter of pure spectacle, the next few hours rival anything I've ever experienced with a fly rod in my hand. The flat is so vast the two of us can't fish it all, and the fish just keep coming. A cast to the leading edge of a school almost always produces a mad scramble for the fly, often won by one of the smaller, more aggressive fish. Even though "small" Andros bones in the 4- to 5-pound range would be nice fish in many locations, I have other things on my mind. By midmorning I've decided to ignore the schools and prospect the

Top: Feeding out line as a bonefish makes its first run, west side of North Andros. Above: Andros Island's juxtaposition of flats habitat and blue water offers anglers a variety of saltwater opportunities ranging from barracuda (above) to billfish.

edge of the flat for bigger fish.

And it doesn't take long to find what I'm after. The first big single's weight must remain a matter of conjecture, as the fish winds up taking my line around a coral head and breaking off. The big cruisers prove choosier than their smaller cousins, but after a couple of refusals I hook and land a solid 8-pounder. Then I spot an even larger fish rooting around the edge of a coral outcropping. The presentation requires a tough cast right into the teeth of the wind, but the fly finds the right place, and at the first twitch from my line

hand the fish turns in pursuit. With tantalizing deliberation, it follows the fly until I have nothing left to strip but leader. But at the last possible moment, it pounces.

I knew the fish was big from the start, but I don't realize quite how big until it puts its weight to work against the drag. Nothing produces a feeling of helplessness quite like a dwindling supply of backing on a fly reel, but the fish finally turns and allows me to work it back through the coral to my hand. Double-digit bones are so special that by the time I've revived the fish and released it, I really don't have another left in me. *No mas,* I tell myself happily, and with that I hook the fly in the keeper and head back to the skiff to spend the rest of the morning following Lori and Felix around with the camera. And why not? This remote Andros flat has given me everything I had a right to ask for.

WHAT TO EXPECT

ANGLING

Almost every island in the Bahamas offers good angling opportunities, but no destination in the country—or in the entire Caribbean, for that matter—can rival the extent and variety of Andros' waters. Furthermore, the island's size, geographic complexity, and general lack of development suggest that it will continue to offer untrammeled adventure-angling opportunities for years to come.

Over 100 miles long by some 30 miles wide and transected by three major bights, Andros offers an incredibly complex coastline punctuated by numerous creeks and channels that create vast inshore marine fish habitat. The island's road system is limited to the north end and western shore. Anglers depend almost exclusively upon boats to reach productive water, which makes it a difficult destination for visitors interested in fishing entirely on their own. On the other hand, the same lack of access ensures the unspoiled, wilderness quality of the fishing experience available to those willing to explore by boat with local guides, particularly on the southern and western sides of the island.

Andros enjoys an important historical role in the annals of modern fly fishing. Founded in the 1930s on the North Bight, the Bang Bang Club was one of the world's first true light-tackle saltwater destinations. Around the same time, a number of wealthy Americans began to develop private facilities in the area, where many of the island's best-known fishing families began their career as guides. Years ago when I fished with famous Andros guide Carl Moxey out of Cargill Creek, he told me stories about growing up among the Andrew Mellon family's entourage on Mangrove Cay. Today, the Mellons are gone, but the Moxeys remain, which ought to tell us something about the enduring value of angling knowledge as opposed to more conventional measures of wealth.

Like most prime flats fishing destinations, Andros offers a variety of game fish species. Although not as well known for permit or tarpon as the Yucatán or Belize, both prowl Andros waters. While anglers may encounter permit on the flats anywhere at any time, permit fishing is best on the north end of the island during summer months. Tarpon are present year-round, and move out of the creeks and onto the flats during periods of calm, stable weather. Mutton snapper enter shallow water during March and April. Barracuda are ubiquitous and Andros waters contain some big ones. Anglers should carry a rod ready for 'cuda (a 10-weight rigged with wire leader and a needlefish imitation) when fishing from a skiff. Fish are present during the winter, although cold fronts can unpredictably compromise the action.

But bonefish represent the heart of the Andros angling experience. Anglers who enjoy wading for bones will find nearly limitless opportunities to do so on hard-bottomed flats scattered along windward shores along the ocean and the major bights. Especially along the southern tip of Andros and the remote west side, bonefish numbers can be unbelievable. In these locations, I've fished for hours without ever being out of casting range of fish, and was often planning my next stalk before I landed the fish I was already playing.

But numbers only represent one aspect of the Andros bonefish story. Once bones exceed 10 pounds in weight, they might as well be considered a different species: solitary, brooding, finicky, and capable of tearing up tackle that would subdue smaller specimens in short order. At some point in every dedicated saltwater fly rod angler's career, big bonefish become an obsession unto themselves, and there is no place to indulge in them quite like Andros.

While double-digit bones can show up at any time, anglers intent on big fish will improve their odds by fishing for them specifically. Good guides will know where to head for big fish, but bear in mind that pursuing them will likely mean seeing and casting to fewer fish over the course of the day. In my experience, the waters near the western end of Andros' Middle Bight offer unequaled opportunities at big bonefish. This means fishing deeper water from a skiff, since most of the flats in this area have soft marl bottoms, and spending long hours studying the water for relatively few fish. But the fish you see are likely to be monsters, and for those interested in the unique challenge of big bonefish the rewards this kind of fishing provides will be well worth the effort.

One of the most enjoyable aspects of Andros as a bonefish destination is the ability to vary the agenda according to whim. I like to alternate between wading the flats for lots of fish and concentrating on areas likely to produce a few big ones. Andros allows both options.

Because of the ever-present possibility of fish big enough to test tackle to its limits, visitors to Andros need to be fussy with their gear. I prefer fairly heavy bonefish tackle here, because of the wind and the size of the fish. Reels and drags should be in perfect working order and capable of holding 250 yards of backing. Change leaders frequently and be meticulous with your knots. Abrasion resistant flourocarbon tippet provides an extra margin of safety when fishing near coral. While all standard bonefish patterns will catch fish on Andros, local guides favor Gotchas for big fish so be sure to pack along an adequate supply.

Dress on Andros is strictly informal. Wear fast-drying, lightweight, long-sleeved shirts and pants while wading. As always, hats and polarized glasses are essential on the flats. Andros offers lots of opportunities to wade for bonefish. Some flats offer delightful wading on hard sand while others contain lots of sharp coral, making tough wading shoes essential.

LAY OF THE LAND

Like many locations about the Caribbean, Bahamian culture reflects a diverse historical background. Although its exact location remains disputed, Christopher Columbus's first New World landfall took place somewhere in the Bahamas in 1492. The islands' original inhabitants, the Arawaks, did not survive a century of Spanish persecution, and immigrants of African descent eventually replaced them. In 1647, a group of dissidents from Bermuda formed the first British colony on Eleuthera. The British formally claimed the islands in 1670, and for the next half century the Crown devoted most of its local efforts to the pursuit of the area's notorious pirates, including Blackbeard and Henry Morgan. The Bahamas remained a British colony until 1969, when it became a Commonwealth nation. The Bahamas became fully independent in 1974. Local ambience still reflects a rich blend of Caribbean, African, and British influences.

Although the largest island in the Bahamas, Andros remains sparsely populated (approximately 8,000 full-time residents) and largely undeveloped. Because of the size of its landmass, Andros historically served the Bahamas as a source of timber and agricultural products, although its economy now focuses largely on tourism, especially fishing.

Several air services offer charter flights to Andros Town from Fort Lauderdale. If your party is large enough to fill a small airplane, chartering might be the most economical way to go and it's certainly convenient. Island Express (954-359-0380) also offers scheduled flights to Andros from Fort Lauderdale. Otherwise, fly by scheduled air service (Delta, American, and Continental, among others) to Nassau and take a scheduled flight on Bahamasair (800-222-4262) to Andros from there. Bahamasair provides regular service to Andros Town, Mangrove Cay, and Congo Town on South Andros. Interisland flights aren't always punctual, so don't plan tight connections.

Visitors with time to spare and an interest in seeing out-of-the-way parts of the islands can also take one of the mail boats from Nassau. Contact the Nassau Dockmaster (242-393-1064) for schedules and reservations. Most operators depend on local taxi service for ground transportation between airports and lodges. Anglers visiting more than one destination on Andros can travel by taxi and utilize free passenger ferry service across the bights. Vehicle rentals are available in Andros Town.

Tap water quality varies with location. Outside reputable lodges, it's wise to drink bottled water. Because Andros contains so much stagnant inland water, biting insects—especially sand flies—can be troublesome when the wind dies down. Sunburn risk is comparable to Florida's. Most flats fishing takes place on sheltered inland water, so seasickness shouldn't be a problem unless you plan to venture offshore. The superb local cuisine depends heavily on fresh fish—heed local opinion regarding the risk of ciguatera poi-

Miles and miles of white sand flats you can wade barefoot after big, unsophisticated bonefish (turn the page for a 12½-pound example).

soning. (See Appendix A for further information.)

Ancillary activities include snorkeling and diving, biking, windsurfing, and sea kayaking.

CONTACTS

MANGROVE CAY CLUB

www.mangrovecayclub.com
Located near the legendary Middle Bight, this new lodge is operated by veteran flats angler Steve McGrath and his Bahamian business partner Liz Bain. Superb guides and ready access to some of the world's best big bonefish water. Book through Frontiers, listed in Appendix C.

BONEFISH BAY RESORT

www.fishabout.com/bone.htm
True wilderness flats angling on remote South Andros, with exceptional opportunities to wade for bonefish. Book through Fishabout, listed in Appendix C.

BAHAMAS DEPARTMENT OF FISHERIES

P.O. Box N-3028
Nassau, Bahamas
242-393-1777

THE OUT ISLANDS PROMOTION BOARD

1100 Lee Wagener Blvd.
Fort Lauderdale, FL 33315-3564
800-688-4752
Information about visitor services on the Bahamas' less developed islands, including Andros.

RECOMMENDED READING

■ *THE BAHAMAS FLY-FISHING GUIDE,* Stephen and Kim Vletas (1999. $29.95. The Lyons Press.) One of the most definitive destination-specific fly-fishing books I know.

■ *FLY FISHING FOR BONEFISH,* Dick Brown (1993. $35.00. The Lyons Press.) A concise sourcebook focused on the Bahamas' signature game fish.

■ *ADVENTURE GUIDE TO THE BAHAMAS,* Blair Howard (1999. $14.95. Hunter.) A basic travel guide, this book contains little authoritative fishing information, but it offers sound background material and many useful contacts.

HEALTH & SAFETY

Acomplete review of first aid and wilderness medicine obviously lies beyond the scope of this discussion, and I would refer interested readers to the brief bibliography at the end of this section for comprehensive information. However, travelers to remote locations face special health issues, including the following topics of particular interest to anglers.

BEARS

Backcountry visitors to the mountain West and Alaska can encounter both black and brown/grizzly bears. (Brown and grizzly bears are both members of the same species, *Ursus arctos*. Alaskans refer to the larger coastal specimens as brown bears in scientifically arbitrary fashion.) Black bears are common in eastern Canada. Eastern Asia contains grizzly bears only. Although grizzlies are generally larger and more aggressive, both species can occasionally inflict serious injury. Bears habituated to human presence, as in national parks, are more likely to behave aggressively than their true wilderness counterparts.

Encounters are especially likely when anglers visit areas of high bear density, such as Alaskan salmon streams. Fortunately, bears fishing for salmon are usually preoccupied and rarely confront human anglers. Nonetheless, all bears are potentially dangerous and need to be treated with the respect they deserve.

Preventing bear attacks is obviously the key to their management, as bears are large, powerful animals. A full-blown attack can result in serious injuries that can prove difficult to treat in the backcountry setting. Although much of the conventional wisdom on the subject makes sense, it remains important to appreciate that unpredictability is a feature of the ursine character, and that no set of human behavior guidelines can guarantee protection against attack in all circumstances.

The vast majority of wilderness bears are even less interested in a human encounter than you are. Although all bears are *potentially* dangerous, they are *predictably* dangerous only under certain defined circumstances: when surprised, when defending a food source, and when sows are accompanied by cubs. The latter situation is especially dangerous, and anglers should always give sows with cubs a wide berth. When hiking along streams in bear country, try to avoid thick brush and other areas of reduced visibility, especially when the wind is in your face. And if a bear acts as if it owns a particular stretch of the river, concede the point and find another place to fish.

Bears that turn toward an angler rather than running away are likely motivated more by curiosity than belligerence, and even bears that appear to be charging are more likely to be engaged in threat behavior than real intent to injure. Nonetheless, these are potentially dangerous circumstances, and how you respond could well determine the outcome of the encounter. Despite the natural impulse to flee, it is impossible to outrun a bear for any distance, and flight can provoke a more aggressive predatory response. If the bear is a grizzly and there is a stout tree nearby, by all means climb it. Remember that black bears climb quite well, and that you would have to reach a height of at least 15 feet off the ground to evade a grizzly. Otherwise, shout to identify yourself, back up slowly while keeping the bear in sight, and avoid direct eye contact (an aggressive message in the vocabulary of bear body language).

In the highly unlikely event of an actual attack, the proper response depends on the species of bear. Active resistance against a grizzly generally proves futile, so the wisest course of action is to assume the "cannonball" position and protect your head and neck as well as possible with your hands. If you are wearing a backpack, try to keep it between you and the bear. Black bear attacks, on the other hand, are often motivated by predatory instinct rather than pure aggression, and fighting back actively with whatever means are available might abort the encounter.

Bears in camp pose a special problem because their presence already implies a certain tolerance for humans. Keeping a clean camp in bear country is the key to avoiding this unpleasant situation. Prepare food away from sleeping areas, and burn scraps and leftovers likely to attract bears. Keep food in odor-proof containers whenever possible. And never sleep in a tent containing food.

The issue of self-defense in bear country remains controversial. I seldom carry a firearm for protection while fishing in bear country, but I usually keep a rifle in camp whenever I plan to spend the night outside in areas of high bear concentration. But then, I know how to use one. In untrained hands, firearms are likely to cause more problems than they solve, and it is illegal to posses them in national parks. I don't have much confidence in pepper spray as a bear repellant, but there are documented cases of its successful use, and it can be a viable alternative for those uncomfortable with firearms or in situations where firearms are not practical.

Although the preceding discussion sounds daunting, it's important to realize that serious bear attacks remain rare events even in places where grizzly bears abound. Benign encounters with bears can provide highlight experiences during any wilderness trip. I have enjoyed hundreds of such encounters over the years without ever experiencing anything truly adverse.

But it's worth repeating: All bears are potentially dangerous. Treat them with the respect they deserve.

BUSH FLYING

Roads and wilderness are largely incompatible. Hence, anglers visiting truly remote destinations often rely on other means of travel. Especially in the north, that often means flights by bush airplane, either on floats or wheels. Bush flying differs substantially from the airport-to-airport flights most of us experience on a regular basis. Bush flights often involve close encounters with bad weather and terrain, landing surfaces can be unpredictable, and load considerations are critical in light aircraft. Although most of the responsibility for a safe and successful bush flight lies with the charter service and the pilot, there are a few things passengers should know before they embark.

The same flight characteristics that make bush planes good at getting in and out of tight places also limit their load capacity. Attention to weight should begin in the trip's planning stages, as no responsible pilot will deliberately take off in an overloaded airplane. Ask your charter service to provide you with a weight limit and stick to it when you pack. Generally, light airplanes are easier to load with a lot of small parcels rather than a few big ones, so pack accordingly. If you plan to carry unusually long or oddly shaped parcels, notify your carrier in advance. If you have some items than can tolerate a bit of moisture, be sure to identify them so they can be loaded into float compartments if necessary.

Airplane propellers needlessly kill people every year. Most of these accidents involve inexperienced passengers who simply walk into spinning propellers when the aircraft is on the ground. Remember that you might not be able to see a moving propeller. Always assume that props are in motion or are about to be.

Prior to takeoff, all passengers on bush

flights should know how to get out of the aircraft and the location of the Emergency Location Transmitter (ELT), survival gear, and flotation devices if the flight will be conducted over water. Pilots should make this information known prior to flight. If they don't, ask.

Most bush plane accidents are the equivalent of fender benders on takeoff or landing, and most occupants survive these mishaps without major injury. However, if you don't have access to the equipment necessary for survival in the bush if the aircraft is disabled, walking away from the wreck won't do you much good. The ability to communicate your situation to rescue aircraft, should it come to that, is essential. When I flew in Alaska, I always gave my regular passengers a brief course in radio operation. In an emergency, remember that Alaska hunting and fishing licenses have a set of standard ground-to-air communication signals printed on the back.

If you are traveling by floatplane, it's usually helpful to wear hip waders in flight so you can help stabilize the aircraft and unload when you arrive at your destination. This might be unnecessary if you are flying to a lodge with a dock. Ask before departure.

Finally, remember that the final responsibility for the conduct of the flight lies with the pilot. Problems often arise when anglers eager to reach a long-awaited destination push pilots to fly in adverse circumstances. The weather might look fine to you, but your pilot knows better. The end result of these arguments is usually nothing but ill will and an unpleasant flight. And remember that the worst outcome of all could come if you win the argument.

No doubt about it—bush flying carries some inherent risk. But the idea of risk-free adventure is an oxymoron. Properly conducted, bush flights to and from remote angling locations should provide an enjoyable opportunity to view the country and the water as well as unique memories once the trip is over.

CIGUATERA POISONING

Although I endorse the catch-and-release ethic as a matter of principle, it's important to realize that in many remote locations the most ecologically sound (as well as practical) dinner entrée might well be fish. Fresh fish from the sea makes a delicious and health-conscious food choice. Anglers visiting secluded locations may no longer plan on hauling home coolers full of fillets, but they should expect to eat some fish during their stay.

Visitors to tropical saltwater destinations must be aware of an insidious health problem called ciguatera poisoning. First described by Captain James Cook during his voyage aboard the *Resolution* in 1774, ciguatera is the most common form of nonbacterial food poisoning from fish in the United States today. The problem begins with a series of toxins elaborated by marine dinoflagellates and passed up the food chain to successively larger predatory fish. Ciguatera is a phenomenon of inshore waters near coral reefs, so bluewater species rarely carry the toxin. Ciguatera occurs at tropical latitudes, generally between 35 degrees north and south of the equator. Cases reported from temperate zones usually involve fish imported from other areas.

Although many species have been reported to transmit ciguatera, groupers, snappers, jacks, and barracuda are the most frequent offenders. Because the toxin accumulates in fish over time, older, larger specimens are more likely to be toxic. There is no practical, reliable means of identifying toxic fish in the field. I generally rely on local knowledge and eat what the locals eat, although this approach is obviously not foolproof. If in doubt, it's wise to avoid eating high-risk species.

Symptoms of ciguatera poisoning usually begin within one to four hours after the fish is ingested. Initial symptoms are nonspecific and include nausea, vomiting, diarrhea, headache, muscle pain, and weakness, all of which resemble gastroenteritis or "stomach flu." Many victims report a variety of neurological symptoms, including numbness and tingling, difficulty swallowing and urinating, itching, and visual disturbances. Short of analyzing the suspect fish in a reference laboratory, there is no conclusive way to confirm ciguatera poisoning even in a hospital. Anyone experiencing these symptoms after consuming high-risk fish should be considered to have the disease.

Mild cases can be treated symptomatically in the field, as outlined in the section on water-borne illness (see page 197), and with acetaminophen for headache and antihistamines for itching. The rate of fatality and serious complications remains low, but anyone suspected of having ciguatera poisoning should seek medical attention if feasible. In-hospital care is supportive rather than specific, but intravenous fluids and respiratory support can be critical in severe cases.

HOOK REMOVAL

Intended for fish, hooks nevertheless have a distressing habit of winding up in all kinds of alternative targets, including trees, fences, shirts, hats, and occasionally human skin. Philosophically, I suppose it does us good to learn what being hooked feels like, but a wayward hook in the wrong place can end a good day on the stream in a hurry, and all anglers should know how to deal with the problem. I earned a lifetime's worth of experience back when I worked as a physician on Alaska's Kenai Peninsula. Every summer, we made a display of all the flies and lures we removed from visiting anglers in the emergency room, and by the end of the season we could have stocked a tackle store.

As always in wilderness medicine, prevention counts far more than cure. Watch your back cast and don't walk up behind someone who is casting without announcing your presence. Several anglers casting at the same time from a crowded boat is a prescription for disaster. Always wear sunglasses or some other form of protective lens over your eyes. And remember that there is no advertisement for barbless hooks as convincing as a big streamer stuck in your forehead.

But assuming the worst, there is a simple trick that allows quick, safe, and relatively painless hook removal in the field. Forget everything you've read about pushing the hook through and clipping off the point and barb. Instead, proceed as follows: 1) Loop a section of stout line or leader around the bend of the hook. 2) Push downward on the eye, forcing it toward the skin. 3) Align the loop so you can pull the rear of the hook backward, away from the eye, directing the force vector downward and parallel to the skin surface. 4) Take a deep breath and give the loop a short, sharp tug. 5) Inspect briefly for damage and keep on fishing.

The purpose of this maneuver is simply to disengage the barb through a combination of downward pressure on the hook eye and backward pressure against the bend. The trick is to be bold when you pull—tentative little tugs won't do the job.

The above advice applies to hooks embedded anywhere other than the eye. A fishhook stuck in the eye requires immediate medical attention and should not be removed in the field.

HYPOTHERMIA

Bear attacks and airplane wrecks might make headlines, but hypothermia kills more outdoor enthusiasts than all these high-profile incidents combined. Because of the time they spend in and about water, anglers are at particular risk. Those headed north need to understand the prevention and management of this insidious, life-threatening disorder.

The human body operates within a remarkably narrow internal temperature range. Hypothermia develops when our metabolic heat production can no longer keep up with the rate of heat loss to the external environment. Although most people associate hypothermia with cold ambient temperatures, it's important to realize that many other factors influence heat loss, including wind, evaporation, and individual susceptibility, such as age and conditioning. That's why hypothermia can affect anglers even though they don't spend a lot of time outdoors in sub-zero temperatures.

Mild hypothermia develops as the body's core temperature falls from normal to 92°F. Signs and symptoms include confusion, loss of coordination, and impaired judgment, all of which might be more apparent to companions than to the victim. Prompt recognition and management are essential to prevent progression. As the core temperature drops into the 80s, frank stupor, impaired ventilation, and cardiac arrhythmias develop. Because shivering usually ceases, the absence of shivering does not exclude the possibility of hypothermia. Once the core temperature drops below 80°F, hypotension, major acid-base disturbances, and life-threatening cardiac rhythm disorders become likely and can challenge resources even in a fully equipped hospital. Obviously, prevention and prompt management of early cases are more likely to save lives than are complex resuscitation efforts under field circumstances.

Begin by recognizing environmental conditions likely to lead to hypothermia. As noted, bitter-cold temperatures are not a prerequisite. Wind greatly increases the risk of hypothermia by raising the *chill factor,* the rate at which internal heat is lost to the environment. Moisture represents an equally important risk factor, especially in damp climates such as Alaska's. Dampness contributes to hypothermia by increasing heat loss through evaporation from the skin and by compromising the insulation value of clothing. This means that an angler with damp clothing after a tumble in a river on a windy day can be at significant risk for hypothermia, especially when faced with a long, strenuous hike back to shelter, even if the ambient temperature is well above freezing.

Proper clothing represents the first line of defense. Anglers in potentially risky conditions should dress in layers. The *inner* clothing layer should serve primarily to wick moisture away from the skin. Polypropylene and silk underwear suit this purpose well because these fabrics are light, comfortable, absorb considerable moisture before they feel wet, and effectively wick moisture away from areas of high concentration such as sweaty skin. The *insulation* layer should provide an effective thermal barrier to heat loss. Polyester and wool serve this purpose well, as they are effective insulators even when damp. Note that down, although an excellent insulator for its weight, becomes virtually useless when damp. The *protective* outer layer should be wind and water-resistant, and nylon works well for this purpose. All layers should be vented around the neck and armpits to allow inner moisture a route of escape.

Although it's not always possible to control environmental factors, paying attention to basic principles can reduce the risk of hypothermia. I'm fairly casual about getting wet while wading under summer conditions close to home, but in the bush it pays to be conservative because it can be difficult to recover from a soaking. Dehydration contributes to hypothermia, so be sure to drink at regular intervals even if the water is cold. In a survival situation, shelter from the wind should be a high priority even if that means nothing more elaborate than huddling behind a fallen log. Avoid overexertion and rest at frequent intervals to prevent excess moisture accumulation from sweat.

In the field, treatment of mild hypothermia should begin with passive external rewarming, which will usually suffice for healthy adults with no complicating injuries or medical problems. Reduce exposure to wind, remove damp clothing, and replace it with dry clothing of high insulating quality. Place the victim in a dry sleeping bag if possible, or improvise with blankets, mattresses, or whatever else is available. Provide liquids by mouth if the patient is conscious. Keep the victim recumbent initially, and don't forget to evaluate and treat any associated injuries. In most circumstances, mildly hypothermic individuals will recover in the field once their rate of heat loss is reduced through these simple means.

Although actively rewarming the victim either externally or internally might seem an obvious step, the task is more complicated than it seems. Applying external heat can result in a shift of warm blood toward the body's surface, away from the critical core, whereas internal heat is difficult to administer in the field to anyone ill enough to need it and can be associated with serious cardiovascular complications. Consequently, active rewarming in the field should be reserved for seriously impaired individuals who do not respond to passive rewarming, and then only when evacuation to a definitive treatment facility is likely to be delayed or impossible. Active external field rewarming can be initiated by placing warmed water bottles against the victim's groin or armpits. Note that sitting in front of a fire is a highly inefficient means of rewarming. Active internal rewarming options in the field are limited to administering warm liquids by mouth. Unfortunately, anyone alert enough to be able to swallow probably doesn't need treatment.

Seriously ill victims who remain unresponsive and hypothermic despite these measures represent a serious medical emergency and should be urgently evacuated for definitive hospital care if at all possible. Handle the victim gently, as minor external trauma can precipitate lethal arrhythmias. And remember that profoundly hypothermic patients often look dead, with undetectable pulse and respiration. Administer CPR if it appears appropriate and make every effort within reason to continue the evacuation. As a grim but profound medical adage reminds us, hypothermia victims aren't dead until they're warm and dead.

IMMUNIZATIONS

An ounce of prevention, a pound of cure...nothing illustrates the wisdom of this old chestnut like the demands of wilderness medicine. Complete, up-to-date immunizations offer a unique, although frequently overlooked, opportunity for the adventure traveler to avoid serious health problems, especially when traveling to destinations where unfamiliar infectious diseases commonly occur.

Immunization prior to travel should begin with a review of standard immunizations most Americans have already received: diphtheria, tetanus, polio, measles, mumps, and rubella. Healthy adults should receive a diphtheria/tetanus booster every ten years. Adequate immunization against measles and polio is especially important in travelers to developing countries, where these illnesses still commonly occur. Travelers born after 1956 who cannot document having received two doses of MMR vaccine (or natural immunity through the diseases themselves) should receive a booster, and revaccination with oral polio vaccine might be advisable for travelers to Third World countries. Consult your physician and review your personal immunization records if in doubt.

Legal requirements are the next concern. Now that smallpox and cholera vaccinations are no longer required for entry into any foreign country, this consideration applies only to yellow fever, a potentially serious viral illness still endemic in certain parts of Africa and Latin America. Although the vaccine is reasonably safe and effective, the risk of acquiring the illness is extremely remote for most travelers even to these areas, and vaccination is seldom medically indicated. Some countries still require proof of immunization upon entry, however, especially for travelers arriving from endemic areas. Yellow fever vaccination is not currently required for those traveling to any of the destinations discussed in this book, but international travelers should review the current state of these requirements well in advance of their departure. Contact the Centers for Disease Control and Prevention (303-221-6400). Should your itinerary require it, yellow fever vaccine must be administered at a designated Yellow Fever Vaccination Center, which could involve some inconvenience in itself.

Travelers should consider specific vaccinations against illnesses encountered more frequently abroad than at home. Although not legally required for entry into foreign countries, these vaccines can offer significant protection against potentially serious illness. The decision to receive any given vaccine should be based on the risk of acquiring the illness, the vaccine's safety and efficacy, and the recipient's health status. Because these considerations are so variable, consultation with one's personal physician, or in complex circumstances with a specialized travel-medicine clinic, should always take place well prior to departure.

Hepatitis A is an uncomfortable although non-life-threatening viral illness transmitted by contaminated food. Hepatitis B, a serious viral infection that can lead to long-term liver disease, including cirrhosis, is contracted through blood transfusion or sexual exposure. Both infections are common in developing countries. Safe, effective vaccinations against both are readily available, and most authorities recommend routine immunization for travelers planning to spend time in Third World countries.

Cholera is a potentially serious gastrointestinal illness of bacterial origin still prevalent in certain rural areas of Asia, Africa, and Latin America. Travelers with largely urban itineraries are at extremely low risk even in countries where cholera is common. Unfortunately, the vaccine is not very effective and most authorities do not recommend it, except for those planning to spend extended periods in very high-risk areas.

Another serious bacterial disease transmitted through contaminated food and water, typhoid fever poses a significant risk to travelers spending time in rural areas in Africa, India, and certain parts of Latin America. Oral and injected vaccines are available in this country, and both are safe and effective. Travelers to high-risk tropical areas, including rural Mexico, should consider vaccination.

Rabies occurs frequently in rural parts of many Third World countries. Although most travelers face little risk, the kind of postexposure immunization regimens we rely on here at home are not readily available in many developing nations. Travelers who reasonably expect extended contact with wild animals might consider elective immunization with the generally safe, effective, and well-tolerated vaccine now available in the United States.

Travelers to eastern Asia should consider vaccination against Japanese encephalitis, a potentially serious viral illness transmitted by mosquitoes, especially if they are planning an extended stay in rural areas during warm summer months when mosquitoes are active. The vaccine is fairly effective, but adverse reactions are more frequent than with the other immunizations discussed in this section. The vaccine is hard to obtain in the United States, so consultation with a travel-medicine clinic might be appropriate.

All of this sounds a bit intimidating, but it's important to remember that a serious infectious illness experienced in a remote setting far from modern medical care can easily become a disaster. For the record, after reviewing the data carefully, I have chosen to receive all the vaccines, except cholera, mentioned in this section.

JET LAG

Rapid travel east or west across lines of longitude disrupts circadian rhythms, resulting in disturbances of sleep, mood, and appetite. Although no one ever died of jet lag, the effect can be unpleasant and is capable of impairing the concentration necessary for the completion of important tasks …like fishing.

The severity of the jet lag phenomenon depends on several factors. Some individuals are far more susceptible than others for intrinsic reasons. Traveling west to east generally produces more unpleasant effects than travel in the opposite direction. The more time zones one crosses, the more severe the jet lag. (Conversely, even long flights north or south do not evoke the jet lag response.) In general, it takes about one day per time zone crossed to recover spontaneously from the effects of jet lag.

There is no specific medical treatment for jet lag. Travelers planning a long transoceanic flight should avoid alcohol and sedative medications, which often make symptoms worse. Eat lightly and try to time meals to coincide with the time of day you would eat at your destination. If possible, try to switch your clocks several hours in the direction of your destination a day or two prior to departure (but don't let this simple measure make you miss your flight!). Melatonin (available over the counter) taken at the time you would plan to sleep at your destination can be useful, although scientific evidence remains inconclusive.

MALARIA

North American travelers visiting tropical areas run the risk of exposure to a number of potentially serious exotic infectious diseases. Although a complete review of tropical medicine lies beyond the scope of this discussion, malaria is so important both in terms of its frequency and potential severity that all anglers visiting endemic areas should familiarize themselves with the basic principles of preventing and managing this illness.

Despite recent worldwide concern over the HIV epidemic, malaria remains the most important infectious disease on the planet, killing more people every year than AIDS and tuberculosis combined. Malaria is a disease of tropical latitudes, including southern Mexico, Central and parts of South America, sub-Saharan Africa, India, and southeast Asia. Angling destinations where malaria is endemic are identified in the What to Expect sections of each chapter. Because

they lack immunity, visitors from temperate climates are particularly susceptible to serious consequences of malaria, as are children and pregnant women.

Malaria is caused by infection with one of four microscopic parasites transmitted by the bite of the anopheles mosquito. These insects are active only at night. Travelers to high-risk areas should wear long-sleeved clothing and insect repellant between dusk and dawn, and cover their beds with netting treated with permethrin when sleeping in unscreened rooms.

Although not 100 percent effective, medical prophylaxis can reduce the incidence of infection significantly. Chloroquine remains the agent of choice in areas where resistance has not been reported, which includes the Caribbean and Central America north and west of the Panama Canal. Chloroquine resistance is common in South America, Asia, and Africa. Mefloquine is the drug of choice in these areas, and doxycycline is the first alternative. Neither of these medications are approved for use in pregnant women or young children, who should carefully consider the risks of travel to areas where chloroquine-resistant malaria occurs. Prophylaxis should begin one week prior to departure and continue for four weeks after return. All these medications require a prescription and have occasional side effects, so discuss the issue with your personal physician well before departure.

The symptoms of malaria include fever, intense chills, headache, backache, and prostration. Febrile illness in travelers to endemic areas should be regarded as malaria until proven otherwise. Microscopic examination of a blood smear by an experienced observer confirms the diagnosis. High-risk visitors to remote tropical areas where health care is not readily available might consider carrying appropriate medications for standby treatment. Consult your personal physician or a travel medicine clinic for current recommendations.

Finally, don't forget to mention your travel history if you develop unexplained illness after a trip to the tropics, even if you have been back for months. North American physicians seldom consider tropical illnesses as a basis for their patients' complaints, and this information can prove invaluable in establishing a proper diagnosis and treatment.

MOSQUITOES AND OTHER BITING INSECTS

Biting insects that feed on human blood cause considerable misery and occasionally severe illness. In addition to the familiar mosquito, troublesome biting insects include blackflies, biting midges (sand flies, no-see-ums), and ticks. Because many species breed near water, anglers are especially prone to unpleasant encounters. Although familiar as a common source of discomfort, it's important to realize that many of these insects can transmit serious illnesses: encephalitis (North American mosquitoes); malaria, dengue, and yellow fever (tropical mosquitoes); Lyme disease, Rocky Mountain spotted fever, and Colorado tick fever (ticks); and leishmaniasis (sand flies). Even when the risk of serious illness is low, biting insects can drive unprotected anglers off the water and make them wish they had never left home.

Protection against biting insects comes in two basic forms: physical and chemical. The former begins with adequate clothing: loose-fitting, long-sleeved shirts and pants, with pants legs tucked into socks, and a brimmed hat. In areas with high tick concentrations and risk of tick-borne illness, impregnating outer clothing with permethrin might be advisable. Because of these insects' enthusiasm for wrists and ankles, tucking pants into socks and sleeves into gloves is especially important in areas with large concentrations of blackflies (including the Alaska version, locally known as white-socks). Rubber medical exam gloves are useful for this purpose when fishing in areas such as Alaska

and Canada during late summer. Although they are a bit cumbersome, face nets might be advisable in areas of high mosquito concentration. A number of outdoor clothing manufacturers now offer lightweight nylon mesh "bug suits" that provide reasonably comfortable total body protection.

My tolerance for mosquitoes is far lower at night (when I am trying to sleep and insects are more active) than it is during the day. Camping out in mosquito country absolutely requires a bug-proof tent. Take along a roll of tape for emergency repairs to torn netting. Avoid unnecessary use of lights inside sleeping quarters at night, as light attracts insects.

Chemical insect repellants are generally more comfortable to wear than is elaborate protective clothing, especially when you are actively engaged in vigorous activities. Numerous insect repellants have been developed and marketed over the years, but none has proven as effective as DEET. Recent improvements in repellant design have largely depended on altering the vehicle to allow lower concentrations of DEET and longer duration of action rather than the development of new active ingredients. Choosing among the numerous commercially available preparations boils down to personal preference for smell, feel, and means of delivery, as DEET remains the active ingredient in virtually all of them. I have a preference for Muskol, not because it works any better than the rest but because the smell—considered obnoxious by some—unfailingly reminds me of good times outdoors in Alaska.

Despite theoretical concerns about applying chemical repellants directly to human skin, DEET appears to be generally safe. Nonetheless, certain common sense precautions apply. Follow manufacturers' recommendations for application. Use no more repellant than needed to prevent bites—the bugs will let you know when it's time to reapply. Avoid contact with cuts, abrasions, eyes, and lips. Remember that DEET can damage some vinyl and plastic surfaces, so keep it away from cameras, sunglasses, and watches. Apply sparingly to small children, and avoid using it on their hands (which frequently wind up inside their mouths). DEET can cause skin irritation and hypersensitivity in some individuals, so avoid it if you develop a rash after application.

The risk of transmitting certain tick-borne illnesses, including Lyme disease, varies with the length of time the tick remains attached. Therefore, those engaged in outdoor activities in areas of high tick concentration should inspect the skin (ideally with the help of a companion) at the end of the day. Despite the extensive lore regarding means of tick removal, no method is superior to direct traction with forceps, which should be part of every first-aid kit in tick country. Grasp the tick gently but firmly near the skin and apply gentle traction, increasing the force slowly if the tick does not detach at once. If mouth parts appear to be left in the skin after the body has been removed, tease them out with a needle as you would a splinter. Antibiotic prophylaxis after a tick bite has not been shown to effectively reduce the risk of tick-borne illness.

SEASICKNESS

Nausea can be one of the most miserable sensations known. Cancer chemotherapy patients who experience nausea during treatment often report that they would rather endure comparable periods of physical pain. So although no one is likely to die from mal de mer, few health mishaps can ruin a fishing trip as quickly.

Individual susceptibility to motion sickness varies greatly. As one of the lucky ones, I'm delighted to report that I cannot speak from experience. But I've watched more than one ordinarily stalwart angler beg to be taken ashore even in the midst of great fishing. And that's about as bad as any nonfatal illness can get.

Even in salt water, the protected areas flats anglers favor seldom produce enough motion to produce seasickness. As the popularity of offshore fly fishing has increased, however, more fly-rod anglers are experiencing the kind of deep ocean swells that put some people down for the count. Susceptible individuals headed to bluewater destinations should plan accordingly.

Eat lightly the morning you plan to set out and avoid alcohol the night before. Distraction helps, so stay as busy as you can during the run to the fishing grounds. If you remain in sight of land, scan the fixed horizon with your eyes at regular intervals. Avoid the temptation to lie down or go below deck.

A number of medications—both over-the-counter and prescription—can help combat seasickness. All work best if taken well before the onset of symptoms, so if you are prone to motion sickness, it's best to medicate before you leave the dock. Over-the-counter antihistamines like Dramamine are modestly effective, although they can cause dry mouth and sedation. Scopolamine transdermal patches, now available without prescription, are effective and have the advantage of being long acting. Although generally safe, they often cause dry mouth, and it's important to follow the manufacturer's recommendations when applying them. Prescription antinausea agents such as Compazine are usually more effective than over-the-counter oral medications but can also cause sedation. Used in chemotherapy patients, the centrally acting antinausea medication Zofran can be effective for those who have failed to respond to other medications. Although generally safe and well tolerated, it is expensive and not approved for this use by the FDA.

Again, all these agents are most effective when taken before symptoms develop. Once full-blown nausea and vomiting have started, the only effective cure is a return to shore. If you're into fish, this is the point at which you will find out just how much your friends aboard really like you.

Sharks

Like snakes and bears, sharks inspire far more human terror than they should. However, many species of sharks are potentially dangerous. Although most adverse encounters between sharks and humans involve surfers and divers, salt-water anglers should treat sharks with respect. Most large, dangerous sharks—such as the great white, tiger, and hammerhead—frequent deep water where anglers are not likely to encounter them. Large sharks do appear inshore in certain areas, however, and even smaller reef sharks can inflict serious injuries.

Principles for avoiding conflict with sharks suffer from a lack of data. Simply stated: The cause of many shark attacks remains unknown. Shark behavior seems to vary considerably with location, but it's difficult to generalize. Although most shark attacks occur within 20 degrees of latitude from the equator, northern California has recently experienced a surge of attacks, mostly by great whites on surfers, who bear an unfortunate resemblance to sea lions when viewed from below. And although sharks in the Indo-Pacific generally behave more aggressively than their Caribbean counterparts, shark attacks in Hawaiian waters are rare. As usual, it's wise to take your cues from the locals. On many mid-Pacific islands and along the river mouths in Costa Rica, for example, local residents scrupulously avoid the water because of sharks, and I'm sure they have good reason.

Despite the uncertainty that surrounds shark attacks and the relatively low risk anglers face, those wading salt water in areas that contain sharks should bear certain principles in mind. Nothing attracts sharks like fish blood, and carrying fish on a stringer in waters sharks frequent is ill-advised. Sharks are generally most active in dim light, so avoid wading at dawn and dusk. Turbid water near river mouths can be an especially dangerous area. Anglers wading flats often see small sharks in the shallows. Although gener-ally benign, I have seen ordinarily placid lemon sharks act aggressively, and they can inflict damaging bites despite their small size. In case of such an encounter, avoid running or otherwise disturbing the water, which could precipitate more aggressive behavior from the shark. Retreat slowly, and if the shark continues to approach, deliver a sharp blow to the snout with whatever is handy. (I have successfully used the butt of my fly rod for this purpose on more than one occasion.)

Fly fishing for sharks has become a popular pursuit. Anglers who have landed one need to remember how quickly a shark can inflict a serious wound. A shark's mouth should be treated like a loaded gun, capable of injuring at any time. I like to think that most fly-caught sharks will be released promptly, but remember that sharks that appear dead after being out of the water for some time can still inflict serious bites without warning.

Massive injury from shark bite is unlikely among anglers, but any shark bite that punctures the skin represents a dirty, contaminated wound. Seek medical attention if feasible for definitive management.

Snakes

Snakes scare a lot more people than they kill. And of the destinations reviewed in this book only a few present any real risk of venomous snakebite—mainland Central America and our own southern seaboard and mountain West. Nonetheless, snakebite is a potentially serious consequence anglers face in certain areas, and all outdoor enthusiasts should be familiar with the basic principles of prevention and management. And as a personal aside, I would note that I have had more encounters with poisonous snakes while fishing than while engaged in any other outdoor activity.

In North America, poisonous snakes fall into four basic families. Rattlesnakes (*Crotalus spp.*) are widely distributed throughout the South and West, vary widely in size and the potency of their venom, and frequently (but by no means invariably) announce their presence and intention to strike by their characteristic rattle. Spend enough time walking the banks of western trout streams during the warm summer months and you'll eventually encounter one. Water moccasins (genus *Agkistrodon*) occur primarily in the Deep South, usually in moist habitat. They can behave aggressively, and warmwater anglers encounter them frequently. Copperheads (another member of the moccasin family) envenom more people in this country than do any other kind of poisonous snake. Small, brightly colored, and shy, coral snakes rarely cause human injury other than to small children who unwittingly handle them.

Rattlesnakes and moccasins elaborate a complex series of toxins that cause local tissue destruction and abnormalities of the blood-clotting mechanism. Coral snakes produce neurotoxins similar to that of Asian and African cobras. Snakes inject venom through hollow fangs in the upper jaw. A substantial percentage of bites do not result in actual envenomation.

As always, management begins with prevention. Visitors unaccustomed to the presence of snakes in the outdoors should remind themselves that they are in snake country and act accordingly. The majority of snakebites occur on the hands. When fishing in areas that contain poisonous snakes, do not put your hands in places you cannot visually inspect. The second-most common bite locations are the foot and lower leg. Exercise caution when stepping over logs and rocks or otherwise placing your feet in locations you cannot see. Although rattlesnakes certainly can swim, they generally avoid water, so the stream itself might be the safest route of travel when fishing in typical western rattlesnake habitat, especially if the banks contain high grass. Heavy waders might guard the leg from snakebite (I've had one rattler bounce a shot off mine), but large snakes can still penetrate them, so don't assume protection.

If bitten by a snake, make a reasonable effort to identify it, but not at the risk of sustaining another bite. Precise identification of the snake species rarely effects medical decision making. Any bite that might have produced envenomation by a poisonous snake should be evaluated promptly by a physician.

The prehospital management of snakebite is easier to characterize by what you shouldn't do than by what you should. Over the years, a number of field treatments, including incision, mouth suction, ice, tourniquets, and even electric shock, for poisonous snakebite have enjoyed popularity. None have proven beneficial and most have turned out to be harmful. So forget about them.

The only field management method shown to be of definite benefit is immobilization of the affected part, assuming the bite involves an extremity, as it will over 90 percent of the time. You won't need anything fancy—a simple splint made from materials at hand will suffice until the victim can reach medical attention. Application of suction to the wound by means of a negative pressure device (Extractor, by Sawyer Products) can result in the removal of a significant amount of toxin, although definitive proof of benefit remains unclear. Otherwise, there isn't much to do except to remain calm and get to definitive medical care as judiciously as possible.

The administration of antivenin involves complex decisions beyond the scope of this discussion. Because of the high incidence of adverse reactions to antivenin, sometimes serious, it should generally not be administered in the field even by qualified personnel.

Remember that in North America –as opposed to Africa, Asia, and Australia, where highly toxic snakes are common—victims survive the overwhelming majority of snakebites, even those by poisonous species in which envenomation occurs. So remain calm if bitten and don't let the occasional sight of a snake ruin a good mayfly hatch. But if you have to reach over a downed log to make your way up the bank, take a good look first.

SUNBURN

For those of us who live at higher latitudes, warm sunlight provides one of the greatest attractions of a midwinter trip to a tropical fishing location. Acute sunburn can ruin a fishing trip in a hurry, however, and cumulative sun exposure can lead to skin cancer, cataracts, and premature aging of the skin. Visiting anglers should treat tropical sunlight with respect.

Solar injury derives largely from invisible ultraviolet (UV) rays, rather arbitrarily divided into UVA or UVB depending on wavelength. Sunburn predominantly reflects injury from UVB. Both forms probably contribute to the long-term effect of excessive solar exposure. Cloud cover does not effectively screen UV rays, so sunburn can occur even on cloudy days.

The risk of sunburn depends on a number of variables: duration of exposure, altitude (greater risk at higher altitude with less filtering atmosphere overhead), individual susceptibility (fair-skinned persons are at greatest risk, especially those of northern European ancestry), prior sun exposure ("tanned" individuals are less likely to burn), latitude (damaging UV rays are more intense near the equator), and time of day (UV radiation is most intense for two hours before and after noon). Water reflects UV radiation. Obviously, a fair-skinned visitor from a northern climate spending a long day wading tropical flats represents a high risk for sunburn.

Despite a myriad of purported topical sunburn remedies, there is no effective treatment for sunburn once solar injury has occurred. Furthermore, painful sunburn symptoms develop progressively for hours *after* the injurious exposure has taken place. This means that the effective management of sunburn depends upon recognizing the risk and taking appropriate preventative measures before problems develop.

Complete avoidance of UV rays represents one obvious way to prevent sunburn, but let's face it: Most of us don't travel to tropical fishing destinations to spend our time indoors. Nonetheless, individuals extremely prone to sunburn, or those with specific medical problems causing allergic photosensitivity, might need to limit their exposure at least during the most troublesome midday hours.

Proper selection of a topical sun-protection product begins with an understanding of the standard sun protective factor (SPF) rating. Expressed as a number, this value reflects the ratio between the amount of time required to produce redness after sun exposure while wearing the product to the time required to produce redness on unprotected skin. For example, an SPF of 8 allows the wearer to stay in the sun 8 times as long before experiencing injury as someone not wearing the product. The higher the SPF rating, the more effective the agent. In general, individuals highly susceptible to sunburn should wear products of SPF 15 on average days and SPF 30 during periods of intense exposure. Those of average sensitivity can usually get by with SPF 8 for routine use and SPF 15 during periods of high exposure.

Commercially available sun-protection products contain a variety of compounds, many derived from PABA (the original chemical sunscreen compound developed in the 1940s). Although generally safe, PABA derivatives can cause allergic reactions in some individuals. Various salicylates and cinnamates provide a "PABA-free" option for those who have experienced sensitivity to PABA-based compounds. The former might not be as effective as PABA derivatives, and the latter might not last as long. Physical agents such as zinc oxide provide another alternative, although because they are opaque many find them cosmetically unacceptable.

In addition to their chemical composition, sunscreen products differ substantially in their duration of action, especially when exposed to water. The FDA maintains objective standards for products labeled "water-resistant" and "water-proof." Anglers should be particularly careful to choose one of these compounds.

Clothing provides significant protection from UV rays—approximately equivalent to SPF 15 sunscreen products. Interestingly, the fabric and weave don't seem to make a lot of difference. When planning a long day in the sun, especially when fishing from a boat, anglers should always carry enough clothing to cover themselves completely at the first suggestion of sunburn. If you have to head back to the dock for a shirt, it will probably be too late. Hats provide important protection to the face and eyes (and hats that shade the eyes make it easier to spot fish). Sunglasses provide important UV protection to the eyes, and hats and glasses should be a standard part of any fishing day in the tropical environment.

WATER-BORNE ILLNESS

North Americans take an abundance of safe, potable water for granted. However, travel in developing countries or remote areas where drinking water often derives from unpurified sources frequently exposes visitors to a variety of infectious water-borne diseases. Although most such exposures result in self-limited illness, some can be serious and most can potentially ruin a trip. Symptoms commonly include nausea, vomiting, diarrhea, stomach cramps, and fever, and distinguishing among specific causes can be difficult or impossible in the field.

The responsible agents fall into three basic categories. Viruses usually cause abrupt, unpleasant gastrointestinal symptoms without long-term consequences. Bacteria are the most common causes of traveler's diarrhea in tropical developing countries. Most bacterial infections produce transient symptoms, but typhoid and cholera can be serious and occasionally fatal. Parasites sometimes produce long-standing symptoms that require specific therapy. Giardiasis represents a particularly important parasitic infection common among backcountry visitors in temperate climates.

Management begins with prevention. As a rule, all unimproved water sources and tap water in many Third World countries should be regarded as contaminated. In urban settings, visitors to tropical locales should rely on bottled drinking water when feasible. Ice from uncertain sources can transmit water-borne illness and should be avoided.

In the backcountry, visitors should purify drinking water themselves whenever possible by one of three basic means.

1. Boiling offers a reliable means of destroying all three major classes of water-borne infectious agents. *Giardia* organisms are particularly sensitive to heat, and even momentary boiling reliably destroys this common contaminant. Boiling water for 15 to 20 minutes effectively kills all agents of water-borne illness.

2. Filtration mechanically removes infectious agents from water by trapping them in a microscopic mesh. Because of their small size, viruses cannot be removed from drinking water by filtration. Filtration devices range in size and complexity from simple filter-containing straws suitable for individual use to large pumps used to decontaminate drinking water for camps. 5-micron mesh will remove *Giardia* and most bacteria from drinking water. 3-micron mesh might be required to remove the smaller *Cryptosporidium* parasite. Filtration devices require careful attention to proper technique in order to ensure a safe final product. Be sure to consult and follow the manufacturer's recommendations for use.

3. Finally, chemical treatment offers a means of reducing the risk of infection when boiling and filtration are impractical. Most commercially available water treatment compounds employ halogen disinfectants—either chlorine or iodine. Both can leave an unpleasant taste in treated water, and many users find one compound subjectively more acceptable in this regard than others. The reliability of any given chemical treatment method depends upon both the concentration of the treating agent and the duration of the treatment. *Giardia* organisms are relatively resistant to chemical treatment, especially in cold water, and treatment times should be prolonged to ensure their elimination. All commercially available treatment preparations are safe and effective if used properly, and choosing among them usually comes down to a matter of personal preference for the taste of the treated water.

There is no specific therapy available for viral gastroenteritis, but most cases of "stomach flu" resolve in 24 to 48 hours on their own. Briefly limiting oral intake to clear liquids and the use of over-the-counter antidiarrheal medications such as Imodium will usually decrease the duration and severity of symptoms. Bacterial traveler's diarrhea due to certain strains of *E. coli*—the most common cause of gastrointestinal illness among visitors to tropical locations—often responds to treatment with prescription oral antibiotics such as ciprofloxacin (Cipro). Although most authorities advise against prophylactic treatment with antibiotics, it seems reasonable to carry a prescription along on visits to tropical destinations

for use should symptoms arise. Less common bacterial causes of gastroenteritis might also respond to specific antibiotic therapy but generally require medical evaluation. Specific treatment also benefits parasitic infections such as giardiasis and ameobiasis. Travelers planning extended stays in remote areas where *Giardia* commonly contaminates drinking water might wish to obtain a prescription for metronidazole (Flagyl) to use on an as-needed basis.

Although most cases of water-borne illness do not require evaluation by a physician, the following signs and symptoms should prompt medical attention: high or persistent fever, severe or unremitting abdominal pain, bloody diarrhea, confusion, or failure of symptoms to improve in a matter of three or four days.

RECOMMENDED READING

- *WILDERNESS MEDICINE,* edited by Paul S. Auerbach (2001. $199.00. Mosby.)
- *GUIDE FOR ADULT IMMUNIZATIONS,* American College of Physicians Available to the general public only through reference libraries.
- *WILDERNESS MEDICAL SOCIETY PRACTICE GUIDELINES FOR WILDERNESS EMERGENCY CARE,* edited by William W. Forgey (2000. $13.95. Globe Pequot Press.)

T A C K L E & F L I E S

Many of the destinations described in this book require specialized tackle and flies for optimal fishing. Where appropriate, I have discussed these equipment issues at least in cursory fashion. However, simplicity has a lot to recommend it in the field, and this is especially true for the traveling angler for whom fishing might be an incidental sidelight on a trip to a distant location primarily motivated by other concerns, whether related to business, family, or other outdoor activities. The more I've traveled around the world, the more I've come to appreciate how much fun a fly-rod angler can have with the kind of basic one-size-fits-all equipment that packs easily into a suitcase or duffel bag at a moment's notice. Although I have great respect for the pleasures and satisfaction afforded by hours at the tying bench and arcane discussions of fishing gear, I sometimes wonder if we haven't collectively taken all this a bit too far. Certainly, the idea that one is not perfectly outfitted should never deter an angler from taking a crack at new water.

Fly rods were never meant for the vagaries of the world's airline transport system. Awkward and fragile, they seem to arouse baggage handlers' worst instincts, and even under the best of circumstances they often arrive in obscure airport corners where they obligate their anxious owners to added inconvenience and waiting time. On an extended expedition, there might be no alternative to a well-constructed rod tube and prayer. But for most routine trips, I've found four-piece rods a far simpler alternative. Modern rod-building technology has made the four-piece models from most of the better manufacturers all but indistinguishable from traditional two-piece versions in the hand. Secured in their metal travel tubes, my four-pieces ride wonderfully in the bottom of my duffel bag, and it's now an exceptional trip that requires me to travel with anything else.

I love good tackle as much as the next angler, and I couldn't tell you how many fly rods I own without counting them. But as much as tackle manufacturers would have anglers believe they can't go near the water without a highly specialized rod for every occasion, that just isn't true. My favorite all-around travel rod is a four-piece Sage RPL 7-weight. This rod will handle line weights from 6 to 9, and I've used it comfortably on everything from trout to tarpon. With the exception of the big offshore saltwater species, I'd be happy to pack it as my sole rod for any destination described in this book.

As much as I appreciate the delicacy of a light spring-creek outfit, it's easier to adjust a large reel to small circumstances than the other way around. Hence, my basic travel kit always includes a reel with capacity for 200 yards of backing. Floating lines are more versatile than sinkers—you can always add a bit of lead above the tippet if you need to fish deeper. Throw in a couple of leaders and spools of tippet in various sizes, and you should be able to take a stab at fishing for just about anything, all with an equipment kit that will barely make a bulge in your luggage.

Fly selection is a complex topic. If you're casting to wary trout in heavily fished water, that complexity might well be justified. But I've found it possible to take most fish, especially in out-of-the-way places, with a few basic patterns. Obviously this approach won't produce optimal results all of the time, but the traveling angler unaware of the exact circumstances at his or her destination should develop a few basic fly selections to cover most of the likely possibilities. I've broken my own preferences down as follows, and have referred to these selections throughout this book.

TROUT

Bead-Head Hare's Ear, #12–16; Pheasant-Tail Nymph #14–16; George's Brown Stone #8–10; Pheasant-Tail Emerger #14–18; Elk-Hair Caddis #12–16; Adams #12–18; Muddler Minnow #2–8; Woolly Bugger #2–6

ANADROMOUS FISH

Skunk #2–6; Egg-Sucking Leech #2–4; Skykomish Sunrise #4–6; Don's Dirty Dog #2–4; Comet #4–6; Single Egg #8–10
Flats: Crazy Charlie #4–8; Snapping Shrimp #2–6; Del's Crab Merkin #2–4; Clouser Minnow #2–6; Lefty's Deceiver #2/0–2; Mylar tube-fly #2

BACKCOUNTRY

Clouser Minnow #2–4; Sea-ducer #2/0–2; Whistler #2/0–2; Del's Crab Merkin #2; Snapping Shrimp #2–4; Lefty's Deceiver #2/0–2; yellow popping bug #2/0 and #8; Spoon Fly #6–8

BLUE WATER

Lefty's Deceiver #2/0; Sea-Ducer #2/0; billfish fly #5/0

BOOKING AGENCIES

Agencies are listed in alphabetical order.

ADVENTURES

P.O. Box 1336
201 S. Wallace, Suite B3B
Bozeman, MT 59715
406-586-9942
Specializes in Central America, especially Costa Rica.

ANGLING DESTINATIONS

330 N. Main St.
Sheridan, WY 82801
307-672-6894 or 800-211-8530
scott@anglingdestinations.com
The Caribbean, Alaska, and Kamchatka.

DESTINATIONS

800-626-3526
www.destinations-ltd.com
Specializes in Montana; exceptionally familiar with the Missouri headwaters and Paradise Valley.

FISHABOUT

P.O. Box 1679
Los Gatos, CA 95030
800-409-2000
trips@fishabout.com
A relatively small agency, but a personal favorite because of its responsive service and the vast experience of owners Howard McKinney and Kay Mitsuyoshi, especially with regard to Mexico and South America.

FISHING INTERNATIONAL

P.O. Box 2132
Santa Rosa, CA 95405
707-542-4242
fishint@wco.com
One of the largest and oldest, with an extensive listing of destinations worldwide.

THE FLY SHOP

4140 Churn Creek Rd.
Redding, CA 96002
800-669-3474
mike@theflyshop.com
Basic selection of fresh- and saltwater destinations.

FRONTIERS

305 Logan Rd.
P.O. Box 959
Wexford, PA 15090-0959
800-245-1950
info@frontierstrvl.com
An especially comprehensive listing of fly-rod destinations worldwide. Large enough to maintain specialized departments with regional expertise.

KAUFMANN'S STREAMBORN

P.O. Box 23032
Portland, OR 97281
800-442-4359
kaufmanns@kman.com
Maintains numerous listings, especially for light salt water.

OFF THE BEATEN PATH

27 East Main St.
Bozeman, MT 59715
800-445-2995
travel@offthebeatenpath.com
Alaska, the mountain West, and Patagonia.

ORVIS

Historic Route 7A
Manchester, VT 05254-0798
800-548-9548
www.orvis.com
One of the giants in the outdoor equipment industry has moved heavily into destination booking. Maintains an extensive selection.

WESTBANK ANGLERS

P.O. Box 523
Teton Village, WY 83025
800-922-3474
wbajh@wyoming.com
Specializes in the Bahamas.

PHOTO CREDITS

INDEX